SELLERS & SERVANTS

SELLERS & SERVANTS

Working Women in Lima, Peru

Ximena Bunster & Elsa M. Chaney
Photography by Ellan Young

PRAEGER

PRAEGER SPECIAL STUDIES • PRAEGER SCIENTIFIC

New York • Philadelphia • Eastbourne, UK
Toronto • Hong Kong • Tokyo • Sydney

Library of Congress Cataloging in Publication Data

Bunster, Ximena.
  Sellers and servants.

  Bibliography: p.
  Includes index.
  1. Women domestics—Peru—Lima.   2. Peddlers and
peddling—Peru—Lima.   3. Women—Employment—Peru—
Lima.   4. Poor—Peru—Lima.   5. Marginality, Social—
Peru—Lima.   I. Chaney, Elsa.   II. Title.
HD6072.2.P42L563   1985   331.4′0985′25   85-6259
ISBN 0-03-060543-1 (alk. paper)

Published in 1985 by Praeger Publishers
CBS Educational and Professional Publishing, a Division of CBS Inc.
521 Fifth Avenue, New York, NY 10175 USA

© 1985 by Praeger Publishers

56789 052 987654321

Printed in the United States of America on acid-free paper

INTERNATIONAL OFFICES

Orders from outside the United States should be sent to the appropriate address listed below. Orders from areas not
listed below should be placed through CBS International Publishing, 383 Madison Ave., New York, NY 10175 USA

Australia, New Zealand
Holt Saunders, Pty, Ltd., 9 Waltham St., Artarmon, N.S.W. 2064, Sydney, Australia

Canada
Holt, Rinehart & Winston of Canada, 55 Horner Ave., Toronto, Ontario, Canada M8Z 4X6

Europe, the Middle East, & Africa
Holt Saunders, Ltd., 1 St. Anne's Road, Eastbourne, East Sussex, England BN21 3UN

Japan
Holt Saunders, Ltd., Ichibancho Central Building, 22-1 Ichibancho, 3rd Floor, Chiyodaku, Tokyo, Japan

Hong Kong, Southeast Asia
Holt Saunders Asia, Ltd., 10 Fl, Intercontinental Plaza, 94 Granville Road, Tsim Sha Tsui East, Kowloon,
Hong Kong

**Manuscript submissions should be sent to the Editorial Director, Praeger Publishers, 521 Fifth Avenue,
New York, NY 10175 USA**

Acknowledgments

This book is based on a study of poor women in the labor force in Lima, Peru: "La Madre Trabajadora," or The Working Mother. The principal collaborators were Ximena Bunster B., Chilean anthropologist; Elsa M. Chaney, North American political scientist; Hilda Mercado Ávalos, Peruvian sociologist; and Gabriela Villalobos, Chilean social psychologist. The latter two investigators have published their results separately in several monographs issued in Peru and cited in chapters 1 and 2.

So far as the research methodology is concerned, a particularly valuable contribution was made by Ellan Young who was responsible for taking over 3,000 photographs used in the construction of the photo-interview kit described in the Epilogue. All of the team members collaborated in the development of the "talking pictures" technique in its different stages. Thus, the methodology is the outcome of a joint interdisciplinary effort.

Valuable assistance in the research design and/or interviewing was provided by Carmen Pimentel Sevilla, Peruvian psychologist; Jeanine Anderson Velasco, North American-Peruvian anthropologist; and Beatriz Basaldúa, Peruvian psychologist and lawyer. Lois Brynes provided editorial comments and assistance.

The original study was funded by the National Institute of Child Health and Human Development, National Institutes of Health; the Social Science Research Council (collaborative grant to Bunster and Chaney); the Smithsonian Institution's Interdisciplinary Communications Program, as well as a grant to Mercado from the local office of the Ford Foundation in Lima.

Contents

Glossary

ama *servant charged with childcare*
ambulante *street seller*
asembleas *meetings*

barriada *shantytown*
barrio *district*
burro *ass*

cama adentro *live in*
cama afuera *live out*
campesino, a. *peasant*
casa poblada *occupied dwelling (hist.)*
club de madres *mothers' club*
colegio *high school*
collectivo *jitney cab*
comadre, compadre *godparents of my child*
compadrazco, comadrazco *god-parenthood*
compañero, a. *mate*
compromiso *engagement, promise*
conjunto *musical band*
conviviente *mate in non-legal union*
costurera *seamstress*
criada *female servant*
crianza *upbringing*
criar *to raise, foster*
cuarto *room in a house*
chicha *corn liquor*
chino *Chinese grocery*
cholo, a. *Amer-Indian (pejorative unless used as technical term in anthropology)*
chompa *sweater*

doméstica *female servant*

empleado, a. *employee (polite term for servant)*
enamorado, a. *sweetheart*
encomendero *landowner (hist.)*
esposo, a. *husband, wife*

esteras *reeds*

fotonovela *illustrated love novel*

gente mala *wicked people*

hacienda *rural estate*
hacendado *rural landowner*

lavandera *laundress*
libra *ten soles*

macho, machista *exaggerated masculinity*
madre, padre *mother, father*
madre soltera *unwed mother*
madrina, padrino *godmother, godfather*
manta *cape*
maquiladora *assembly plant*
mercadillo *small marketplace*
mercado *market*
mestizo, a. *Amer-Indian/Spanish*
minga *work party*

obrero, a. *factory worker*

paisana *person from one's home province*
paradita *temporary selling site*
patrón, patrona *master, mistress*
pensión *roominghouse*
propina *tip*
pueblo jóven *young town, polite name for slum*

residencial *large, luxurious residence*
ropa chica *hand laundry*

sala *room; also livingroom*
salida *holiday*
serrano, a. *person from mountains*

sierra *mountains*
sirvienta *female servant*
sol, soles *Peruvian dollar, dollars*

terreno *building site*

tía *aunt*
tierra *one's home province, literally "land"*
trabajador, a del hogar *household worker*

Introduction

Program's and projects to incorporate Third World women in economic development, and to blunt the negative effects of male-oriented agricultural and industrial modernization,[1] may depend, paradoxically, on a recognition that women to a great extent already are "integrated in development." Their productive labors often are not included in national account statistics, and censuses categorize them as "non-working." Yet women perform many essential economic activities in the household, in smallholder agriculture, and in the urban sector. The most constructive way to assure their participation in development may be to support and enhance the productive activities in which women already are engaged. At the same time, such a strategy may assist in restructuring the development enterprise so that it accomplishes its stated goal of reaching the poor.

One approach to women's situation in Third World economies is through a recognition that women's resource base is shrinking, yet their responsibilities are increasing. Many women are forced to migrate to urban areas, leaving behind failing subsistence agriculture and disintegrating kin networks that no longer provide the minimum for a decent life to growing rural populations. In the towns and cities, even women with male partners must produce some income to supplement their menfolks' meager wages. Many others become economically responsible for their families—worldwide, about one-third of urban households are headed by women.[2] They must devise strategies to provide for themselves and their dependents who may include other adult females, their children, old people who no longer can bring in much cash and, occasionally, adult men who are unable or unwilling to work.

The urban household deploys some of its members, if possible, to wage labor; others to informal sector activities or to what Jamaicans call "scuffling": wheeling and dealing; trading and bartering; performing odd jobs such as carrying parcels, or watching and cleaning parked cars; scavenging and begging. Still other family members are assigned to productive work at home: sewing and repairing, preparing food for sale on the street, or artisan activities. Elder daughters and older women may cook, wash, clean, and take care of children full time so that other household members can devote themselves to their cash-earning activities or, in the case of young men, stay in school or enter an apprenticeship program. Help from relatives and neighbors bridges the gap in emergencies.

Guiding all these initiatives, the female household head also must allocate her own labor time, sometimes shifting her work from one category to another that looks more promising, and balancing cash-earning activities and necessary domestic tasks that cannot be delegated: taking a sick child to the free clinic, or going to the parish to sign up for milk powder and cooking oil.

Thus, Hermalinda, a live-out household worker in Lima, rearranged the *esteras* (reed panels) to accommodate her cousin who came to live with her in the *barriada* (shantytown) where Hermalinda had gained title to a small parcel of land. Hermalinda helped her cousin to become a street vendor of *chicha*, a fermented corn drink, accompanying her to sell on her own day off. The daughters of Hermalinda and the cousin, both nine years old, traded off staying home from school to look after Hermalinda's two younger sons, four years and six months old. About the same time, Hermalinda had to buy more esteras and construct another room for her three younger brothers who arrived from the country; she sent one, who refused to go to school, out to earn wages as a carpenter's helper to his uncle. The middle brother also worked to keep the youngest in school so that "one, at least, will have a profession."

At one point, Hermalinda quit her servant's job and started selling chicha full time, but she decided that she was not earning any more money, and her old *patrona* (employer) took her back. During this same period, Hermalinda was giving food to a neighbor and her small daughter when she could; the neighbor was trying to find enough clients to fill her week of laundering by the day, after failing in her attempt to become a beauty salon helper. Sometimes the father of Hermalinda's children gives her money, but she cannot count on any set sum since he has another, "official" family: a legal wife and five children.

Why are so many Third World women and men still earning their livelihood seemingly in such haphazard fashion, after more than two decades of intensive development activity? Development planners face the Third Development Decade with numb ears. Few need to be told again that agricultural development has in large part benefited the wealthier farmers; that capital-intensive strategies have failed to generate the promised employment in industry, and that rural development schemes have not been effective in keeping the rural poor from setting out for the towns and cities of their own countries and, in increasing numbers, from migrating across international boundaries in search of a better life.

Added to all this, evidence is accumulating that development projects often have proved detrimental to women—by leaving them out altogether, by eliminating their income-earning activities, by adding many extra hours of work for already overburdened women, or by depriving women of any control over the benefits or income from the projects.

From the other side, there also is evidence that even when Third World women achieve jobs in the modern sector, development exploits women's labor: those who work under crowded, unsanitary, and noisy conditions at repetitive jobs in the branches of multinational industries (sewing garments, packing pharmaceuticals, assembling electronic components) may have achieved modern sector employment, but sometimes it is difficult to see how they have benefited in the long run. In the *maquiladora* (assembly) industries on the U.S.–Mexican border, for example, mostly young, unmarried women are employed, for an average of three years (Fernández-Kelly 1983, pp. 216–20). After that, their prospects are bleak; unwilling to return to their villages or farm homes where there is no opportunity for employment, many drift into day work, crime, and prostitution.

What one author has called "development under monopoly socialism" also often exploits women's labor, sacrificing women's participation and progress to the exigencies of the state's larger development goals. Socialist countries have provided, on balance, much more opportunity for women to engage in productive work on farms and in the urban industrial labor force. However, women in these countries continue to face, as do their counterparts in countries undergoing dependent capitalist development, the "double day": a range of unpaid household tasks at the end of their shift of paid work. Women's unpaid housework continues to subsidize development, whether in capitalist, socialist, or mixed economic systems. Thus, at no cost to their governments or to industry, women's labor in the home reproduces the labor power of the wage earners, including their own labor power. As Croll (1981, pp. 398–99) remarks (in a study of development programs in the Soviet Union, Cuba, the Peoples' Republic of China, and Tanzania):

> The emphasis on attracting women into the collective waged labor force has outweighed the concern for redefining women's reproductive and domestic roles. The limited development of the service sector, the existence of a large private subsistence sector of the economy, and the persistence of a traditional sexual division of labor within the household have meant that the burden of subsistence and domestic responsibilities continues to devolve upon peasant women, who in effect subsidize rural development programs with their intensified labor.

In the cities, women's situation sometimes is better under socialism; household and child-care activities have been taken over by the state at least to some degree, although such services are far from universally available.

To argue for enhancing the integration of women in development may, under the conditions outlined above, appear perverse. If the major development efforts of the past 20 years have produced so few gains for women (and even have been negative in many cases), why should anyone suggest that women become more involved? For three principal reasons, among others that could be cited:

(1) Development efforts will go forward, and women already are involved. We must ask ourselves if, on balance, it is better for women to be present, conscious, and articulate, both in the administration and at the grass-roots, as these agencies strive to increase agricultural production and reduce malnutrition; improve health, water, and sanitation; preserve forests and other natural resources, increase employment—or to continue to be silent and ineffectual, unable to reap the benefits of conscious participation in development, while continuing to suffer its negative effects.

(2) Development planners are putting increasing emphasis on the world's poor, and many programs have moved away from an almost exclusive emphasis on macroeconomic approaches, toward at least some attention to people's needs and their potential for solving their own problems if they are provided a modicum of resources and technical assistance. Along with the questioning of development models, the small farm and the household are being seen as entities that not only are viable, productive economic units, but refuges of the poor against the large business, industrial, and state enterprises and bureaucracies.

(3) As we look more closely at those settings where the majority of the world's poor work out their survival strategies, women are becoming more visible. Their economic activity is being recognized as vital to these subeconomies. It is becoming easier, more natural, and even inevitable that women are taken into account. There is beginning to be concern, too, that there are more women in the lowest-prestige, lowest-paid jobs, in both the formal and informal labor markets. But we lack detailed information about them, their work and family life, and their aspirations for the future.

Our study looks at women in two specific traditional occupations. Most often, sellers and servants are part of the formal sector, but at other times their labors are unregulated and uncounted, and they may slip into the shadowy world of the casual labor market. In many world areas, migrant women arriving in cities and towns from the countryside find their greatest opportunities for employment as sellers or servants (or as servants *and* sellers, since many women first work as domestics, then move to street vending after the birth of a first child). Women born in the city also engage in these occupations, but their numbers are fewer. In Lima, according to 1972 census, only 11 percent of domestic servants were natives of Lima (Martínez, Prado, and Quintanilla 1973); a survey in 1976 of vendors revealed that only 8.2 percent were born in Lima—all the rest were migrants (Österling 1981, p. 77). Sellers and servants in Lima account for nearly one-half of all economically active women (see Table 1.3).

Yet, in spite of their importance, we know very little about women in these occupations: why and how women enter them; how long they remain, and how many are heads of household; whether they initiate daughters and sons into their occupations, or steer them toward other kinds of work; if they depend on other sellers and servants when they need credit or a helping hand in an emergency, or whether they count on family and community networks where they live for such assistance; to what extent they avail themselves of urban services to make up full family income; their participation in community associations, labor unions, and civic/political organizations, and the degree to which they maintain ties to their *tierra*, or home provinces.

The lack of information on women is partially a defect of the way studies have been carried out; often migration and labor force surveys have concerned themselves exclusively with male respondents. It has been customary to view women as passive in migration. The literature often describes the typical migrant as a young, single male. If women participated at all, they were thought simply to accompany their fathers, brothers, male partners, or sons to the cities and towns. They were supposed to have little to say in the migration decision, and little to do at the destination outside the household. Now evidence is accumulating that women play a much more active role in migration, both international and internal. If women do not want to migrate, the family probably will not go, and the male has to decide whether to go off and leave his family behind. In nearly every world area, however, if women do not predominate in migrant streams, their proportions are increasing faster than men's. The greater numbers of women migrating internally within Latin American and Caribbean countries, and from Latin America to the United States and Canada, is a phenomenon now nearly two decades old.[3]

Many women do go along with, or to join, their menfolk. Many others go alone, often with dependent children. Sometimes it is the woman who goes first, either to establish a beachhead for other family members, or simply in search of a better life for herself and her children if she has been abandoned by her male partner. Sometimes it is easier for women to find work quickly in the urban environment—study after study shows that whether one is talking about women in the Senegambia moving towards Dakar or Abidjan, Colombians going to Caracas, or Central Americans migrating to Washington, D.C., women find jobs as domestic servants.

Whether she is accompanied or not, the migrant woman will most likely work in paid employment either upon her arrival or soon afterward. Employment data show that migrant women consistently work outside the home in proportions exceeding the rates of women born in the place. One study of women in the urban labor market in Peru (Del Valle 1976) shows that factors explaining women's labor force participation are less considerations of education, training, and work experience, and more such questions as civil status (with high participation rates for women never married, separated, and widowed, all often with dependents) and income per hour. Such variables as number of children and age of last child did not correlate very highly with women's participation—underscoring the fact that many women desperately need to work.

In addition to the need to earn money, the woman newly arrived in the city has many complicated tasks to perform, all at once. She must reconstruct what one expert has called "survival networks," that is, all those links to kin and community that make the difference between what people can earn and what they need to live successfully in the city: schools, churches, medical and health care facilities, commercial establishments, *barrio* (neighborhood) associations. The man goes to and from his place of employment. The woman must quickly master an often-complicated bus system to get around the new environment. Moreover, she may have to do so while still learning the rudiments of the language and fighting hostility if she and her children are ethnically and racially distinct.

Because there are so few detailed studies of migrant women and their fate in the urban labor market, we undertook the present survey in the city of Lima, Peru. Sellers and servants are a key group to study not only because of their numerical importance, but also because their jobs occupy the lower tiers of the traditional labor market both in terms of wages and conditions of work. Within domestic service, as well as market and street vending, women as a group receive the lowest salaries, perform the least desirable activities within each occupation, and work in the worst districts and locations. For example, men occupy the public posts in domestic service, chauffeuring the cars and waiting on tables, in the houses of the wealthy and in the fine restaurants, while women are relegated to scrubbing pots and laundering clothes. Fewer women sell in the desirable areas of Lima, and they handle the perishable commodities: fresh fruits and vegetables, and prepared foods. Thus, while we know that most sellers and servants, male and female, are poor, women form a subgroup within each occupational category; they are the poorest of the poor.

Moreover, the occupations of seller and servant are theoretically interesting because they are extensions of "women's work." Domestic servants share in or replace the domestic labor of other women in the home, while the majority of female vendors specialize in the sale of fresh or prepared foods. As Henríquez (1980, p. 108) remarks:

> A significant part of these [women's] occupations contributes towards lowering the costs of the reproduction of the labor force in the total society through, for example, non-paid family work, the selling of food on the street and the work of domestic servants.

It is important that feminists begin to confront the implications of the fact that their domestic servants take over, or at least collaborate in, the most disagreeable tasks of the employer's double day, while servants often have a second "shift" in their own homes.

The appropriate level of analysis is a particularly difficult problem for investigators doing research on female participation since women's presence in demographic, labor force, and other statistics first needs to be "unveiled" (Pérez-Ramírez 1978). Women must become statistically visible before macrolevel data are very useful in providing a valid basis for analysis and program planning. Conversely, studies that focus directly on individual women may not give an accurate picture of their situation because most women live in households and work in collaboration with other household members. The household also is the entity that stands between the individual and the larger society, mediating the members participation in economic and social life, and making it possible for them to escape from complete dependency on wage labor. For this reason, the household—as the key production and consumption unit in developing societies—is being viewed by researchers as a promising unit of analysis.

Our study attempts to combine several current conceptual approaches. First of all, at the macroeconomic level, it is situated in the context of those studies that link the individual worker in Third World countries into relations of dependency on developed economies. In the long run, we do not see how the position of the world's poor, and particularly that of poor women, will improve without deep structural changes in the capitalist world system: it is functional for capital accumulation that an informal labor market provides cheap services (and subsidies through subcontracting) to industrial manufacturing and commerce, and it is essential that women's unpaid domestic labor continues to produce and reproduce the labor force for both the formal and informal labor markets (Beneria 1979).

Nor can socialist systems continue to let the demands of production and economic development take priority over women's interests—as Croll (1981, p. 399) remarks, "In the absence of well-defined, long-term policies concerning the reproductive sphere, the present inequalities in the sexual division of labor will continue, despite important achievements in socialist development experiences."

The Peruvian economic system, in spite of attempts at restructuring during the Velasco era, has reverted to a classic dependent capitalist model of development. This means that there may be only limited room for maneuver and only limited gains to be made by poor women in improving their situation. Yet, it is still important to document their work and family lives, and to try to discover ways in which they can be improved and strengthened, if only incrementally. So far as the family is concerned, as Safa (1976, p. 80) has pointed out, though women and men in Latin societies may be alienated in their work role, they have a domestic sphere to which they can retreat. Several other scholars recently have been discussing the fact that even though poor Third World households by sustaining their members at low cost have subsidized industrialization in developed countries, there is another side to the question. The household, whether in a city slum or on a small semisubsistence farm plot remains an important point of resistance against the advance of capitalist penetration (Nash 1982). Certainly such structures are extremely vulnerable. Yet, the household has demonstrated a certain ability to support its members outside the capitalist system, and a resilience in its ability to adapt constantly to new challenges in sustaining them.

In our own study, we have used whatever statistical data are available to link women's situation to the national and international economic systems, without, of course, being able to make any direct connections. So far as women's work life is concerned, we have here used our survey case study data on individual women—for most, their work for cash is carried on in the urban setting away from the household, so it makes sense to study women's employment separately from their family life. However, the analysis would be incomplete without a separate chapter that sketches women's lives in relation to their children, male partners, relatives, neighbors, and friends, and traces the degree to which they are inserted in community organizations. Another chapter explores the special relationship between the working mother and her children, as she combines the traditional tasks of childcare with a socialization into their future roles as workers.

In addition, our study—built on in-depth interviews with 50 women each in domestic service, street selling, and market vending—employs a new survey methodology using photos of women in similar occupations as an interview tool. Ximena Bunster describes the construction of the interview albums of "talking pictures" and tells how they were used in the Epilogue. For a greater understanding of the intervening chapters, the reader interested in interview techniques may like to refer to this epilogue first.

Considering the large proportion of economically active women who are sellers or servants in Peru, little research on either group exists, except for some doctoral studies. Smith (1971) did the pioneering study on household workers in Lima. Sagasti (1972) examined domestic servants in relation to their social, economic, and political socialization, especially in terms of literacy. Testa-Zappert (1976) interviewed a subsample of maids in a study of children's socialization in Lima. Burkett (1975) touches on the historical antecedents of both selling and servitude in Peru, demonstrating that urban women were engaged in very similar tasks to those they carry out today as early as the sixteenth century. Schellekens and van der Schoot (1984) did a joint master's study on maids in Lima. Babb (1981) has produced a thesis and several articles on market women in Huarás. An exception to the lack of attention to these women is Figueroa Galup's study of domestic servants in Lima, issued in 1983 and cited extensively for purposes of comparison in the first chapter of this book.

It is our hope that in the future more attention will be paid to women in the two occupations that account for about one-third of all employed women in Latin America. Our study is offered as a modest contribution to that end.

NOTES

1. Boserup (1970) was one of the first to draw widespread attention to the detrimental effects of modernization on women, particularly in rural areas. Tinker (1974 and 1976) widened the discussion of how Western development practices have undermined the position of women in many traditional societies, as did two early articles by Nash (1975 and 1976). Many other researchers and women-in-development experts have joined in the critique; the most extensive treatment is Rogers (1980). An early, still valuable "classic" is Youssef (1974).

2. Massiah (1982) has produced the most complete study on the Caribbean, while the International Center for Research on Women did the pioneering work and produced three studies that include Latin American and Caribbean data: Buvinić and Youssef, with Von Elm (1978); Buvinić and Sebstad (1980); and Youssef and Hetler (1983). Studies documenting the poverty of women-headed households in the region include Merrick (1977); Merrick and Schmink (1983); and Sant'Anna, Merrick, and Mazumdar (1976). One study contending that women-headed households are not always so disadvantaged is Brown (1977).

3. There are good reviews of the literature on women in migration in Chaney (1980); *Migration Today* (1982); Orlansky and Dubrovsky (1978); and Youssef, Buvinić, and Kudat (1979). Suárez (1975) considers the issue specifically for Peru.

1   *Agripina*

The large household still sleeps. After lighting the fire for the morning coffee, Agripina[1] slips out the side door—only when she is serving does she step onto the mirror-like floors of the family living quarters unless she is cleaning or polishing them—and walks hurriedly through the damp Lima dawn to the corner bakery to buy the breakfast bread. If the bread man had arrived early enough, she would have loped down the walk at his whistle, saving herself one of several trips she will make today to the corner *chino* (Chinese grocery store), bakery, or drugstore on errands for different family members. Agripina buys two dozen French rolls, still warm from the oven, and slips them into her string bag.

Agripina's day has begun. It will last from 5:00 or 5:30 a.m. to at least 10:00 p.m., and often past midnight if she has to open the gate for a late-arriving family member. Except for a short period after washing the lunch dishes from the large mid-day meal, she will be on her feet and on call to cook, launder the *ropa chica* (hand laundry), serve, wash dishes, sweep the walks, water the garden, and run errands. This morning she has had time only to splash cold water on her face (the servant's small bathroom does not have hot water, since it is believed that servants waste it; her toilet lacks a seat, and her shower cubicle does not have a curtain) and slip into her faded uniform of striped cotton. It has been only three years since Agripina cut off her long braids, but her bronze skin and dark hair still proclaim her Quechua ancestry.

Agripina is 18 years old, and she has completed 3 years of primary schooling—probably all that she will attain because, although she herself does not yet know it, she is pregnant. Ahead of her lies a hard year when her furious *patrona* (employer)—"*¿Cómo lo te ocurría que te ibas a quedar acá con niño?* Whatever made you think you were going to stay on here with a child?"—will fire her, she will give birth at the free Lima Maternity Hospital, be turned away by other patronas who will not hire a maid with a child, and finally in desperation, will try her hand at street selling. Soon you will find her at a busy downtown intersection, her three-month old baby slung over her back in the colorful *manta* of the sierra. Shyly, she will offer the small leather coin purses she had made from scraps begged at a shoe factory. She will have to keep a sharp eye out for municipal police who will chase her away, or at least confiscate her wares, for selling on a forbidden corner and without a license.

For Agripina, there is no going back. She arrived in Lima five years ago with her *madrina* (godmother), leaving home at her mother's suggestion to ease the situation on the small peasant holding where there never was enough of anything: food, clothing, space, opportunity for schooling, salaried employment. Her education was cut short because her parents could not afford to buy her notebooks and school supplies. Her home is near a remote sierra village, two days and two nights by bus, another day by horseback. Her present job is her third employment in Lima; the other two also have been in housework.

In her first job, which lasted two years, Agripina was not paid because she was apprenticed to her madrina, a fictive or sometimes real aunt or female relative who initiates the young sierra woman into Lima ways, teaches her Spanish, and gives her a first instruction in housekeeping tasks. Now Agripina earns the equivalent of U.S. $30 per month, and she has been working since she was 11 years old.

Agripina is a composite, a demographic profile of the typical maid-of-all-work in urban Peru. She has been created from data gathered from several sources: Figueroa Galup 1983; Gianella 1970; Rutte García 1973; Sindicato de Trabajadoras del Hogar, Cusco 1982; Smith 1971; Vargas de Balmaceda 1981, and my own study carried out in 1975–76. But Agripina's sisters—similar in age, rural origin, and work history—climb the rain-slicked hills of Bogotá's residential districts or walk the shady, gracious old streets of the middle and upper-middle-class residential areas of Santiago.[2]

Agripina is the only composite in this study; the other women are among 50 interviewees whose stories told here are their own. Of these case studies, 28 are of general household workers (*todo servicio*, or maids-of-all-work); 11 of laundresses, 10 of cooks, and 1 of a full-time seamstress employed by a single family. Among recognized specialties, therefore, the group lacks the *ama*, or servant dedicated exclusively to childcare, although several of the interviewees worked as amas in the past. Relatively few families can still afford an ama, in addition to other servants, and among the 50 workers interviewed, only 1 would change her present specialty to exclusive child-care responsibilities, while 3 list ama as the specialty they most dislike. In some cases, this is because they have been abused by the children of the household (lack of respect, and even blows and kicks) without being able to fight back.

While the number of interviewees in the present study is relatively small, the group matches closely the age distribution, employment histories, and migratory characteristics of maids in a systematic sample taken in metropolitan Lima by Figueroa Galup in 1974, as well as migrant women in several other studies carried out in recent times.[3] For an account of how the methodology used in the study was created and employed, see the Epilogue.

Agripina is a significant figure. Aside from the intrinsic drama of her life, she symbolizes the persistence in Latin America of a traditional or secondary labor market of large dimensions which, or so conventional development theory told us, should long ago have begun to atrophy. While persons in the traditional sector are counted in labor force and census surveys, and their jobs are covered by labor legislation (even if enforced only sporadically), nevertheless they typically work at jobs that do not require much capital investment, use rudimentary technology, and do not demand high level skills. Many persons who work in the traditional sector are therefore underemployed and less productive than those in more highly capitalized and skilled modern sector jobs.

On the positive side, the traditional sector provides employment to many like Agripina who otherwise would not have any way to earn income. In some cases, wage workers in the traditional sector—for example, men in some blue-collar manual specialties—earn more than salaried workers in the modern sector (MacEwen Scott 1983).

The secondary labor market, where Agripina and at least a large proportion of other servants and sellers work, should not be confused with the informal or casual labor market where workers are uncounted in official statistics and escape state-enforced labor legislation (Portes, forthcoming). While the informal sector is the subject of intensive interest and study at present, as well as reappraisal as to its value in terms of development, the casual labor market is outside the scope of our study. There are, of course, continuities and complementarities between the traditional and modern, as well as between the formal and informal labor sectors. Sometimes people work in both formal and informal sector employment; often the boundary between formal and informal occupations is difficult to establish, since sometimes unregulated, low-income jobs may be included in the formal occupational structure, and at other times not (Arizpe 1977, p. 25).

Agripina also symbolizes the disadvantaged place of women *within* the secondary labor market; pressure on the traditional sector by men who cannot find modern sector employment forces women into the least desirable jobs in both commercial and service occupations, and pushes many over into the shadowy world of casual labor. As noted in a recent study of women's employment published by the Oficina Internacional de Trabajo (1978, p. 74):

> In practically all of the countries, more than one-half of the feminine work force in Latin America works in the service sector. Within it, between 50 and 70 percent of women work in domestic service, which constitutes between 30 and 45 percent of the total urban female economically-active population. This female role constitutes a transition between the socialization of the woman in rural life and her new adaptation to the urban.

Agripina's situation also has important implications for development because the presence of so many Agripinas in the urban traditional sector may be an important factor in continued population growth. One of our findings is that women in urban marginal occupations are not exposed to modern values, attitudes, or information and do not adjust their fertility downward at the rate many demographers assumed would be the case. Jobs in the traditional sector pose much less of the role conflict analysts assumed would accompany women's entry into the labor force, conflict that was supposed to induce women to have fewer children. Some domestic servants, for example, are allowed to live in with a small child, or to bring their preschool children with them if they work by the day. Street sellers or market vendors commonly have their small children by their sides as they sell, with older children joining them, often still in their school uniforms, in mid-afternoon.

Another factor is suggested by Safa (1983) in a comparative study she carried out with Heleieth Saffioti in São Paulo, Brazil, and in a New Jersey factory town. She hypothesizes that women in Third World countries continue to have large families in urban settings because they need children to earn cash. In Brazil, she says (1983, p. 104), there is no advantage in reducing family size, since the individual working-class family has "only its labor to sell." Infant mortality also is high, and thus many children are needed to assure that some grow to adulthood. In Peru during the first year of life there are 114 deaths per 1,000 births; only Bolivia has a higher infant mortality rate among the South American countries (Chaney 1984, Table 7.7, p. 142).

The present study is not, however, focused only upon the potential developmental or demographic effects of women's incorporation into the economy, but on their own status in work, family, and community. An attempt has been made to approach the problems of these women from the perspective of the women themselves; our central concern has been that the women's lives be revealed as fully as possible in the women's own words and from their point of view. Hence, the elaborate methodology, detailed in the Epilogue, designed to center the interview around the work, family life, and community participation of the women, and to record their reactions to photos of women like themselves, confronting the same problems as the interviewees face every day. In the present study, we wish to give a voice to women, especially poor women, and to reveal their lives (insofar as we, as outsiders are able) as they themselves define their problems, fears, desires, and hopes for the future.

This study deals with the situation of migrant women in Lima, the capital and largest city of Peru. However, recent studies of women in several other metropolises reveal that rural female migrants to other Third World cities face the same sets of limited options and the same experience of being relegated to the lowest-paid, lowest-status jobs in the traditional sector as their Peruvian sisters.[4]

What stands out in these studies, and is confirmed in our own investigation, is the fact that the migrant experience for women differs in significant ways from that of men. It is a central hypothesis of the present study that modernization, particularly in urban environments, far from increasing female opportunity, actually narrows the number of options for women in Latin America, especially for migrant women, and further, that their options are more restricted than for either migrant or native-born men. Indeed, a well-documented demographic fact is that, as a group, migrant men often fare better in the city than men who were born there. As will be demonstrated, the migrant woman's initial employment possibilities are reduced to domestic service, street vending, market selling (for a relatively small number, if/when they accumulate sufficient capital), factory work (again, for a small proportion), and begging.[5] It is interesting to note that the occupational opportunities for women who are recent migrants to Mexico City are very similar (Arizpe 1977, pp. 33–36). MacEwen Scott (forthcoming) recently has analyzed extreme gender segregation of women in the Lima labor market:

> Unskilled and service work constitutes 52.6 percent of female manual employment compared with 17.4 percent of male employment, and office work provides jobs for 51.9 percent of nonmanual women compared with 34.3 percent of non-manual men. Women are over-represented within these lower ranking occupational classes. The situation is particularly acute in the case of unskilled and service worker occupations which are dominated by women absolutely and receive nearly twice their proportional share of female employment. On the other hand, women are under-represented in the occupational classes which rank highest both within manual and non-manual groups.

Not only are more women found in the lowest-paid, lowest-status jobs in the traditional sector (while men dominate the modern sector with its better salaries, greater job security, pensions, health services, and trade union protection), but they are more likely to remain there. Some males—among them significant numbers of migrants—move out of the traditional sector to better employment; any movement of women tends to be lateral (Suárez 1975, Cuadro 32, p. 61). For example, several studies (de Sagasti 1974; Mercado 1978; Testa-Zappert 1975) show that women move from domestic service to street selling or begging, but rarely to factory employment and almost never to white-collar work (domestic servants in the survey often could not identify the secretary photographed in a typical office setting and used in a question on women's aspirations; the problem was many had never been in an office nor seen a secretary at work). In the studies carried out in conjunction with my own, Villalobos (1977, p. 3) found that 77 percent of the factory workers she interviewed had begun their work in the industrial manufacturing sector, an indication of the lack of mobility into factory jobs. Only 3 *obreras* (blue-collar workers) in her study had ever been domestic servants, but 24 of the 50 street vendors interviewed for our study worked as domestic servants on their arrival in Lima (Mercado 1978, p. 28).

A second hypothesis to be explored in this study is a corollary of the first: not only do modernization and the associated phenomenon of rural-to-urban migration narrow the opportunity structures for

women, but the inability of poor women in most Third World countries to control their fertility also accounts for their relegation to
the lowest jobs in the traditional labor market. To better explore
these questions, we chose to study women in four occupations who
are mothers, many of them the major providers for dependent
children. Of the domestic servants studied, 11 are married (one had
separated); 11 are living in consensual unions, and the remaining
are single mothers (26 *madres solteras*, 1 separated, and 1 widow)
supporting their children, even though some maintain sporadic relationships with men, often with the same man over a long period of
time (see Chapter 3 for an analysis of the relationship of the interviewees with husbands and children).

The situation of these women illustrates a problem of growing
dimensions in the Third World: mothers who must provide for their
children with little or no help from an adult male. Sometimes to
carry out their responsibility they must put their children to work.
Women left behind in the rural areas face similar problems—sometimes seasonally, sometimes for years on end, sometimes for good
—as men migrate to plantations, mines, oil fields, or cities in search
of work. Estimates place the female-based household at one-third of
all households world wide (Buvinić and Sebstad 1980, pp. 40–42;
Youssef and Hetler 1983, pp. 230–31). In Peru, Violeta Sara Lafosse
(1980: 315) estimates that 40 percent of madres solteras are domestic servants, a statistic which challenges our stereotype of the
domestic service worker as young, single, and unencumbered.

Women get locked into traditional jobs because, sooner or later,
most women become pregnant whether or not they are in stable
unions. As in Agripina's case, this fact further shuts off the slim options they had in the first place. The woman does not have any
choice in the matter; in lands where poor women have little access
to or knowledge of contraceptives, one accepts the number of
children God sends. It is therefore not surprising, as noted above, to
discover that so many street vendors first worked as domestic servants; practically the only opportunity for a servant-mother whose
patrona refuses to keep her is to take to the streets either to sell
some kind of commodity, or to beg.

Another factor must be taken into account: the prejudice
against hiring *cholas* or indigenous women for modern sector occupations.[6] Testa-Zappert's 1975 study attests to the difficulties indigenous women have in securing employment, not only because of
their lower educational qualifications, but because they do not exhibit the "buena presencia," i.e., the proper appearance demanded

not only for office jobs, but for clerking in stores, working in the post office, and in other petty bureaucratic positions.

Before going on to explore in more detail the servant's life in contemporary Lima, domestic service will be discussed in relation to development, then examined in historical perspective.

DOMESTIC SERVICE: A TRANSITIONAL OCCUPATION?

Some years ago Coser (1973) characterized domestic service as an "obsolete vocational role," and showed how the servant gradually disappeared as Western societies modernized and as formally free labor replaced ascriptive assignment to work roles. In Latin America, it had been assumed not only that domestic service was a traditional occupation happily fated to disappear with increasing industrialization, but also that domestic service was transitional for the person, especially the migrant, who would be socialized through it, learning new attitudes and behaviors appropriate to the urban culture. In a few years, the typical domestic would move on to a better job in the modern sector or marry a factory worker, lower police officer, or even a petty bureaucrat, passing occasionally into the upper strata of the lower class, but rarely into the middle class (see especially Smith 1971, Chapter V).

Indeed, the whole topic of domestic service has been regarded as transitory and unimportant, even by those engaged in women's studies. No matter if presently it is the largest occupational category for women in the Third World, if it is rapidly disappearing, why bother to study it?

But to what extent is domestic service actually diminishing? In most developing countries, according to Chaplin (1969, p. 19), because mining and agriculture are becoming more mechanized, while manufacturing sectors remain weak, the proportions of domestic servants are much greater than for comparable periods in Western societies. We forget that even in so industrialized a nation as the United States, domestic service was the leading occupation for women in every census from 1870 through 1940 inclusive; only in 1950 did stenographers, typists, and secretaries outnumber paid household workers among U.S. women in the labor force (Baxandall, Gordon, and Reverby 1976 pp. 406–07). Figueroa Galup (1983, p. 3) and Nett (1966, p. 439) concur in characterizing domestic service as a "permanent" occupation under current conditions in Latin America. These conditions are not likely to change in the near future because even if some countries are able to accelerate their industrialization, capital-intensive modes of production do not generate sufficient employment. As Jelin (1977, p. 134) observes, the continuous supply of young migrants replenishes the pool of domestic servants for urban households. MacEwen Scott (forthcoming) notes that domestic service in metropolitan Lima almost trebled in absolute terms, contributing one-third of the net increase in female employment between 1940 and 1972, even as its relative position as a source of female employment has fallen. The 1980 census confirms this trend (Ferrándo de Velásquez 1984, Cuadro 30, p. 70).

Not only do the numbers of those engaged in domestic and other low-status service occupations remain high, but the persons doing this work do not appear to be "transitionals," on their way to becoming "modern"; rather, they form a new subuniverse of workers, most of whom will never escape from their low-income, low-status jobs.[7] Thus, our investigation adds to the accumulating evidence that Third World development does not replicate all the historical stages of modernization as it occurred in the advanced Western nations.

The complex factors generating rates of world-wide unemployment and underemployment, and the growth of the traditional service sectors of developing countries have been analyzed by many scholars. Capital-intensive technologies in agriculture and mining push people out of traditional occupations with no possibility of more than a small number being absorbed either by the new mechanized agricultural enterprises or by the modernized urban manufacturing and service sectors. In Peru, most *campesinos* (peasants) who have land at all are smallholders, excluded from the benefits of the new cooperatives created by the agrarian reform. A highly unequal distribution of income also persists; whatever reforms the Velasco government carried out were primarily in the modern sector which accounts for two-thirds of the gross national product but employs only one-third of the labor force (Fitzgerald 1976, pp. 94, 105).

Several studies confirm that about 60 percent of the urban labor force works in traditional employments. Women are found disproportionately in this sector, and they earn less than men — facts often overlooked in development studies. Webb's (1974, p. 29) analysis of Lima and seven other cities shows that the urban traditional sector has a much higher proportion (40 percent female) even when domestic servants are excluded from the count, than the modern sector (18 percent female). He attributes this not only to the flexibility and easy entry that characterize the traditional labor market, but to the "social discrimination that reserves more stable and higher-wage modern sector jobs to men."

Table 1.1 shows the distribution of the economically active population by sex and principal economic activity in Peru in 1981, while Table 1.2 gives the participation rates for women and men in the Department of Lima-Callao in three recent census years.

TABLE 1.1 Distribution of the Economically Active in the Total Population by Sex and Principal Economic Activity in 1981 (Six Years of Age and Over)

Economic sector	Total (100.0) 5,281.7	Women (100.0) 3,937.7	Men (100.0) 1,344.0
Agriculture, forestry fishing, mining	38.2	21.6	43.9
Manufacturing industries	10.6	10.1	10.7
Construction, electricity, water, gas	4.0	0.4	5.3
Commerce, banking	14.5	19.1	13.0
Transportation, storage, communication	4.0	1.0	4.9
Services	19.9	32.1	15.7
Other or not specified	8.8	15.7	6.5

Source: República del Perú, Instituto Nacional de Estadística, Censo de 1981. Compiled by Ferrándo de Velásquez 1984.

TABLE 1.2 Numbers and Percent of the Economically Active in Lima and Callao by sex in 1940, 1961, and 1972 (Six Years of Age and Over)

Years	Total	Women	Men
1940	372.1 (100.0)	107.5 (28.9)	264.6 (71.1)
1961	817.5 (100.0)	220.1 (26.9)	597.4 (73.1)
1972	1,225.4 (100.0)	332.8 (27.2)	892.6 (72.8)

Source: República del Perú, Instituto Nacional de Estadística, Censos de 1940, 1961, and 1972. Compiled by MacEwen Scott, forthcoming.

In Lima, about one-third of the total labor force is concentrated in two occupations in the lowest strata of the commercial and service sectors, both characterized by low productivity and low income: sellers, mainly ambulantes (street sellers) and service workers, principally domestic servants. Women are in a slight majority in the first occupation (53 percent of ambulantes in Lima are women), and overwhelmingly in the majority in the second; about 47 percent of service workers are domestics, and of these, 92.8 percent are women (República del Perú 1976; Villalobos 1975, Cuardros III-3 and III-4, pp.35–36; Vargas de Balmaceda 1981, p. l). Besides those who are counted in the official statistics, there are many thousands of both sellers and servants who form part of the informal economy, and who are not captured either by census or labor force surveys. Table 1.3 shows women workers in the total country and in Lima by occupational status in 1972.

TABLE 1.3 Distribution of Economically Active Women by Occupational Status in the Total Country and in Lima in 1972 (15 Years of Age and Over)

Occupation	*Peru*	*Lima*
	100.0 (763.2)	100.0 (327.4)
Empleada (white collar)	28.3	42.2
Obrera (blue collar)	8.5	9.7
Trabajadora independiente (independent worker)	31.1	17.9
Trabajadora del hogar (domestic worker)	17.4	27.9
Trabajadora familiar (family worker)	7.9	—
Other	6.8	2.3

Source: República del Peru, Oficina Nacional de Estadística y Censos, VII Censo National de Población, 1972.

It is difficult to get an exact estimate on the numbers of domestic servants in Lima. According to the respective censuses, in metropolitan Lima they totaled 26,200 in 1940 and 66,100 in 1961 (Smith 1971, pp. 61–62), and 79,186 by 1972 (Testa-Zappert 1975).

This works out to be about one-quarter of the female labor force in the Department of Lima, compared to 1 percent of the male labor force in 1972. In the country as a whole, 202,000 persons worked as domestic servants, and of these, 85 percent were women (Ferrándo de Velásquez 1984, Cuadro 30, p. 70). Smith (1973, p. 193) estimates that the total number of Limeñas who have been engaged in this occupation to be perhaps as large as 250,000 women, but this figure probably is low.

Women also are disadvantaged when it comes to wages in the urban traditional sector. In 1970, one-third of persons in urban traditional sector occupations earned an equivalent of U.S. $23 a month or less, while only 12 percent earned $116 or more. In contrast, a third of those in the modern sector earned $116 or more (Webb 1974, p. 39). Women, however, earned less than their male colleagues in the urban traditional sector. Among the self-employed, for example, women's incomes averaged only $30 per month, versus $70 for men. Domestic servants earned an average of $31 per month, versus the $50 per month average wage for the sector (ibid., pp. 33–34).

Among those who have carried out studies in other countries, there is general agreement with our own findings that servants are not—either as individuals or as a group—moving out of the household either into industry or to become the "servants in the office," as women workers did in the years between the world wars in the United States (office workers represent 15.4 percent of all women workers in Lima). In Brazil, for example, between 1872 and 1970, estimates of women employed as household workers oscillated between 27 and 33 percent (Saffioti n.d., p. 3). García Castro (1982, p. 103) cautions that the apparent declines in the numbers in domestic service appear to be related to economic cycles; contrary to expectation, participation in this sector may rise in response to hard times because more women (and children) have to work to keep their families afloat. Suárez, Vargas, and Jurado (1982) have noted the same tendency in Lima. The category unpaid family worker in Colombia includes, in García Castro's view, many young women and girls who work without pay and who are not registered in the official statistics. She concludes that since 1979–80, the annual percentage increases in domestic service in Colombia have been about 0.9 percent. There also is a marked trend among household workers to do daywork and to work on a part-time basis—both more difficult to capture in employment statistics. Suárez, Vargas, and Jurado (1982, p. 5) note that in metropolitan Lima,

... in the years of greatest economic growth, 1970-1974, the woman decreased her labor activity from around 36 percent to 29 percent. The contrary occurred in the years of crisis and economic contraction, where the activity rate of woman was significantly increased from 29 percent in 1972 to a little more than 40 percent in 1981.

Domestic service thus turns out not to be an occupation in transition. From the domestic's own objective situation, neither does domestic service appear to be transitional for the person who exercises it, although she herself may feel that she is better off when she marries if she does not have to go out to do housework for pay afterwards (Smith 1978). We do not know the distribution of women in terms of years on the job, not the destiny of those who leave the labor market. Yet limited data from my own and Figueroa Galup's study (1983, p. 11) put us in disagreement with Smith's 1971 findings that women in domestic service better their position *within* the occupation itself—either by calculating their job moves to better neighborhoods and/or moving from maid-of-all-work to cook or ama, which they believe pay better, or by using the occupation as a vehicle for upward mobility out of the servant class. Moves occur much more haphazardly, and for the group interviewed for this study, are dictated by other considerations than upward mobility (see pp. 63 ff. for a more detailed description of the servants' aspirations). As Figueroa Galup (1983, p. 11) notes,

Comparing the location of the first household and the first job with the present job, we can corroborate that from the middle-class areas ... there is a flexible social mobility towards other levels. The step from an upper-class residential area at the beginning to a present position in a young town (slum) is fortuitous, and household workers who have started out in barriadas simply do not succeed in obtaining later employment in upper-class residential neighborhoods.

The classic view, characterizing domestic service as a "bridging occupation" which facilitates first horizontal, then vertical mobility, may not fit the situation in developing countries (Chaplin 1969, p. 12). Even in Europe and the United States, the function of domestic service as a modernizing agent may have been exaggerated, as Katzman (1981, pp. 275-76) points out:

The private home and family were organized as conservators of tradition, and especially in homes with servants they proved remarkably resistant to modernization. There is no evidence to suggest, for instance, that women actually adopted the widely advocated systematized work organization urged by reformers. The presence of servants probably retarded modernization in the household, and domestics would benefit little from its belated appearance in the home. . . . There is also the strong possibility that the selection process among women workers left as servants the groups most resistant to modernization. . . . The selection of traditional women's work within the household probably indicated their desire for work least associated with the tide of modernization and industrialization . . . and schools were probably more of a modernizing agent than service.

The servant role may persist for reasons that are outside economics. As Nett (1966, p. 439) observes, servitude is not solely a function of economic conditions, but a complex institution of Latin American societies that exists for reasons other than the "vast reserve of unskilled human labor" available. Theories of social stratification suggest that to feel superior to some others may be a basic human need; Figueroa Galup (1983, p. 5) points to the psychological and cultural functions of the servant; "the presence of the 'chola'," she says, "reaffirms in an unmistakable way the superior status of her employers." Figueroa Galup (1983) goes on to speculate that a dominance/dependency syndrome may exist not only in terms of Peru's economic relationships, but also in response to the need to dominate or be dominated which she sees as a basic pattern of the Peruvian personality.[8]

Rubbo and Taussig (1978, p. 22) touch on the same theme: the presence of servants serves to confirm in the growing child his or her superior social position. A servant is the badge of a lower-middle-class family's upward mobility, and the sign that the middle-class family is maintaining its status.

At the same time, indigenous women from the sierra have been socialized to remain subservient, at least toward the outside world (within the rural environment and within their own homes, they may exercise power within well-defined boundaries having to do with the home and children). While the male peasant also has been dominated, the campesina has been subordinated not only by the Hispanic society, but also by her own father and uncles, brothers, male partners, and, oftentimes, her own sons.

Other authors point to the persistence of servitude as a function of the unique relationship established between the household worker and the family, particularly with the patrona. Because the nature of her service is personal, just as is the housewife's, the domestic worker's activities incorporate feeling and sentiment into the relationship (García Castro 1982, p. 101). As Katzman (1981, p. 146) also notes, "What set domestic service apart from other occupations was the mistress/servant relationship, a highly personalized one in which the worker herself was hired, rather than just her labor supply." Many maid servants in the present study emphasize the personal bond that links them to their patronal family, and particularly to the patrona herself, and give this as a reason for being content with their present occupation.

In sum, the consensus among those who have carried out studies since Smith's is that while domestic service may be declining, it is not slated to disappear. In many countries, while the proportions of women in this occupation are diminishing, at least in the official statistics, the absolute numbers of domestic servants continue to increase (as is the case in Peru).

THE SERVILE STATE IN HISTORICAL AND JURIDICAL PERSPECTIVE

Neither in its historical nor contemporary aspects does the reality of the servant role in Peruvian society (or in most of Latin America for that matter) bear much resemblance to the cosy world of down below in the British Broadcasting Company's popular series, "Upstairs, Downstairs." Nor does the female servant's daily life much resemble the adventures of Latin America's most popular heroine of the lower classes, the Indian servant María, diffused through the *telenovela* (soap opera) and the *fotonovela* (photos with captions) and comic book versions as "Simplemente María." In this modern fairy tale, a servant from the sierra of an unidentified Latin American country, after much suffering—including giving birth to an illegitimate child fathered by an upper-class medical student who abandons her—becomes a seamstress, learns designing, and finally emerges as an international figure in *haute couture*, meanwhile finding happiness in marriage with a humble, honest, upright, and handsome school teacher who had befriended her through her years of struggle.[9]

In order to understand the position of the servant in the Lima labor market, it is necessary to review the historical and juridical background of the servant's position in Peruvian society. Such an exploration does not at all negate the demographic, social, and structural reasons for the persistence of the servile state, which remain primary; yet such a consideration does serve to round out the picture.

The basic fact about the servant in Peru and other countries of Latin America is that she (since only about 1 percent of servants in Lima are male, the feminine pronoun is appropriate) still is linked far more to the patrimonial dispensation of Peru's past than to the modern system of contract labor. My study and Figueroa Galup's demonstrate that all but a few privileged servants live, for all practical purposes, in a preindustrial, patriarchal society. This world is inhabited to a degree by all women, minors, indigenous persons, and imbeciles, but the maid servant is very near the bottom (only prostitution and begging are perceived by women themselves to be lower occupations; see Heyman 1974, p. 81).

Thus, the servant throughout Latin American history—most often racially and/or culturally distinct from the master class—has subsidized the classes above her, permitting even modest Spanish households to live in a style which would be beyond their means if there were not a servant class. As Chaplin has observed (1970), any measures to upgrade servant status and to bring servants under legislation governing the modern labor sector are resisted by the dominant classes.

In 1956, for example, Peru's first woman senator, Irene Silva de Santolalla, introduced legislation that would have provided training, including literacy, to young women arriving from the sierra in "Hogares de Paso," temporary shelters that would have assisted them in their first difficult months in the cities. The senator also suggested regulation of salaries and hours, and that the appelation "sirvienta" be substituted by the more dignified "trabajadora del hogar," measures that would not be accepted in law until nearly 15 years later in the Velasco regime. The opposition to Irene Santolalla's bill was immediate and vociferous, and the debate in the Congress heated. The legislation did not pass, and she herself received many complaints that her efforts would put ideas into the heads of servants and make them too expensive.

In the last few years, one might add, the new feminist organizations among Latin American women have all but ignored the contradiction that professional women have their freedom to pursue their careers and feminist activities through another woman who at least shares, if not altogether replaces her employer in, the duties of the second shift in the "double day."

Lockhart (1968, p. 150) notes that even though Spanish women were not numerically a large group in the first two generations after the conquest of Peru (1532 to around 1560), there were sufficient numbers to give a "Spanish mold" to Peruvian society. In the early 1540s, there was only 1 Spanish woman for every 7 or 8 men; by

1555, they numbered about 1,000, including the thoroughly Hispani-sized *moriscas, mulattas,* and *mestizas* (Spanish-Arab, Spanish-Negro, and Spanish-Indian women) who "passed" because of the shortage of women in the colony.

The wives of Peru's *encomenderos* (those to whom a group of In-dians literally had been "recommended," from whom the Spaniards extracted work in return for "civilizing" them and instructing them in the Catholic faith) early set the tone of the society with their large staffs of servants. Central to the duties and ambitions of the en-comendero, says Lockhart (*ibid.*, p. 21) was the *casa poblada*, literally, an occupied or peopled dwelling, where his obligation was to main-tain a perpetual open house: "A large house, a Spanish wife if possi-ble, a table where many guests were maintained, Negro slaves, a staff of Spanish and Indian servants, and a stable of horses." The casa poblada was the largest single element in the dream of lordly life to which all Spaniards aspired.

According to Lockhart, however (*ibid.*, p. 159), "even artisans' and merchants' wives could come nearer that ideal than might be imagined." None of those persons who, in Spain, would have been considered poor and plebian, were without servants in Peru "to call them señora and relieve them of the burden of daily housekeeping," he says. Even humble women had servants to whom they taught Spanish ways: "The household of one almost indigent Spanish woman of Lima could stand as a paradigm of Spanish Peru: herself, her Negro slave, her Indian servant, and a mestiza orphan girl" (*ibid.*, p. 169).

Indeed, it was the fate of many mestizo children to enter the ser-vile state; according to Lockhart (*ibid.*, p. 164), illegitimate children "received sustenance, education, and affection, but were seen in the light of servants." The term *criada* from *criar*, to raise or foster, to-day used exclusively to mean "servant" (and considered demeaning by household workers themselves) originally meant a person adopted into a colonial family and reared as a family member; in Latin America, the criada appears to be somewhat analogous to Ariès' young servants of the same period:

> At the heart of this complex network of the "big house" of the 17th century [big in the sense, he says (p. 395), that it was always crowded and had more people in it than little houses] was the resident group of children and the servants. The progress of the concept of childhood in the course of the 16th and 17th centuries and the moralists' mistrust of the servants had not yet succeeded in breaking up that group. It was as if it were the living, noisy heart of the big house. Countless engravings show us children

with servants who themselves were often very young. . . . There was not a great age difference between the children of a big house and the servants, who were usually engaged very young and some of whom were foster-brothers and members of the family. . . . The servants and apprentices were placed on the same footing as the children of the family. Sons of the houses went on performing domestic functions in the 17th century which associated them with the servants' world, particularly waiting at table (1962, p. 396).

Such a practice appears also to have been very common in colonial Peru, where the wives of encomenderos (no orphanages existed) often took in many children to raise who were not their own. Lockhart (1968, p. 164) documents the collection of doña Francisca Jiménez who by 1548 had

ten children alive and with her; two by her first husband, three by her second, and five by her third. She also was raising the mestizo daughter of her second husband, who acted as her maid.

It may be that, just as in medieval Europe at that time before the idea of service had become degraded [from the 17th century onward, according to Ariès (1962, p. 396)], the servant who so often had blood ties with the family upon which he or she was dependent, was not yet regarded as the menial the person in service would later become.

As the *hacienda* system developed, it was a regular practice for the landowner to exact labor in the fields from both men and women, but the latter also were required to serve by turn in the hacienda's big house, or in the houses that the landowner maintained in the nearby provincial town and/or in Lima. One source has suggested that domestic service today can be considered in some sense as an extension of the "unavoidable pressure on the campesino to hand over his daughter. . ., and her work in the patrón's house a prolongation of the social relationships of her parents and the family with the landowner" (Sindicato de Trabajadoras del Hogar del Cusco 1982, p. 19).

The "lordly dream" of Spanish colonial Peru never has been relinquished by Peru's dominant classes, only scaled down. It still is possible for even modest lower-middle-class or upper-lower-class homes to have at least one servant.

Today, the anomaly of the servant's status persists. Other investigators also have pointed to the fact that domestic service is not congruent with modern work relationships. On the one hand, as García Castro (1982, p. 101) points out, domestic service is governed by precapitalist work relationships. At the same time, whether the housework is done by the mistress herself, or by the household worker, it is necessary to modern industrial society because domestic work renews the labor force for its daily tasks outside the home. There exists here an interesting interplay between the domestic servant's relationship to the production and reproduction of the labor force, a theme that so far has not been very much explored by scholars.

Legislation enacted by the Velasco government in 1970 at least officially lifted the servant (renamed "trabajador del hogar," household worker) from the exploited position she or he had occupied for centuries. Weekly holidays (24 consecutive hours) and yearly vacations (15 days with salary) were mandated, and servants for the first time came under social security legislation. Yet few provisions were made for enforcement of the new laws, and the only recourse servants had at the time of this survey (if they knew of his existence) was one lone, harassed male lawyer in the Ministry of Labor who, with no support staff, tried to deal with the complex professional and personal lives of Peru's household workers. This office had no power to sanction infractions of the domestic service laws; factory workers, in contrast, had an elaborate juridical structure within the ministry for their protection. Nor can anyone satisfactorily explain why, in law, the obrera is entitled to an eight-hour work day, one month's paid vacation, the minimum wage, and maternity leave, while the domestic worker has none of these things. Ironically, the most important provision of the new legislation regulating domestic service, that the servant is entitled to 8 hours rest in each 24, has been widely interpreted by patronas as a license to exact 16-hour workdays from their maids!

While the weekly *salida* (day off) appears to be rather widely observed and many servants now also demand and receive their yearly vacation, the new social security legislation is not enforced. For one thing, the patrona must go with her maid to arrange the enrollment, and the bureaucratic process is time consuming. Maids often do not ask to be enrolled in social security because one-half the payment would be deducted from their already small salaries. Others do not wish to carry a social security card that would confirm their identity as servants. Enrollment also requires one's birth certificate, a document often not easily accessible to a woman from a distant province where records, in any case, may not be kept with much care, or where her birth simply never was recorded. The refrain, "Recién estoy scando mis documentos—I've been getting my documents together recently" was a common response to the query about whether an interviewee was insured. Only 7 of my 50 interviewees had been enrolled, and this reflects the findings of Figueroa Galup (1983, pp. 41-43), who also found that not 1 of her 170 interviewees could explain social security.

Many servants themselves resist the "contractualization" of labor-management relations (Chaplin 1970, p. 1). This is partly because they prefer the fiction that they are family dependents rather than employees, particularly if they perceive the treatment as kindly, and if they have been with the family for a long time. Figueroa Galup (1983, pp. 41–49) has a section in her study on the complete gamut of legislation related to domestic servants, and the degree to which they are aware of their rights and obligations, as well as the extent to which they are prepared to demand and fulfill them.

A logical question to ask at this point would be: why have servants not organized themselves and long ago rebelled against the conditions of servitude under which such large numbers of persons have lived? There have been in Peru several efforts, inspired in great part by the work 20 to 25 years ago of Peruvian priests inspired by the French Catholic lay movement, the Juventud Obrera Católica (JOC) (Young Christian Workers), and these initiatives persist at least in Lima and Cusco, although the leaders formed in the days of the JOC do not have, at present, any formal ties with the church. But the associations are very small and weak. Schellekens and van der Schoot (1984) have documented the history of these organizing efforts.

What militates against organization is the isolated nature of the servant's work—each one, or each small household staff, separated from the others' workplace. Servants have few opportunities to meet together because they do not have the same free days and there are few meeting places. Moreover, a household worker often has difficulty in conceptualizing his or her fellow and sister servants as a class; Figueroa Galup and I both noted in our interviewing that questions asked about the general situation of servants often would be answered (even when the questions were framed in terms of servants-as-a-group) in the singular. Many of our interviewees had never thought in terms of shared problems and shared solutions as a way to ameliorate the conditions of servitude. Most of the women interviewed in my study say they prefer to work alone, and few report having friends they trust. They like to stay in the house, and if they go out on their days off, they generally visit relatives in one of the barriadas (see Tables 1.15 and 1.16 in this chapter).

However, the major reason the situation does not improve is structural. A constant supply of young indigenous women, uneducated and untrained for any occupation, arrives from the sierra; the servant maid remains a readily available commodity purchasable for a very small price. Jelin (1977, pp. 132–34) speculates from existing data that large numbers of young women in the age groups 14-29 arrive in the cities of Latin America looking for work; from the other side, domestic service in Latin America is an occupation filled principally by recent young migrants. So far as my own interview group is concerned, 70 percent are in this age group. [Studies of the supply/demand for servants in the Lima labor market have been carried out by Del Valle (1976) and Vargas de Balmaceda (1981).]

In the next section, we turn to a more detailed examination of the migrant situation, especially as it affects the woman migrant's employment opportunities.

LIMA, CITY OF KINGS AND MIGRANTS

Lima, called the City of Kings because it was founded in 1535 on the religious festival commemorating the arrival of the Three Kings at the Manger in Bethlehem (Epiphany, January 6), might today more accurately be called the City of Migrants. As Martínez, Prado, and Quintanilla (1973, p. 34) observe, those who live in the central part of the city have the sensation they are moving in an environment dominated by dark-skinned provincials. Older women often keep their distinctive hairstyles and dress, even after long years of residence in the city.

About 40 percent of Lima's present population comes from other parts of the country (Chaney 1984, Table 3.10, p. 35); yet the Lima workforce is 61 percent migrant (Gianella 1970, p. 28), reflecting the fact that so many people come to the city in their working-age years. Jelin (1977, p. 131) has reviewed the major migration studies, and concludes that for Latin America as a whole, more women migrate to the cities than men, reversing earlier trends. Since the great bulk of the migrants who came in each decade were in the 15 to 25 year old age group, and since over one-third of all migrants living in Lima today arrived since 1961, they also are over-represented in the workforce because they still are overwhelmingly in the economically active age group. Table 1.4 shows the migrant population of Lima by decade of arrival, while Table 1.5 gives the composition of the population by age group, comparing the Lima-born to the migrants (one caution in reading the tables: the fact that one-third of the total population of Lima is shown as dependent persons 14 years of age or younger tells us nothing about the relative fertility of the Lima-born versus the migrants, since all migrant children born after their parents arrival are, of course, "native born," i.e., counted with the children of Lima natives).

TABLE 1.4 Migrant Population of Lima Showing Decade of Arrival

Population	To 1940	1941–50	1951–60	1961–70
Total 1,249,600	217,200	248,400	348,300	435,700
percent 100	17.4	19.9	27.9	34.8

Source: Martínez, Prado, and Quintanilla, 1973, Cuadro 3, p. 21.

TABLE 1.5 Native and Migrant Population of Lima by Age

Age	Native	Migrant	Total
0–14	33.1	5.8	38.9
15–29	19.3 { 13.8	27.8 { 15.8	47.1 { 29.6
30–44	5.5	12.0	17.5
44 and over	4.1	9.9	14.0
Total	56.5	43.5	100.0

Source: Martínez, Prado, and Quintanilla, 1973: Cuadro 9, p. 35.

Not all migrants to the city come from the remotest rural areas; only about 13 percent do so (Martínez, Prado, and Quintanilla, 1973, pp. 79–80).[10] Nearly 40 percent were born either in a provincial or departmental capital. Another 45 percent, however, do come from district capitals; since these often are very small places (more than 70 percent have fewer than 600 inhabitants), then it is not inaccurate to say that the majority of migrants to Lima are rural (*ibid.*, p. 81).

The fact that large numbers of these migrants are campesinos from the Andean sierra known as the "Mancha India," literally the Indian stain or blemish, greatly affects their fate and prospects after their arrival in the city. More of my interviewees, who come from 20 of Peru's 24 *departamentos* (in Peru, the larger divisions are departamentos; the subdivisions within the departamentos, *provincias*), come from the sierra than the migrants to Lima documented in the extensive national survey of migration of Martínez, Prado, and Quintanilla (1973); some 60 percent come from there. As Table 1.6 shows, domestic servants (the same tendencies are reflected in the Smith and Figueroa Galup studies) also tend to come from more remote Andean areas. The town of Cusco, for example, accounts for the highest proportion of servants in both the Figueroa Galup and my own study, while it was thirteenth in terms of the percent of migrants it had contributed to the general population of Lima by 1970.

TABLE 1.6 Department Origin of Migrants in Two Studies of Domestic Servants, Compared to Migrants in the General Population, Lima, Peru (1970)

All migrants (male/female)				Domestics (female only)					
Martínez et al. study				Chaney study			Figueroa Galup study		
Department	Type[a]	Rank	%	Department	Rank	%	Department	Rank	%
Ancash	(TR)	1	10.3	Cusco	1	14.0	Cusco	1	14.6
Ayacucho	(S)	2	8.0	Ancash	2	10.0	Ayacucho	2	10.9
Lima	(C)	3	7.9	Arequipa	3	8.0	Ancash	3	10.3
La Libertad	(TR)	4	7.5	Ayacucho	3	8.0	Cajamarca	4	10.3
Arequipa	(S)	5	7.0	Lima*	3	8.0			
Piura	(C)	6	6.6	Apurímac	4	6.0			
Junín	(S)	7	6.3	Junín	4	6.0			
Cajamarca	(S)	8	5.5	Cajamarca	5	4.0			
Apurímac	(S)	9	5.4	Huancavelica	5	4.0			
Lambayeque	(C)	10	4.7	Huánuco	5	4.0			
Ica	(C)	11	4.6	Ica	5	4.0			
Huancavelica	(S)	12	4.2	La Libertad	5	4.0			
Cusco	(S)	13	3.9	Piura	5	4.0			
Huánuco	(S)	14	3.6	Amazonas	6	2.0			
Puno	(S)	15	3.0	Lambayeque	6	2.0			
Balance			11.5	Loreto	6	2.0			
				Pasco	6	2.0			
				Puno	6	2.0			
				San Martín	6	2.0			
				Tacna	6	2.0			
				Unknown	6	2.0			
Totals			100.0			100.0			

*Lima department; three interviewees from Lima city.

[a]*Source*: Martínez, Prado, and Quintanilla 1973, Cuadro 32, p. 75. (Note: TR = transitional department; S = sierra department; C = coastal department)

Many fewer women born in Lima become domestic servants; indeed, there is a marked tendency for women migrants themselves to make a distinction between work for serranas and work for Limeñas (for hillbillies and women native to Lima). "Soy serrana, y por eso soy empleada—I'm from the mountains, and so I'm a servant" is a typical phrase, while the three coastal women who are among the domestic servant interviewees in this study are ashamed to say what work they do. "This work is for little hill girls," one explains. Figueroa Galup remarks that representatives of the coastal or jungle areas of Peru among Lima's domestic servants are few.

Of the domestic servants in Lima, 80 percent are migrants (Vargas de Balmaceda 1981, p. 1), and by this calculation are somewhat underrepresented in my study and the one by Figueroa Galup. Vargas de Balmaceda's estimates may be a little high. Jelin (1977, p. 133) documents the proportions between migrants and city-born women among household workers for other Latin American cities, showing a similar pattern. In Bogotá, the percentage is around 85 (García Castro 1982, p. 108).

For the past 40 years, the migration pattern for both women and men has been the "salto directo" (literally, "direct jump"), that is, the migrant has set out directly for Lima from his or her place of origin. This has been the tendency no matter whether the place were a remote sierra village, an intermediate-sized town, or a provincial capital (Martínez, Prado, and Quintanilla 1973, p. 55). Women are slightly more inclined than men to go directly to Lima, probably reflecting their perception that their employment possibilities are even more restricted in the provinces than in the capital. In Martínez, Prado, and Quintanilla (1973, Table 19, p. 60), only 26.6 percent of the women had first tried out another place, and had worked outside the home before migrating to Lima. My *domésticas* match this national sample almost exactly: 27.6 percent had made intermediate stops on their way to Lima, usually only one. Of those who did stop, in every case but one they worked for a time in the district or provincial capital nearest to their home. Macisco (1975, pp. 68–69) found that three-quarters of the women who had worked as domestic servants before their arrival in Lima had gotten their experience in relatively small towns.[11]

About one-half of the women in my survey group come from agricultural families; most of their fathers farmed (and many still do) a small subsistence plot or, in several cases, were attached to haciendas. Of Figueroa Galup's domésticas, 39 percent had campesino parents (1983, p. 14). Hewett (1974, p. 3) also found that half of her domésticas were daughters of agriculturalists. So far as other occupations of parents are concerned, among the fathers of my interviewees there are several chauffeurs, construction workers, and laborers, plus a miner, street vendor, policeman, hotel busboy, stevedore, two weavers (of sweaters and ponchos), and a member of an Andean *conjunto* (band). Figueroa Galup's fathers, in contrast, included a few professionals (a judge, a justice of the peace, and a teacher); this is understandable, she says, when one takes into account the high rates of illegitimacy in the sierra (*ibid.*).

Although 34 percent of their own mothers are reported by my interviewees also to work or to have worked in agricultural tasks, another large percentage (22 percent) are said to have been housewives only. It is highly probable, however, that many of the mothers also engage regularly in farm labor. Only six mothers of interviewees had been domestic servants. The others are reported as "occupation unknown"; in 7 cases this is because the mother died, or abandoned the interviewee in her early life.

Over one-quarter of the father's occupations (and/or present residence) are unknown to the respondents; Figueroa Galup, (1983, p. 14), who observed the same ignorance about their fathers among her interviewees, believes that this accurately reflects the disconnection that often ensues after some years, in spite of the fact that many migrant women try to preserve their links to their "tierra" (literally, "land"—the popular name for one's province of origin). Among my own group of domésticas, well over one-half have never journeyed back to their native towns, or have only gone once, a fact that would seem to belie the notion that servants return frequently enough to become role models or even change agents in their own rural communities (Smith 1971, pp. 402–10). Of the interviewees, 16 indicate they go home with some regularity, and the remainder either are Limeñas (3) or did not respond to this question.

One reason many domésticas do not visit their tierra more often is that many live in places separated from Lima by at least two or three days' journey on an inter-provincial bus; the fare represents a large sum for servants, a crucial ingredient in their decision to postpone and postpone again a trip home. Distance is only one factor; there is also the fear servants (quite justifiably) have of losing their jobs if they go off on vacation. Some patronas routinely hire replacements for vacationing maids because they do not want to bother taking on temporary household help.

The greater number of ambulantes who visit their tierra (see Chapter 2, p. 91) may be explained by the fact that they have more freedom than domésticas, and will not lose their posts if they are away for a few weeks.

Contact with one's native place may, however, be preserved in other ways; it is the rare servant who does not have at least some "familias" (many use the plural term to mean both near and distant relatives) in the city. Most often these do not include parents; in both the Figueroa Galup sample and in my own group, parents most often did not follow a daughter to the city. Of nine with one or both parents in Lima, eight had come to the capital with their families as small children. Of the household workers in my group, ten have brothers and/or sisters in the city; seven, uncles and/or aunts, and four have other relatives. Only 12 of the 50 are completely alone in the city without any "familias."

Links also are kept alive through the provincial clubs and through the folkloric dances and other social events held in the Lima Coliseum or in the Campo de Marte (a large, open park in Jesús-María, one of the lower middle-class districts of Lima). Only one of my own group (all, it must be remembered are mothers) frequents any of these gatherings, but evidence from other studies shows that many maids without children do so.

Finally, even if not as many migrants do go directly to the barriadas or marginal shantytowns on their arrival in Lima, as once was supposed [only 10 percent of my interviewees and 12.7 percent of Figueroa Galup's (1983, p. 11) first went to live and/or work in a barriada], almost all aspire one day to acquire their own *terreno* (building lot) there; one-half of my 50 interviewees already have a stake in land either on their own, with their *compañero* (male companion), or relatives (see Chapter 3). Migrants gravitate to marginal areas of the city when they are ready to build, often seeking out relatives or friends from their home province in order to cushion the worst features of city life. Lomnitz (1975) has demonstrated that this penetration of the city by groups of campesinos who hang onto their cultural values is, in fact, from the migrants' perspective not regressive, but an adaptive strategy for survival in a new environment that provides no welfare, unemployment insurance, adequate health care or day-care facilities. As my chief informant, Hermalinda, put it one day, "When we don't have anything to eat, we go down to my uncle's or down to my sister's to eat." ("Down" is literal for Hermalinda. As one of the latest invaders, she lives near the top of the hillside, about a half-hour's walk to her sister's house near the highway.)

The poor have thus outwitted those development experts who saw the extended family as a brake on change, and the nuclear family as the ideal. The constant demand that what one earned should be shared with kin, it was thought, would prevent the poor from accumulating savings. Instead, the importation of the rural world to the city, including the continued existence of the extended family, may be the key to why the poor are able to survive in the city against such terrible odds.

Macisco (1975, pp. 64–68) points out that the employment situation of migrants before they set out for the city gives certain insights into their economic situation and, indirectly, their motives for moving to the city. In his own study of migrants to Lima, he found that 60 percent of the male, but only 25 percent of the female migrants had been employed before arriving in the city (although he cautions that many more women might have been looking for work in their home place). Of the latter, 37 percent had worked, chiefly in the small towns, as domestic servants. Immediately before setting out to Lima, however, 80 percent of the males were unemployed.

My own group is not typical in that 21 of the 47 women migrants *had* worked before coming to the city (and 18 of these had done domestic service of some kind). Three did other work: one hauled potatoes, put to work when she was only five years old, and two helped their mothers sell fruits and vegetables. In addition, many say they helped their parents on the small landholding, although the most typical answer of those who had no outside paid employment is "helped my mother in the house." My group also is atypical in that most migrated at a very early age specifically to become domestic servants (the median age of first job in Lima is 12 years old). Among both men and women, those in the younger age group (20 to 24) are much more likely to be single, and to arrive in Lima unaccompanied by relatives [except for the madrina or "god-mother," or *tía* (aunt) who often brings a young girl to the city to go into domestic service; this recruitment system is described below]. Men and women in the 25 to 34 year old age group are most often accompanied by both spouse and children; one interesting finding in the Macisco study (1975, pp. 65–66), however, is that a fairly large number of older women came to Lima with children but without husbands.

Most of my domésticas come from large families; the average number of children in their natal families is 5.6. As in Hewett's study (1974, p. 3), birth order appears to have little to do with migration; about one-third of my group are the eldest in the family, another third are middle children, and the final third are the youngest. Sometimes an elder daughter had to wait until a younger sister could take over the care of the smaller children in the family before she could migrate.

Hewett (*ibid.*, pp. 70–72) disagrees with Boserup's (1970, p. 187) notion that fathers send their daughters to town to work as domestic servants because there is not enough to occupy them in their native place. Women, she says, can keep busy because female tasks are always plentiful: the preparation of food; washing and caring for the clothing; looking after the animals; helping with the ploughing, sowing, and harvesting, as well as collecting firewood, carrying water, and looking after the younger children. Why, then, do they leave if they have plenty of useful work at home?

It is true that women in the countryside, single and married, young and old, are engaged in productive work. Indeed, because of the heavy out-migration of men, there often is a shortage of laboring hands in rural areas. However, several recent studies indicate that even when women do engage in productive labor, they do not necessarily gain control over their earnings even when their men are absent. Often when husbands migrate, they leave their affairs and land in the hands of male relatives who do not migrate.

Unmarried daughters could keep busy enough in the countryside, but they are the least likely to earn either recognition or wages for their work. It has been suggested that rural families may encourage their daughters to go to the city not only to earn cash, part of which they expect to be sent back to help the family, but also because the basic subsistence needs of the young women for food and shelter will be covered (Jelin 1977, p. 136). Since my interviewees all need their wages for their children, my own data do not give many hints about whether daughters do, in fact, send significant remittances back home. Several say that they did so in the past. Considering the difficulties in communication and the unreliability of the mails in Peru, it seems doubtful that much money gets back on a regular basis, even from maids who are single. What does happen is that the young woman going to her tierra on a visit saves up so that she can take with her the many gifts she will be expected to bring.

In recent years, increasing attention has been given to the negative effects of urbanization on women's economic, social, and political status. When women migrate to the city, many of their productive functions are taken away, to be carried out in factories, food processing plants, laundries, and dry cleaning establishments. Even their primary role in providing their family's educational, health, and recreational needs, is drastically reduced. The argument is made that women in preindustrial hunting and gathering societies, as well as in peasant cultures, have a more equal, if still secondary status because their contributions to the household economy are so crucial—and are recognized as such.

This view is tempered by other studies that show it is not the amount of work women do that determines their status, but the extent to which they control resources and earnings. Several recent studies on women in peasant communities, two of them on women in the Peruvian sierra (Bourque and Warren 1982; Deere 1977) argue that concern over women's greatly diminished participation in production under modern Western capitalism has been accompanied by a tendency to romanticize and idealize the women's position in precapitalist modes of production. As Deere (1977, pp. 52–55) documents the women's situation in Cajamarca, Peru, the appropriation of women's labor time only appeared less severe than the appropriation of the time of the male sharecropper on the hacienda. Besides the obligation of serving, by turn, two to four weeks in the hacendado's house (which oftentimes meant cooking for 20 to 30 workers, a task requiring the women to rise at 3:00 a.m. to begin the long process of grinding the maize for the noonday meal), the women also often had permanent charge, assisted by the children, of the hacienda's animals. As well, they were on call to help out in *mingas* (work parties), for example, to shuck the hacienda corn. Additionally, they could be required to grind and prepare the corn or barley flour for the hacendado's house, make chicha (a fermented corn drink), butter, cheese, and often were expected to spin the hacienda wool into thread.

For Deere (1977), the situation of women under modernization thus remains contradictory:

> That the transition from servile to capitalist relations of production should both improve and deteriorate the socioeconomic condition of the women directly and indirectly involved, is the logical outcome of an uneven process of social and economic change.
>
> For the mass of rural women who rid themselves of servile obligations, principally the unlimited commitment of their labor time, there is an absolute decrease in the potential and effective length of the working day as the surplus labor time which was appropriated by the hacendado is eliminated. It was noted, however, that women's servile obligations were the last to be done away with, either as wife or as worker.
>
> For the women who are proletarianized with the development of capitalism, the form of exploitation changes, but continues, as the value of what they produce in the production process is appropriated by the nascent capitalist class. There is little doubt, however, that the wage relationship is superior to the unlimited demand on women's time which took place under servile relations of production. The most important advances for women's work are the right to remuneration and the right to legal recourse for abuses of the length of the working day (Deere 1977, p. 66).

The Bourque-Warren and Deere studies both note how women's prestige and power did increase in community affairs in two rural areas of Peru from which men had migrated in such numbers that there was no alternative to women's assuming some degree of control over the land and even taking on political responsibilities. However, Bourque and Warren (1976, p. 95) conclude that, even so, "the critical nature of women's contribution to the economic unit is not sufficient to accord her an equivalent place with men in the enjoyment of wealth and status in the community."

Under these conditions, it is not difficult to understand why women desire to leave the countryside and go to the city. For younger women such as those in my interview group, there is no question about their chief motive for leaving home: the desire to work in paid employment; the decision to go directly to Lima reflects this. Not only is Lima perceived to be the center of opportunity, but for women and men alike the shrinking opportunities in the countryside, coupled with population growth, mean that the decision to seek employment "almost automatically carries with it the decision to migrate" (Figueroa Galup 1983, p. 9).

Only one of my doméstica group arrived in Lima on a lark; she came with relatives who visited the city after the harvest and decided to stay behind. Seven other migrated, most at an early age, with their natal families, and one recent migrant had come with her husband after the earthquake in the Central Sierra. Another three fled maltreatment: one the sexual advances of her stepfather after her mother's death, and the other two the beatings of their male "employers" to whom their mothers had given them at the ages of seven and ten years. Many sierra families, it should be pointed out, give away their children because they cannot afford to take care of them, and hope they will have some opportunity in the city. Several of my interviewees came to Lima because they were pregnant and the need to work was particularly urgent:

> *Alicia*: I had separated from my husband because he ran off with another women. That was the reason I came to Lima. In the sierra I couldn't support myself, my husband didn't give me anything. I came alone. . . .
>
> *Victoria*: I came to Lima with the señora's aunt (the aunt of her future employer). I came because I had my baby, and it seemed to me hard to raise it there, so I asked the señora to bring me, and she brought me.
>
> *Edelmira*: I came with a señora from Lima, I came because I didn't have anything. I didn't have the means to support my little

son. I didn't have anything, my husband went off with another woman. I came here when I was two months pregnant.

The remaining 35 of my interviewees who migrated came with the intention of working. Revealing is the fact that only three mention that they also came with the hope of combining study with work:

Eusebia: I wanted to work and to earn a little more.

Regina: I came because I wanted to work, my parents were poor, and I wanted to earn something. As a matter of fact, we're working now to observe my father's anniversary, to celebrate a mass on the first anniversary of my father's death.

Hermalinda: My aunt brought me in order to work. Because up there I was studying, and my parents didn't have any money to buy my school notebooks, you see? And so they sent me here to work and to find out if it was possible to continue studying and working.

Emilia: I came with the señora who brought me here to work for her. I was 15 years old then, and the señora put a pile of ideas in my head. She told me that life was better here, and I came with the illusion of earning money.

One-half of the migrants (24 of 47) in my group already had their positions as domestic servants assured before they arrived in Lima because they came with their madrinas; the 3 Limeñas also were placed in their first jobs by their madrinas. It is common for city women who have rural connections to go to the provinces to recruit very young girls to work for themselves and their friends; two-thirds of the 27 who were sponsored were 11 years old or younger at the time they were put to work. In times past, servants from a provincial hacienda or "big house" were promoted to serve in their employers' Lima residences. These young women travel to the capital with the tías (aunts, in most cases a title of courtesy only), their future patrons, or their madrinas. Godmothers are the female sponsors at baptism and marriage, but the term often is used for any women who "adopts" a little girl and initiates her into the servant role. Sometimes the adoption is formalized, and several of my interviewees spoke of the "paper" that had been executed, providing that the girl would work as a domestic servant in exchange for her education and upbringing or *crianza* (and thus, later, the term criada became synonymous with servant maid, although the meaning of the word is broader).[12] Ten of the other interviewees secured their first positions through relatives, or through friends and teachers (six cases). Only six found their first jobs through the impersonal sign on the door, "Se necesita muchacha" (Maid needed), or through an agency. One woman found her job by consulting a policeman in the neighborhood where she wanted to work.

Hardly any of my group migrated alone, and this is the standard pattern; as Hewett (1974, p. 88) observes, the notion that prostitutes are recruited among innocents who arrive at the inter-provincial bus stations probably is a myth. While we know little of the history of prostitutes, the scant evidence suggests that women may turn to prostitution as other job opportunities are closed. "The life," however, simply is not open to many migrant women at any stage, since indigenous women are not perceived as attractive. What our evidence does show (confirmed by Figueroa Galup's 1983 study, p. 11) is that girls rarely leave their native villages without sponsorship:

> *Alberta I*: I came practically alone in the company of an aunt, or rather, a señora. I grew up abandoned, without a family. My mother gave me to Señor _____ at 7 years of age, and he abused me badly.
>
> *Carmen*: I came with an aunt, the sister of a señora of San Martín. I arrived in San Martín (a Lima suburb) from my province with an aunt, well, not really a relative, but I'll call her "aunt" anyhow. My mother sent me. I came by means of a paper that was signed by the civil guard, you see, a document or something like that. My mother knew the family.
>
> *Alberta II*: I was at the hacienda, and the señora (the owner) ran into me there. I met her and she talked to me about coming, and then talked to my mother . . . I didn't live with my father, he lived on another hacienda.
>
> *Barbara*: I spent my childhood in Sicuani, but when I was 9 I went to Arequipa. My madrina raised me, she didn't put me in school. I helped her out in everything, and for this reason, I haven't studied.
>
> *Faustina*: I went to Arequipa when I was 7 years old to be with a married sister. And from there when I was about 11 years old a señora kidnapped me and brought me to Lima.

Girls who come to Lima are put to work at an early age. The median age is 12 years old for the 50 women in my group, but the 27 who were recruited for their first employment by their madrinas started work at a median age of only 11 years. Typically, the women arrived with little education; by the time of the survey some had managed to advance somewhat; a further discussion of the women's educational experiences and aspirations is more properly included in the next section. Once she arrives in the capital, the young woman is immediately taken to her new home. Almost all work as live-in maids at first. The next section explores in detail what happens to the young maid servant in Lima.

THE DOMESTIC SERVANT IN THE LIMA LABOR MARKET

There are good reasons for migrants to go directly to Lima; the city is not only perceived to be, but is the center of whatever opportunity exists in Peru—not only for work, hopefully steady work in a factory, but for education, health care, housing, and other amenities of modern life that have become the aspirations of the poor throughout the world.

Almost three-quarters (71.6 percent) of the industrial establishments employing five or more persons are located in Lima-Callao, and 65 percent of all industrial workers in Peru are employed in the greater Lima metropolitan area. In 1970, 90 percent of banking, 65 percent of retail trade, and one-half of the national wealth were centered in Lima (Weiss 1976, p. 22).

Many studies show that what migrants most want is a factory job. Some succeed in finding one; while almost two-thirds of the economically active residents of Lima are immigrants, 73 percent of the industrial labor force is made up of migrants, confirming again the now well-established demographic fact that migration, until recently, was selective, that is, the most capable and energetic persons tended to migrate. The high success rate of migrants versus natives in the industrial manufacturing sector must be interpreted in the light of two facts: the small size of the sector and its relative stagnation and the consequent restricted opportunities for migrants and natives alike to find jobs in industry.

It is true that during the 1960s and 1970s the economically active population in metropolitan Lima grew slightly faster than the overall population. But it is important to note the sectors in which workers find job opportunities and to estimate the degree, not so much of outright unemployment, as of disguised unemployment and underemployment, and of income differentials.

Even though the industrial sector in Peru has grown, it is very weak, even incipient (Suárez 1975, p. 28). As has often been noted, some urban blue-collar activities classified as "modern" pay less than some jobs in the urban traditional sector. Productive capacity is centered mainly in soft and intermediate goods. While these sectors are indeed labor-intensive, still the capacity of the industrial manufacturing sector overall has been too limited to absorb the tremendous numbers of both native Limeneans and migrants who would like to work in it.

Moreover, Suárez (1975, p. 4) has characterized at least 60 percent of industrial manufacturing activities as "artesenal" in character, that is carried on in very small workshops with rudimentary equipment. Coupled to the large numbers of people who are forced into unproductive service occupations and street vending, she estimates that these workers accounted for an incredible 42 percent rate of un- and underemployment in metropolitan Lima in the mid-1970s.

Table 1.7 shows how the industrial labor force is distributed, contrasting Lima workers to workers in the rest of the country by present occupation and place of birth. Table 1.8 shows the distribution of natives and migrants in the industrial, manufacturing, and other sectors by sex. The tables do not reveal the thousands upon thousands of migrants who cannot find the urban job of their dreams, but survive by picking up a few days' casual work here and there, mainly in construction, or who are underemployed in one of the many jobs that have proliferated in recent years in the service sector.[13]

TABLE 1.7 Peruvian Industrial Labor Force: Location of Present Occupation by Place of Birth

Regions/(born in)	Presently working in Lima	
Lima	Natives	27%
	North	22
	Center	37
	South	14
	East	—
		100
Country	Presently working in:	
	Lima	65
	North	10
	Center	12
	South	9
	East	4
		100

Source: República del Perú 1975; Vol. 1, Cuadro 11–16, p. 75.

TABLE 1.8 Natives and Migrants by Economic Activity and Sex, Lima and Eight Principal Peruvian Cities[a]

	Lima				Eight cities			
	Natives		Migrants		Natives		Migrants	
	Men	Women	Men	Women	Men	Women	Men	Women
Industrial manufacturing	27.3	25.7	35.6	16.6	27.8	23.5	29.0	15.4
Construction	5.0	1.4	7.1	—	9.6	0.2	10.5	0.3
Commerce	24.4	17.7	20.6	22.2	21.5	28.2	18.2	27.6
Transport	11.0	2.8	8.6	0.6	9.2	1.6	9.1	0.8
Services	27.3	40.4	23.7	26.0	22.9	35.1	23.5	24.9
Domestic service	1.3	10.5	1.4	33.2	—	8.4	1.6	27.3
Others[b]	3.7	1.5	3.0	1.4	9.0	3.0	8.1	3.7

Source: Martínez, Prado, and Quintanilla, 1973, Cuadro 83, p. 171.
[a]Trujillo, Chiclayo, Piura, Arequipa, Cusco, Puno, Iquitos, and Lima.
[b]Agriculture, mining, and energy.

What the last table does reveal is the fact, central to our study, that the industrial labor force is dominated by male migrants. The industrial sector itself is 86 percent masculine. Not only do many more male than female migrants find opportunities in the industrial sector, but the relatively small size and low absorptive capacity of industrial manufacturing also has the effect of pushing men into the better-paid, more secure service jobs, thus forcing women into the lower echelons of the tertiary sector, and specifically into domestic service and street vending. In other words, women migrants have almost no opportunity to land factory jobs; at the same time, the condition of the Lima labor market means that the opportunities are also restricted for women because they are competing with men for jobs in the service sector. [In Latin America as a whole (Arizpe 1975, p. 42), 64.5 percent of the working women are in the service sector, yet they constitute only 34.1 percent of service workers, and are overwhelmingly in domestic service.] (In Peru, the figures are 68 percent and 38.7 percent, respectively, for 1970.) Thus, Arizpe contends that "male labor that should in theory have entered industrial employment, has instead pressured the sector which in developing countries is predominantly female: the services."

It must also be remembered that while 16 percent of migrant women who work are in industrial manufacturing in Peru, female factory workers tend to cluster in the smaller establishments or function as piece-workers in their own homes (Sara Lafosse 1981). A study of the occupational status of men and women in nonprofessional jobs, chiefly in the service sector, shows that there is one woman for every two men; however, if the lowest status jobs are taken into consideration, then there are two women for every man (COTREM 1974, p. 2).

It is true that both women and men migrants share common disadvantages related to their indigenous background, their rural origin, and their lack of skills and education. Moreover, both sexes suffer from the same disadvantage that they were not socialized to city ways; this makes it difficult for them to compete for the scarce jobs with those who were born and/or grew up in Lima.

Yet women and men do not start out exactly equal when they compete for jobs in the Lima labor market. The female/male ratio of percent literate in 1972 was 0.65, that is, there were only 65 literate women for each 100 literate men in Peru (Chaney 1984, Table 4.1, p. 56).

Many women when they arrive in Lima speak only their native Quechua or Aymará, while most men know at least the rudiments of the Spanish language; it is the male who traditionally deals with the dominant society, insofar as the indigenous family has been obliged to do so at all. Many Amer-Indian men also have served in the armed forces where they learned to read and write.

Another disadvantage of women in the Lima labor market, as was noted above, is the fact that women lack opportunity in the city. Modernization and urbanization tend to segment the job market ever more rigidly into a relatively wide range of "male" occupations in both the modern and traditional sectors, and a much narrower range of "female" occupations, mostly in the traditional sector. Overall, 19 percent of all Peruvian women who are ten years of age and over are in the labor force, but only 8.4 percent of persons in higher administrative and managerial posts (governmental and nongovernmental) are women (COTREM 1974, p. 2). In nonprofessional occupations, however, the proportion of women rises to 32.5 percent. A young woman from the provinces consequently has hardly any choice but to go to work as a domestic servant, and 42 percent of female migrants 14 to 29 years of age were found in this occupation at the time of the survey (Martínez, Prado, and Quintanilla, 1973, p. 170).

In the interview group, a wider range of ages is represented, with interviewees aged 18 to 49 years, although nearly one-half of the women are below the age of 25. Other characteristics of the survey group at the time of the study are as follows: median years of education are three years of primary schooling. Two-fifths of the survey group have served less than 1 year in their present post, and another 15 have served only 1 to 2 years, although the median number of years in Lima is 13. They work in 28 different barrios of the city (which, for the purposes of this study have been stratified in five socioeconomic groups): 28 are maids-of-all-work, 11 are laundresses, 10 are cooks, and 1 works as a fulltime seamstress for a single family. Median number of households interviewees have worked in is four, with a range of one to ten-plus employments. Table 1.9 shows the interviewees by specialty and type of barrio where they work.

TABLE 1.9 Interview Group by Specialty and Where Employed

Barrio	Maid-of-all-work	Cook	Laundress	Other
Upper-upper	2	3	1	
Upper-middle	11	2	2	1
Middle	8	2	3	
Upper-lower	5	2	2	
Lower	2	1	3	
Totals	28	10	11	1

Barrios are classified as follows: Upper-upper: La Encantada, La Planicie, Monterrico, San Antonio, San Borja; upper-middle: Chaclacayo, Miraflores, Orrantia, Santa Cruz, San Isidro; Middle: Breña, Chorrillos, Ingenería, Jesús-María, Lince, Magdalena, Pueblo Libre, Surquillo; upper-lower: Barrios Altos, Chota, La Victoria, Lima Centro, Rimac; lower: Atacongo, Canto Grande, Ciudad de Dios, Huerta Perdida, San Juan de Miraflores.

So far as the interview group is concerned, their employment histories demonstrate that women do not easily break out of the servant role once they are in it (except for the transition, already mentioned, from servants to sellers). Only 11 of the women had ever tried anything other than domestic service after arriving in the city, and for all but 1, their forays into other fields were one-time-only experiences. Two tried work in factories, both short-lived employments (one replaced a vacationing friend for two weeks, hoping to be taken on herself, and the other was in an apprenticeship program for one week). Two became street sellers for short periods, one of chicha, and the other of toasted peanuts. Three worked in restaurants as waitresses and dishwashers. One was employed in a nursing home, and another as a helper in a beauty salon. There was only one domestic servant who had more than one employment outside a household; Carmen, a 26-year-old (presently with two children), who has been in Lima for eight years and has completed primary schooling, worked (in addition to her employment as cook and laundress in five to six houses), as a seamstress in a small factory, a helper in the Parque de Leyendas (a children's amusement park), a vendor of prepared meals, and a cleaner in a supermarket.

Occupational histories also confirm that not a single interviewee has been able to dedicate herself to one specialty *within* domestic service, that is, to remain exclusively a cook, ama, etc. as she moved from job to job. Many mention with nostalgia the time when a household helper was hired to "do only one thing," when there were many more large establishments with multiple servants than today. Nevertheless, 45 percent of the interviewees are in situations with at least one other household worker; in households in the two upper and upper-middle-class districts, 56 percent have more than one servant, while in the other three middle to lower-class districts, only 36 percent work with another servant.

Within the interview group, cooks are the most specialized, but they now are often called upon to perform other duties as well. The kitchen had been the one place where a domestic might exercise some degree of autonomy over her schedule, and some degree of creativity. Moreover, as Agripina puts it, "In the kitchen, one eats well, and it's more peaceful there." Now "you end up doing anything and everything, even when you enter (a house) as the cook," says Eusebia. Juana adds that patronas "hire you for one thing, but in reality they make you do everything." Domitila, a cook, says that she will do laundry or pitch in on other tasks "when they ask me please to attend to it."

As to what they would rather be doing within the domestic service field, 22 of the 50 say they like cooking best—by far the favorite occupation (these include 8 of the present cooks, 10 of the maids-of-all-work, and 4 of the laundresses). Maid-of-all-work is desired by only 9 of the 28 who already are doing it, and by no one else. Of the 11 laundresses, 4 want to continue that specialty, but only because they have discovered what is not general knowledge, even among domestic servants themselves: laundresses can earn more than those in other occupations. Of the others, two want to sew (including one who already is a full-time seamstress); one wants to be an ama, and one wants to "work where the family is considerate." Ten do not know that they would rather be doing.

What do the women earn in domestic service? Pay is low, understandable because so many uneducated, very young women are available. For the survey group, the median pay is 1,500 soles* per month, with a range of 0 to 4,000 soles per month, or U.S. $1.29 per day, if a weekly *salida* or holiday is allowed. In 1975, the living wage in Peru was set at 3,000 soles per month. Only 14 percent of the interview group received 3,000 soles or above. Vargas de Balmaceda (1981, p. 7), calculating wages and payment in kind, arrives at a proportion of 49 percent of domésticas who receive the living wage or better in a survey conducted in 1975 by the Ministry of Labor. But she adds that not all household workers receive the same type of nonmonetary remuneration, nor have the same work hours or working conditions. If maids do not have a day off, or go out only once or twice a month, their daily salary rate is, of course, proportionately lower.

Patronas justify low wages because, they say, maids and their children receive food, clothing, shelter, and other benefits in kind. There is a rough correlation in the survey group between those who receive 1,000 soles or less in wages and live in (*cama adentro*), and those who receive 2,500 soles or more, almost all of whom live outside the patronal home (*cama afuera*). Table 1.10 shows the salaries earned by live-in, live-out status.

TABLE 1.10 Household Workers by Wages and Live-in, Live-out Status

Wages	Live-in	Live-out
1,000 soles and less	8	4
1,200–2,300 soles	11	16
2,500 soles or more	2	8
Unknown		1

There are a few other correlations. As the Table 1.11 shows, starting pay is not uniform—those with less than one year of service are almost evenly divided between those receiving less than the

*The *sol* (plural: soles) was valued with the time our study at 43.16 to one U.S. dollar.

median wage and those receiving the median wage or above. Nevertheless, with length of service, there is a tendency for domesticas in the interview group to receive at least the 1,500 soles median salary.

TABLE 1.11 Wages by Length of Service (in the same household)

Wages	Less than one year	One to two years	Three years or more	No reply
Less than 1,500 soles	11	5	4	
1,500 soles or above	9	10	9	1
Unknown				1

Curiously, prior experience in other houses does not appear to count for much in the interview group, in that less than the median wage is being earned by 42 percent of the 31 women with experience in 4 or more houses; in other words, there is little chance of bettering one's salary by gaining experience in moves from household to household. Table 1.12 shows salaries by the number of positions held.

TABLE 1.12 Wages by Number of Positions Held

Wages	First employment	One house	Two houses	Three houses	Four or more	No Reply
Less than 1,500 soles	1	1	3	2	13	
1,500 soles or above	1	3	4	3	18	
Unknown						1

There is a strong belief that better salaries are paid in the more affluent districts, and there does appear to be some basis for such a notion in relation to these particular interviewees. Of the 22 who work in the 2 more exclusive neighborhoods, 17 receive the median salary of above, while only 12 of the 27 who work in the other 3 barrios earn 1,500 soles or more. Interestingly, 5 of the 6 servants in the poorest neighborhoods also earn the median or better.

The real surprise, at least among these 50 cases, is the fact that cooks do not earn the highest salaries, contrary to general belief;

three-quarters of the interviewees say that cooking pays the best of any domestic service specialty. Cooking may be the preferred occupation for so many not only because, as was suggested above, the women perceive it as the one domestic service occupation in which they may gain some measure of autonomy, but also because of the mistaken idea that cooks earn more. While this interview group is too small to generalize on salaries throughout the Lima metropolitan area, it is the laundresses in the present study who are the top income earners. For the interview group, the average wage for cooks is 1,630 soles per month; maids-of-all-work average 1,375 soles, but laundresses in the survey group earn an average of 2,500 soles.

Washing and ironing as a permanent occupation is hard and unpleasant work; nevertheless, calculating a monthly salary at the daily rate charged by the laundresses among the interviewees results in most of them being at the top of the salary scale.[14] Of the laundresses in the survey only two realize that laundry potentially pays better: "I prefer to be a laundress because you earn more," says one. The going rate for laundresses is 60 or 70 to 150 soles per day, depending upon the amount of clothes. A laundress thus can earn 2,500 to 3,000 soles per month, and have two days off per week. Again, it must be emphasized that the work is very hard, and not all women have the strength to wash and iron every day. Of the 11 laundresses in the survey, 5 do their work by hand, as no washing machine is provided, and only 1 patrona has both a washer and a drier. Yolanda says that, at times, "I can't continue. I ache all over, and I am damp through and through." Table 1.13 shows what the interviewees earn, by specialty.

TABLE 1.13 Wages by Specialty within Domestic Service

Wages	Maid-of-all-work	Cook	Laundress	Other
Less than 1,500 soles	15	3	2	
1,500–2,500 soles	13	6	2	1
3,000–4,000 soles		1	6	
Unknown			1	

Before leaving the subject of salaries, a word should be said about those who receive no pay for their work. Among the interviewees, there is only one currently in this position. María I, who is 28 years old, came to the house of the employer for whom she still works at the age of 11 and has never received a salary. The señora, María says, always claims that María is just like a family member, and has everything she wants and needs. It is difficult for persons not acquainted with the servant situation to understand the passivity and fear of a woman like María who to this day has never gotten up the courage to demand a wage or to look for another position, although she long ago realized that other servants *do* receive a salary, and she would like to earn one herself. Although she continues to live in, María has managed to form a stable union and has one child. What María receives she calls "propinas" or tips, a common recompense for younger servants just beginning their work life, and still found here and there among older women. María says:

> Well, they don't pay me anything, I don't earn anything. The señora buys my clothes, shoes, and apart from that, sometimes gives me a tip. Every month she gives me ... sometimes 500 soles, sometimes 200 or 300, according to what she has. Well, I am happy here because I have become accustomed to the house, and she is good to me and she also loves my little boy.

But María also says that she would have liked to study hairdressing, and several times during the interview reiterated that she would like to be paid, "even if it were only 1,000 soles a month so that I could buy what my son needs."

Younger servants often are not paid a regular salary in their first years of work. It is assumed that they are amply recompensed by receiving food, clothing, and shelter while they learn their trade and the ways of Lima. Among my interviewees, it was typical to receive no more than 200–400 soles for a first job ($5 to $9 per month). These tips recall Ariés (1962: 396) observation that in earlier centuries servants were not paid, but rewarded.

> *Barbara*: Well, I came here when I was already big, I came at about 15 or 16 years of age. I realized that I ought to be earning something since my madrina didn't pay me anything (she worked from the age of 9 in Arequipa with her madrina). I didn't know any better and for that reason I came. A señora gave me my bus fare and her address, and that was how I came, and that was in San Isidro.

To earn their meager salaries, long hours are required of domésticas. Perhaps one of the most difficult features of the household worker's day is the necessity to rise early, and to stay up very late. The hour of awakening is 5:30 or 6:00 a.m. in most cases, and earlier for some live-outs. Most servants are on duty until the cleaning up and putting away from the evening meal are completed, after which many face a long bus ride home. Because they must care for their own children, often in stolen moments, between their household duties or late at night after returning to their own homes, their days are long. It is not uncommon for live-in servant to be obliged to wait up for a household member who is out in order to open and close the gate for the car, or simply because family members do not always remember to carry house keys and it is convenient to have someone at hand to unbolt the front gate and door.

The median number of hours worked each day for the interview groups is 11.5, with a range of 5 to 6 hours, to 17, 18, and even a 19-hour day. Those who earn the larger salaries have a longer average work day than the median, 12.1 hours per day. Average hours worked do not change greatly from specialty to specialty, except for laundresses, who work an average of only eight hours day, well under the median. Nor does the average change by barrio in any systematic fashion.

Rest is important in a long workday, and it is the custom that a servant have an hour or two in the middle of the day, particularly if she is a live-in who is expected to cook and serve an evening meal, likely to be almost as elaborate as the large mid-day meal that is standard in every affluent Peruvian home. Two-fifths of the maids in the survey customarily receive a rest period during the workday, two-fifths never have any rest, and the others rest sometimes. There is not any particular pattern: those in the lower salary brackets are as evenly divided among those who can rest and those who have no rest period, as those in the higher–waged group. Nor is the privilege more common to the better residential neighborhoods than to the poorer ones. Specialty does have a definite effect, at least for these interviewees, on opportunity for a daily rest period; while only one-half of the maids-of-all-work have time off during the day, three-quarters of the cooks do. Live-in maids often cannot use their time off for personal relaxation and recreation, in any case, because they are busy washing, ironing, feeding, and caring for their own children in their free time (in Chapter 3, the strategies for fitting childcare into the workday are described in more detail). When maids do get free time, they report that they use it to knit, read magazines, or catch up on sleep. Two do their school homework during their rest period.

Besides requiring that servants be granted 8 hours of rest in each 24, the law also provides 24 hours of rest each week; that is, the employee is supposed to be able to leave the patronal house at whatever day and hour have been agreed upon, and to be absent overnight, arriving back to the place of work at the same hour the following day. Other than the laundresses, most of whom do not work a full week and also control their own weekends, there are 39 women who have the right to a weekly salida; however, only 21 report that they receive their weekly free day (in 2 cases, maids get the weekend off). Others get their day off twice a month, monthly, or in 5 cases, not at all. Again, cooks have the advantage, in that 8 of the 10 have their weekly holiday, while only one-half of the 28 maids-of-all-work do.

Sometimes household workers do not take advantage of the weekly salida, even when it is extended. A few use the time to catch up on tasks related to their own or their children's needs. But it is sometimes difficult to go out because there are no relatives nearby to visit, or the women do not feel like taking a long bus ride. A few appear simply to be "housebound": "I have Sundays off, but sometimes I don't leave the house," says Maruja. Zunilda says that she "probably will go out and walk a few blocks, then return."

More than three-fifths of the interviewees work in uniform. Considering that the uniform is the identifying badge of the servant, it is perhaps surprising that about one-half of the interviewees either like to work in uniform or are indifferent (but many of these say they do not care to wear a uniform out on the street). For those who are positive about wearing a uniform, the reason overwhelmingly is one of convenience: "to save my clothes," "to stay clean." There are slightly more uniformed maids among those who earn 1,500 soles or more per month, and a clear association between uniformed maids and the socioeconomic level of the barrios in which they work. Table 1.14 shows this correlation.

TABLE 1.14 Interview Group by Uniform and Where Employed

	Uniformed	
Barrio	*No.*	*%*
Upper-upper	6	(100)
Upper-middle	12	(75)
Middle	7	(54)
Upper-lower	4	(44)
Lower	3	(50)

Rosa, who does not wear a uniform, says that it is the señora who decided: "She doesn't like uniforms. She thinks everyone is equal, and that it is not good for people to distinguish between the señora and the employee." For the 16 interviewees who work in street clothes or would like to do so, the theme of not being singled out as inferior was often mentioned.

Another indication of more equal status is where the employee eats. Seven of the interviewees eat their meals at the family table; of the rest, all eat in the kitchen either alone or with other servants, except for Yolanda who is given enough food each day to take home for herself and her daughter. One who does sit at the family table would prefer to eat uninterrupted in the kitchen after the family meal, "as it would be more peaceful. Now I have constantly to get up and down to serve." A domestic service organizer, who is herself still a full-time household worker, remarks that such privileges are fine, "but should not substitute for low wages. Whenever a wage is paid for housework, a situation of inequality is set up in any case. I myself would prefer to eat in the kitchen and receive a just wage."

Meager salaries are supplemented by gifts in kind, or other privileges, but not all servants in the study enjoy the same range of goods and services. Six of the live-ins do not have even the maid's small room to call their own, but sleep in the señora's room, and one has to roll out her mattress each night in a corner of the kitchen. Most often, a very small room is provided at the back of the house, opening either onto the patio or kitchen. The standard equipment for the maid's room is a bed and mattress, with a household worker customarily providing her own bed linens and towels. A few rooms have wardrobes and dressers, but the space often is too small to accommodate more than a bed. In many cases, the maid keeps her few possessions in her suitcase under her bed (for a more complete description of the physical arrangements of a typical *residencial* and its servant quarters, see Smith 1977).

In five cases, household workers are expressly forbidden to use the hot water; additionally, many of the maid's bathrooms are equipped only with cold water. Often, too, maids are not allowed to sit in the chairs or use the furniture, although they sometimes are invited to look at television in the living room if they sit on the floor. Toribia says "they don't allow me to sit on the furniture, that is only for them."

On the positive side, 11 patronas of live-in maids do provide milk and/or food for the children of their domestic helpers. Most patronas also give their maids old clothes. Hermalinda remarks that all of her clothes and those of her three children were given to her by her patrona. In other cases, food is provided to the servant, but she must buy her own children's provisions, although she is allowed to prepare their meals in the kitchen. Bertha II laments that her patrona "instead of giving the extra food away, throws it in the garbage, and they burn the old clothes. If there is rice left over, the señora says, 'Throw it out.'" Questioned about whether she ever asked for leftover food or old clothing, Toribia says, "No, never. I am ashamed to beg for these things, but I would take them if they were offered."

Another important privilege is the opportunity to study (until the young woman has completed her 15th birthday, it is a right under the law). So far as the interviewees are concerned, they have a median of only three years of primary education. Only four had studied beyond primary school, and none had completed secondary education. However, 7 had managed to finish primary school, and 16 had at least 3 years of schooling—probably the minimum to retain literacy. Two-fifths of the interviewees, or 21, either are illiterate, or nearly so, even though 8 of these had attended first grade.

Aside from formal schooling, many had begun short courses, the majority in sewing and dressmaking. A typical pattern, however, is not to complete the course because of illness, becoming pregnant, the pressure of looking after their own children, or work responsibilities. Still, most of the interviewees are anxious to continue learning, and this is a recurring theme. Carmen, who had to give up after six years of formal schooling, mourns for her lost opportunities:

> Our teachers taught us very well. I was taking five subjects, including Spanish and mathematics. . . . I would like to know everything! I was so sorry to leave off studying, I came home crying over my studies, and was always talking about them. . . . Before, I had my notebooks, I kept them beautifully. But now they are lost.

Ana Juana says that apart from one patrona who "saw to it that I completed primaria," the others told her that there was no reason to study. "They said, 'You're always going to be a maid, and therefore, what use is it for you to study?'" Regina's patrona, "la doctora," tells her: "You should study to be a good mother to your children, nothing more."

In spite of the fact that patronas complain that household workers these days always demand time off for school in the afternoons, this may be one more myth. Only seven among my interviewees presently are studying; they range in age from 23 to 49—three of the students are, in fact, in their 40s. Nor do the students necessarily come either from the more affluent neigborhoods nor are they among the more highly paid; the seven range over the entire pay scale and work in a variety of neighborhoods, as well as specialties within domestic service.

Many of the others want to go on studying: ten want to learn to read and write, six would like to study beauty culture, and three nursing. But study often involves a costly trade-off. Juana says she wants to "learn many things, everything, but if they give me time for school, they'll pay me less."

Besides formal schooling, the women in the survey group are eager to learn whatever their patronas can teach them, and generally give their employers high marks on this score. Only eight say they never learned anything from their patronas. Over one-half learned to cook, and other skills mastered include sewing by machine, cake baking and decorating, childcare, and home management skills (to be orderly, to do things in an efficient manner), as well as moral training and good manners (mentioned 15 times). "I learned how to sit at table." "I learned good Spanish—the señor is always correcting me." "My señora taught me how to intervene in a conversation." One might argue that little of this training is altruistic, since it redounds to the employer's benefit. Nevertheless, the interviewees want to go on "learning in the school of the kitchen," as one puts it. What they most want to do, besides perfecting their cooking (mentioned 16 times), is to learn dressmaking (19 times). Mercedes, who speaks of cooking as "always my hobby, my profession," learned to cook "by going to the kitchen whenever I could to help the señora. I would watch with attention, recording everything I saw." Another learned to cook by having her children read her recipes from the cookbook.

More important than the material rewards or privileges to the servant—and more crucial to the household—is the relationship between the household helper and her patrona. Of the women in the survey, 20 express themselves quite positively about the dealings with their mistresses, even with those whose behavior is not always perceived as ideal. For example, four women reporting good relations mention that their patronas have quite variable temperaments. Manuela says that "la doctora has her moments of bad humor because she is having problems at the Academy." Aurelia reports that her señora "sometimes has a problem, sometimes she's happy—but that's life, everyone has problems." Maruja says that her mistress also is having problems at work, "and because of this, she sometimes is very irritable when she comes home, but I don't pay any attention." Hermalinda complains that her mistress, with whom she has an excellent relationship after 12 years of work in the same household, "sometimes is nervous and shouts, not at me, but at her own children." She cannot think of any improvements she would like in her mistress's behavior toward herself, but would like to see her employer "more understanding of her children." Many patronas might be surprised to learn that their maids are as understanding and perceptive as the above statements reveal.

Of the interviewees, 11 are ambivalent about their relationships to their mistresses, and 18 characterize their relations as negative. Those who feel positive say that what they like most about their employer is the fact that she is good (mentioned by 15 of the 20), cheerful, kind, and considerate; that she is understanding and does not pressure unduly to get the work finished, but is tranquil and patient. Those who feel negative find it difficult to work for patronas who are nervous, temperamental, nasty, and ill-humored, who don't keep their promises, or who are violent, hard, or cruel. One recurring theme of the mistress-servant relationship is respect; servants want their mistresses to treat then with courtesy, and not to insult them or scold them in public. "If my mistress has anything to say to me, I don't care that she says it frankly and plainly," remarks one interviewee, "but not in front of visitors or the other employees."

Another theme is communication. Those who are positive say that the fact that their patronas talk to them contributes greatly to the relationship; among those who are negative, mistresses who refuse to converse are a difficulty. One of the great sorrows of Juana's life is the fact that days sometimes go by when she doesn't set eyes on her patrona (she is in a large household with three other servants): "She stays in bed until 11 o'clock, then calls me on the intercom to discuss what I am to cook, but I don't see her face to face."

When one considers all the negative aspects of the servant role: the low pay, the long hours, the short holidays, etc., what may be surprising is the fact that such a large number of the interviewees are so positive about their relations to their patronas. What may be happening here is that servants sometimes don't blame their mistresses for the bad conditions that prevail in lives of servants, and they are aware that they won't necessarily improve their lot materially by changing households. What they can do (and what the work histories of this particular group prove that they, at least, have done) is to change households to improve their work conditions psychologically, that is, until they find a mistress to their liking. The quality of their patrona may be the only variable over which they have some control. Because of the demand for servants, women with some experience can move from household to household with relative ease. Osoria does not think she has to put up with a patrona who screams at her:

> Sometimes patronas are scolders. Only one time where I went to work did they shout at me. I said to the señora: "Since my childhood, nobody has screamed at me, and this is the first and the last time that this is going to happen." And I packed my suitcase and left.

Of course, it is not so easy to change households when one has a child, and the fluid servant market also works against household workers in that patronas know there is an endless supply. If a maid leaves today, there will be five to take her place tomorrow. Still, it is always a chore to break in a new servant, and for this reason, many patronas may prefer to keep a pleasant atmosphere in the house. This is not to be construed as a strategy only; many patronas no doubt are genuinely kind and considerate, and do not understand their complicity in an exploitative system.

Would the interviewees themselves like to be patronas and have their own servants? About one-third say yes, and another third a definite no. The final third are not able to take the question seriously. "I doubt very much with the life I have that I ever would become a patrona!" "How would this ever be that a poor woman would be able to have an empleada?" Indeed, many reacted with hoots of laughter that they would ever be in a position to employ a servant. Among those who say yes, reasons center around having a solution to childcare, having time to rest or to continue studies, or to go into business. They all say that they would treat their empleada well, incorporate her into the family, and help her with her children. Those who do not like the idea of employing a servant are definite in their reasons:

> *Juana*: No, I wouldn't like to be a patrona. It doesn't seem to me human to have an empleada and treat her like a little animal. Sometimes patronas even send the empleada to sleep with the dog, and treat her like a *burro* good for carrying heavy loads.

> *Mercedes*: To live happily, I don't need to become a patrona; only to better my situation and earn a daily minimum for my children.

> *Rosa*: Even if I had the opportunity, I wouldn't have an empleada. For what? Why do I need an empleada when I can take care of all my own things?

The empleada's relationship to her patrona is important because the work itself does not bring the household worker into contact with very many people. One of the main characteristics of the servant's working environment is its isolation. Curiously, for the interviewees, this isolation is not always mitigated even when there are several empleadas. Over three-quarters would prefer to work alone, and do not make friends either with their work companions or with household helpers in the neighborhodd. Table 1.15 shows these work relationships and preferences.

TABLE 1.15 Household Workers by Number of Employees and Preference for Working Alone/Accompanied

Actually working	Prefers working alone	Prefers working with others	Unknown
Works alone	21	6	
Works accompanied	11	10	2

The preference for being the only empleada differs to some degree by specialty: almost all of the cooks want to be on their own, while two-thirds of the maids-of-all-work and only one-half of the laundresses want to work alone. Preferences are not much affected by age, but there is a definite tendency in the better districts for maids to prefer to work accompanied—perhaps because the households tend to be larger and there is more work to do. Preference for working alone does not appear to be associated with whether or not one is completely dependent upon other household workers to converse and exchange confidences; one-half of those without compañeros still prefer to work alone. Only 18 of the 50 empleadas regularly talk with someone during the workday; most often, those with whom they interact are other empleadas or the patrona.

Over one-half of the interviewees specifically mention that they do not have any friends, either in the workplace or in their barrio of residence. This is most often a definite policy on the part of the interviewees themselves, a conscious decision not to cultivate friendships because it is dangerous to do so, rather than because of the lack of opportunity to make friends:

Merçedes: I don't have any friendships, and I have always been like that wherever I've worked—very far from making friends. My mother always said that friends could induce one to make a wrong turn, or advise one badly. If you go through life alone, you can take better care of yourself.

Victoria: No, I don't have friends. I don't want to have friends, because the first thing you know you could get blamed for something. I don't have good luck with friends.

Clodoalda: In the past, yes, I had friends, but now I have distanced myself from them. I count on my children, no one else. I don't like to meddle in anything.

Eusebia: I don't have any friends, because I don't have confidence in anyone. Not anyone. Not even in my own shadow!

Juana: I don't have friends at work. The empleadas gossip with the patrona and play up to her. I don't like to join in this adulation. I think that everyone should stay in her place, and win appreciation through one's work.

Domestic workers have little opportunity for contact with anyone else during the work day, aside from other empleadas or the patrona. Nearly one-third never leave the house. Moreover, three-quarters say that they do not like to go out, and would prefer not to have anything to do with persons in the street, even when they are obliged to deal with the milkman, go for bread, go to the market, run errands, etc. Because of their isolation—working alone, or with human contact often limited to other servants and to the patrona only when she is giving orders—many women in domestic service apparently never develop the capacity to form friendships. Their limited language ability and lack of spending money makes them fearful to venture very far out of their immediate neighborhoods. When they are sent out on errands, they are always under pressure to return quickly and get on with their work in the house. If they are caught loitering or gossiping with servants from other households—or conversing with men on the street corner—they are liable to be scolded. The patrona will be likely to read improper behavior into even the most innocent exchanges with tradesmen, repairmen, policemen; therefore, it is better to go about one's business with as little to do with others outside the household as possible. Table 1.16 documents the preferences for staying in the house during the work day, or for going out.

Reasons for exchanging one household for another center around what the empleadas perceive as mistreatment, in most cases verbal,

TABLE 1.16 Household Workers by Contacts During the Work Day with Persons Outside the Household

Whether interviewee actually goes out or stays in	Likes to go out during the work day, or to go out "sometimes"	Does not like ever to leave the house, or is ambivalent	Unknown
Goes out during the work day	8	22	
Stays in house during work day	2	13	5

but in some five to six, physical as well. Some 40 percent mention that they left a previous post because the señora (in 13 cases) or other family members (8 cases) either didn't respect them, constantly scolded them, or were hard and cruel. In two cases maids said they left because of the sexual advances of the patrón. Another 19 percent left posts because of disagreements over pay, days off, or vacations. Ten percent left because they were not able to go to school. Another 20 percent left some previous employment because when they traveled to their provinces on vacation, or because of illness of family members, they were replaced. Sixteen percent had to leave employment at one time because they could not find a solution to their child-care problems. Almost one-third left a prior employment because their employers left Lima or left the country. Six empleadas left when they got married, but later returned to work as domestic servants. (The percentages do not add to 100 percent because of multiple reasons for leaving various employments.)

An important question, in the light of their difficult work situation, is that of organizations and associations of domestic servants to improve their salaries, hours, and work conditions. What is interesting in the replies is the vast differences between what the interviewees, in the past, have done and what they believe would be the appropriate response to an opportunity to work with others to address some of the urgent questions in their work lives.

So far as manifestations, strikes, and protests are concerned, most of the interviewees recognized photographs of women marching and carrying banners as scenes of mass protest, although only two of the interviewees had ever participated even once in such events: one had joined in a march for higher salaries, and another "when the teachers asked us to join in a march to demonstrate to the authorities how many illiterates there are in Peru." Almost three-fifths recognized a photograph of the Ministry of Labor, and ten actually had gone there to complain—mainly over back pay that was owed. Nothing much came of these efforts; indeed, one worker could not get past the guard to enter the ministry, so was never able to present her petition.

Nevertheless, when asked whether they believed that women ought to participate in marches, strikes, and protests for their rights, only 11 of the interviewees flatly say "No." Their reasons range over a wide spectrum from fears that they would get themselves, their children, or their employers in trouble, to a conviction that organizing is a privilege of factory workers and or a "cosa de hombres" (men's affair). Of the 50, 35 are, somewhat surprisingly considering their almost complete lack of participation, strongly in favor of organizing to demand their rights. "Yes, because sometimes the employers don't pay, and that is an abuse." "Yes, I'm in favor, that they would pay the legal wages." "When it's necessary, when there is some injustice, one ought to participate, and I would like it that they were protesting." "Yes, the woman has a right to protest, just as much as the man."

The women in the study were asked what they would put highest on their list if there were some possibility of associating themselves with others to demand their rights. Almost one-half say a raise in salary; 20 percent want "better treatment," and fourteen percent their social security inscription. Eight of the women say they would demand back pay due for work, vacation time, or the indemnification that employers are obliged to pay when a worker is dismissed. Other items on the list include opportunitiy to get help or to know their rights and assistance in securing a building lot or building a house (see Chapter 3). Only one interviewee says she would demand schooling, and only two would protest their working hours. One wants a reinstatement of the "Hogar de Domésticas," (Domestic Workers' Home) a place that received domestic workers when they were fired, sponsored talks and entertainments, and found new positions, but which closed some years ago.

What other kind of work would domestic servants like to do, if there were a possibility to change to another occupation? Only one-half say they would like to change; of these, seven believe that factory work would be preferable; six would choose selling; three dressmaking, two hairdressing, one cake decorating and four would change within domestic service: one to cooking and the other three to "something easier, even though it still is in housework." One does not know what she would prefer.

Of those who would not change to anything else, 15 express themselves as content: 5 say the family is good and kind; 4 that the señora is good, or is a friend; 2 that they have "food, clothing, and a roof over my head"; 2 that they do not have to work too hard and earn a good salary and 2 do not know why they are content. Of those who would not change but are *not* content in their present occupation, five say they stay because they don't have any way out; two that they don't really care in what occupation they work; and one that she would not be able to get used to another house/family.

Conditions in the Lima labor market pose the question of upward mobility, touched upon earlier. The issue is complex, but a careful evaluation of the data we have, and the conclusions of other studies, leads us to conclude that there is little movement out of the traditional labor market. The study by Martínez, Prado, and Quintanilla (1973) cited above shows that for women migrants as a group, longer residence in the city is correlated to holding higher level jobs. For those who have been in the city one year or less, fully one-half work in domestic service, while less than 16 percent find opportunity in industrial manufacturing. Conversely, women migrants with ten or more years' residence in Lima are much less likely to be found in domestic service if they work: only 20 percent work as domestics, while 33 percent are in the industrial sector. The proportion also is, of course, influenced by age and education levels.

However, such percentages must be interpreted with caution. They cannot be taken to mean that there is a great deal of job mobility for the individual migrant. This is the erroneous interpretation Martínez and his colleagues (1973) make of their own data, and Smith (1971) and Figueroa Galup (1983) also commit the same error of mistaking such figures to indicate intra-generational job mobility. For one thing, such percentages do not show the occupational history of the individuals and thus we do not know what those living in the city for longer periods did as first occupation. Many may have been among the better educated, or from the larger towns, and gone immediately into factory work.

A more accurate picture emerges when we look at the data from a labor force mobility study of Suárez (1975). This study asks the same respondent what he or she did as a first occupation on arrival in Lima, and what his or her present occupation may be. These data are given in Table 1.17. Table 1.18 gives the Suárez stratification scheme and the median income for each occupation.

What becomes clear is that the domestic servant probably will not move out of household work of his or her own free will, nor will this movement come in the near future. For one thing, the economic

TABLE 1.17 Mobility between First Occupation and Present Occupation According to Sex

Strata of origin: first occupation	Strata of present occupation	Total	Sex	
			Men	Women
Highest	Highest*	83.3	83.6	82.3
	Medium high	7.6	6.4	11.8
	Medium low	4.2	5.4	—
	Lowest	4.9	4.6	5.9
Medium high	Highest	11.6	16.5	3.3
	Medium high	73.5	63.3	91.0
	Medium low	9.5	13.1	3.3
	Lowest	5.4	7.1	2.4
Medium low	Highest	2.9	3.1	1.8
	Medium high	9.7	10.3	6.6
	Medium low	70.7	71.0	69.5
	Lowest	16.7	15.6	22.1
Lowest	Highest	3.5	4.6	1.6
	Medium high	9.2	12.0	4.7
	Medium low	24.3	35.6	5.7
	Lowest	63.0	47.8	88.0

*See Table 1.18 for classification by occupation.
Source: Suárez (1975) Cuadro 32, p. 61.

structures give them little opportunity for doing so. If female domestic servants like Agripina do move, they will either leave the labor force entirely to set up housekeeping with husband or *conviviente* (common law spouse); they will move laterally into street vending, or they will drop out of the statistics into the shadowy world of the informal labor sector.

There is little evidence that the domestic servant makes any rational calculations about learning her trade in order to move to a better neighborhood to improve her position or to increase her

TABLE 1.18 Stratified Occupational Groups (with median income 1975), Lima

Occupational groups	Percent female	Median income
Highest		
1. Professionals	27.7	$177
2. Managers-administrators	15.4	179
Medium high		
3. Technicians	42.8	119
4. Office workers	43.9	83
Medium low		
5. Conductors	1.7	78
6. Skilled and semiskilled workers	24.0	68
Lowest		
7. Unskilled workers	2.9	67
8. Sellers	52.4	53
9. Workers in service occupations	71.0	38
10. Agricultural workers*	19.5	not available

*This group comprises agricultural, hunting, and fishing occupations, which, in Lima, includes very few persons (hardly 1.8 percent of the labor force).
Source: Suárez (1975) Cuadro 2, p. 16.

prestige. Figueroa Galup's 1983 study shows that servants by and large continue to work in or near the neighborhood where they first "land" after migration. In my own study, servants say they would like to work in San Isidro or Miraflores, but their actual moves are more likely to be made by chance. They move to a nearby household because a señora stops them on the street and offers them a few more soles. Or they move to another house simply because conditions have become intolerable in the first—"The señora yelled at me too much."

In my own study, 18 of the 50 interviewees are satisfied with their barrio of employment, and 2 did not answer this question. Of the 30 who are not satisfied with their present barrio, several say they would like to go "wherever they would pay me a little more," but others want to move for reasons having little to do with upward mobility for themselves: "someplace nearer to my house"; "wherever there is a stable employment"; "near a hospital because my child may get sick"; "a place nearer my mother who is not well." Several say that they will work "wherever they give me a job."

So far as their actual behavior is concerned, 16 of the interviewees who changed jobs (immediately prior and present employment) moved from a lower to a higher status district; however, 14 moved from a higher to a lower, while 15 changed to a household located either in the *same* barrio (11 cases) or to one of similar social status (4 cases). Five are in their original employment, several for many years.

What would these women's lives be like if they had been born in different circumstances? If they could go back in time and begin again, what would they choose as an occupation? And what occupations would they like for their daughters and sons?

Nursing heads the list of aspirations for both self and daughters among the interviewees, followed by dressmaking and hairdressing. However, the latter two occupations are desired far less for daughters than for self. Women are apt to choose much more prestigious occupations for sons than for daughters: medicine is chosen 19 times for sons, but only 4 times for daughters, but teaching (a far less prestigious employment) is desired 14 times for daughters, but only 5 times for sons. Table 1.19 shows the occupations that women would choose for themselves, their daughters, and sons.

Topping the list of most disliked occupations, for the interviewees themselves, are farm work (mentioned 27 times) and street vending (24 times). For daughters, least desired occupations are farmwork (22 mentions) and vending (26 mentions). Although six of the women would choose domestic service for themselves as their preferred occupation, even if they could go back and start over, none designates it as suitable for either a daughter or a son. Among the interviewees, 13 single out domestic service as the most disliked occupation for themselves, and 28 specifically mention that they do not want their daughters following in their own footsteps into the domestic service occupation.

Most of the interviewees realize that these aspirations are not realistic, either for themselves or for their children. So far as their own occupational preferences are concerned, the question itself was couched in terms of "if you could live your life over again"; when asked the more immediate question of what occupations would be more suited to their circumstances as worker/mothers, they mention such things as selling, sewing at home, and factory work (see Chapter 3, p. 148). Whether children, particularly sons, can fulfill the much higher aspirations their mothers have for them, is an open question for most of the interview group. The usual response is "If God wills." Many also say that success will depend on the children's own desires and efforts, but that they will do all in their power to help:

Hermalinda: I don't know if she can [become a nurse]. At all cost, I want her to succeed, and for my daughter I will work all my life that she can be something more than I, that she is not a domestic servant like me or a dressmaker or a seller.

Rosa: I'd like for my daughters any of the professions. I want much more for them. That the mamá has been like this, a servant, is no reason that they must be one.

Eugenia: So expensive! One would have to make an enormous effort. If God gives me life, me and the father, I will make such a great effort!

Osoria: If God gives me life, I will sacrifice that my daughter makes something of herself—she is more studious than my sons.

TABLE 1.19 Occupational Aspirations for Household Workers for Themselves, Their Daughters, and Their Sons

Occupation	For self	For daughters	For sons
Nursing	22	28	—
Dressmaking	25	12	—
Hairdressing	15	5	—
Domestic service	6	—	—
Vending	6	—	—
Farm work	5	—	—
Secretarial, accounting	4	17	7
Teaching	3	14	5
Medicine	1	4	19
Factory work	1	1	1
Law	1	1	7
Engineering	—	—	11
Other	a	b	c

[a] Psychology, craftwork: 2 mentions.
[b] Some profession, whatever it may be: 1 mention.
[c] Mechanics: 7 mentions, investigation or policework (3), carpentry (2), tailoring (1), driving (1), military (1).
Note: Numbers add up to more than 50 replies because of multiple answers.

In the next chapter, the work lives of sellers in Lima are described and analyzed, followed by an exploration of the women workers in their relationships to compañeros, children, community, and nation.

NOTES

1. Only first names are used here to protect the respondents' identities. However, we always used the formal "Señora" and "usted" in our interviews with domestic servants. The nomenclature also poses a difficulty: household workers themselves do not like to be called maid or servant (*criada* or *sirvienta*), but usage differs from country to country. In Peru, probably the term in widest use is *empleada*, but the translation as "employee" in English is confusing. The official title in law in Peru at present is "trabajadoras del hogar," or household workers. For variation, all of the above terms are employed.

2. For a historical treatment, see Lauderdale Graham 1982 (on Rio de Janeiro from 1860 to 1910). A general overview is Jelin 1977, and Butler Flora (1982) has written about the image of the domestic servant in the *fotonovela*. Case studies of various cities include: d'Ajuda Almeida et al. 1979 on Rio de Janeiro; Ary Farias 1983 on Fortaleza, Brasil; Chaney and García Castro, eds., forthcoming, a collection of case studies on household workers; Duarte 1976 and 1983 on Santo Domingo; FEM 1980–81 on Mexico; Figueroa Galup 1983 on Lima; Gálvez and Todaro 1983 on Santiago de Chile; García Castro (1982) on Bogotá; Gogna 1981 on Buenos Aires; Goldsmith 1983 on Mexico City; Nett 1966 on Ecuador; Prates 1983 on Montevideo; Rubbo and Taussig 1978 on the Cauca Valley, Colombia; Rutte García 1973 on Lima; Sindicato de Trabajadoras del Hogar 1982 on Cusco, published in Mexico in an edition edited by Gutiérrez 1983; Saffioti 1978, a theoretical treatment with a study of Araraquara, Brasil.

3. The criterion for the selection of the interview group was the workplace, but an attempt also was made to secure women living in a variety of barrios. The interviewees could not, however, be interviewed where they worked, since it was decided that the conversations should not take place in the presence of the patrona. In all cases, we were able to interview the household worker alone.

In order to find interviewees, we set out to discover where domestic servants congregated, outside their work. We found them in hospitals (both at the time they themselves had come to give birth to a new baby, or at the outpatient clinic with their children); employment agencies; afternoon schools with household worker students; childcare centers, and at the Ministry of Labor's offices where several had come to complain. This does not afford a representative sample, but by comparing the demographic characteristics of the interview group with one such sample (Figueroa Galup's 1983 study) and other studies, we are reasonably confident that our group at least represents a gamut of women in various situations and life-stages: young and mature; doing various kinds of work; living-in and already established as dayworkers; with compañero and single mothers.

An attempt was made to interview the women, if possible, in their homes, and we were able to do so in 25 cases. Most interviews took two sessions, and lasted an average of 2.3 hours. The interviews were carried out by the author and by Beatriz Basaldúa, who was able to converse with the interviewees in Quechua. All of the interviewees spoke Spanish, but at times, a translation into the indigenous language was helpful in clarifying a question. Often we worked in tandem, but some of the interviews were done on our own.

4. There are good reviews of the literature on women in migration in Chaney 1980; *Migration Today* 1982; Orlansky and Dubrovsky 1978, and Youssef, Buvinić, and Kudat 1979. Suárez 1975 considers the issue specifically for Peru. Studies documenting the disadvantaged position of women in both urban and rural areas are covered extensively in the articles and bibliography of the volume on women and poverty edited by Buvinić, Lycette, and McGreevey 1983.

Several articles with a comprehensive review of the issues of women in the urban labor force include Arizpe 1977; Jelin 1977 and 1982; Safa 1977 and Schmink 1982. Pioneering studies on urban women were carried out by Arizpe 1975 on indigenous migrants to Mexico City; Bolles 1981 and Standing 1981 on working-class women in Kingston, Jamaica; García, Muñoz, and de Oliveira 1982 on households in Mexico City; Lomnitz 1975 on survival strategies of poor households in Mexico City; Moser 1981 on women in Guyaquil; Piho 1975 on textile workers in Mexico City; Safa 1983 on factory workers in New Jersey and Brasil; Schmink 1977 and 1979 on urban women in Venezuela and Brazil; Scott Kinzer 1975 on Buenos Aires professional women. The recent volume edited by Nash and Safa (1985) has several articles that deal with urban women, as does the Standing and Sheehan collection (1978).

Finally, Villalobos de Urrútia published some results of her collaboration with our research project in 1977, dealing with urban factory workers.

5. Perhaps prostitution might also be included here, for the few migrant women who are considered attractive. Data on prostitution are hard to come by, however, and no studies have yet been done in Lima to the authors' knowledge. Prostitution is legal in Peru and classified as an occupation; the numbers are, however, hidden in the category "other services" in the census.

6. The term *chola* denotes a woman of rural origin who has put off at least to some extent Indian ways, yet is not fully acculturated to the dominant Hispanic society's standards. The term is pejorative in some contexts, but is used also as a technical term by anthropologists.

7. Quijano 1971, p. 1. Webb (1974, pp. 30–31) challenges the assumption that the traditional sector acts as a "receptacle" for migrants in search of modern sector jobs. He uses data for Lima and seven other Peruvian cities surveyed in 1970 to show that average length of residence is similar for migrants whether they work in traditional or modern sector employment (15.3 and 16.9 years, respectively). Moreover, both the urban traditional and urban modern sectors had the same proportion (63 percent) of migrants in their labor force. Where Webb disagrees with most interpretations, including Quijano's, which he specifically criticizes, is on what he regards as their overly pessimistic view of opportunities and incomes in the traditional labor market.

8. Servants in Western Europe and the United States did not, of course, disappear because of changes in the French, German, or North American character. New economic needs, giving the servant class other options, transformed the rigid social hierarchies in these world areas. Still, one might argue that nothing *else* except change in economic structures has been effective in doing away with servitude. Even a Civil War did not better the lot of blacks in the United States who had to wait for the economic opportunities generated by World War II to move in significant numbers into modern sector occupations. Legislation, introduced in Peru in 1972 to improve the life of servants, has had little impact; measures to form labor unions of domestic workers or to make the upper classes more conscious of conditions in which their servants live have been no more effective.

9. The popularity of María and her wide influence are shown in, among other manifestations, the number of servants who (when asked about their aspirations for themselves or for their daughters) put *costurera* (dressmaker) at the head of their list by a wide margin over other occupations. This topic is explored below. For a recent exploration of the image of the domestic servant in the fotonovela, see Butler Flora (1983).

10. Remote rural areas are defined as an isolated house in the country, a shack on a hacienda, or a *caserio comunidad* (outbuildings on a hacienda for farmhands, grouped together). According to this survey, only 2.7 percent of the migrants to Lima are of foreign origin.

11. Macisco notes that close to one-quarter of the women 35 years of age or over in his sample came to Lima without husbands but with one or more children, the proportion being about the same regardless of the size of the place of previous residence. This compares to only 5.8 percent of males in the same age group who migrated to Lima without wives.

12. Rutte García (1973, p. 62) observes that papers "permit the patrones an almost absolute domination over the employee. . . . for them, the papers have an almost magical character that binds them to their employers. . . . since many do not know what the documents say, nor moreover, do they have any elementary legal knowledge to be able to evaluate their documents. They sometimes feel bound by papers that certainly, in whatever circumstance, will prejudice them."

13. This assertion flies in the face of conventional economic wisdom that assumes such jobs come into existence because the people who do them are simply responding to real demands, real needs. Yet I tend to agree with Arizpe (1977, p. 34) who observes that "a street vendor who sells what she just bought in the market two blocks away is not fulfilling a real demand. It is reasonable to suppose that if they had other alternatives, these women would not engage in such activities."

14. Laundresses may not work every day. In the survey group, several worked two or three days a week, and only one worked all five days. In order to be able to compare laundresses' salaries to the rest of the domestics, their monthly income was calculated at their daily rate multiplied by 20 potential working days. Laundresses choose this occupation despite its hardships precisely because they can earn as much as other domestic servants in a much shorter work week, or they can earn substantially more by working every day. Moreover, they have more flexible work hours. Fandila, even though she would prefer to cook, says that she cannot "because you have to go very early in the morning to make the breakfast, and I can't because of my children."

LIST OF PHOTOGRAPHS AND CAPTIONS

1.1   Many sellers and servants are migrants from the Peruvian sierra, particularly from Cusco, Ancash, Arequipa and Ayacucho.

1.2   Most sellers and servants in the survey worked on the land as children, a life they were glad to leave behind.

1.3   Some household workers find their jobs through posted notices, "Girl Needed"; but most first jobs are arranged through intermediaries.

1.4   The maid-of-all-work cleans, shops, takes care of children, and often cooks and launders as well.

1.5   Cooking is the preferred occupation; in the kitchen, there is some autonomy and "you eat better."

1.6   Of maids in the survey, 60 percent leave the house to deal with trades, delivery persons, or market sellers.

1.7   Off to market with the señora and child; 70 percent of household workers in the survey would prefer never to leave the house.

1.8   Marketing is one of the most time-consuming duties of household workers; many will themselves later go into selling.

1.9   In summer, household workers socialize in the parks while caring for their charges. Yet over one-half say they do not have any friends.

1.10   Most household workers prefer to eat alone; if they sit at the family table, they must get up and down to serve.

1.11   Disagreements over salary, time off account for fewer job changes than lack of respect and bad treatment.

1.12   Household workers enjoy carefree days before they have their first child.

1.13   With one or two children, the servant must use all her free time to attend their needs.

1.14   Maids at afternoon school. This one taught not only high school subjects, but workers' rights.

1.15   Maids often form close relationship with the children of the patrona, and sometimes are the chief influence in their upbringing.

1.1

1.2

1.3

1.4

1.5

1.6

1.7

1.8

1.9

1.10

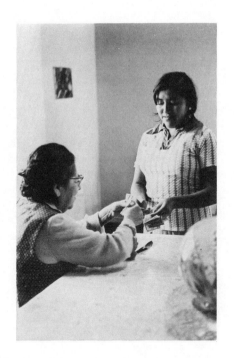

1.11

1.12

1.13

1.14

1.15

2   María

It is 3:00 a.m., María is startled into the day by her second-hand alarm clock. Still half asleep in her dark one-room dwelling, she gropes for silence; the toddler Chabelita, huddled against her body, will perhaps sleep for a few more minutes. Teresa, seven years old, asks quickly if it is time for school, and, as quickly, falls back to sleep. Another long hard day starts for María. She is an *ambulante* (street peddler) selling potatoes in the San Juan de Miraflores market. There are many such markets in the city of Lima, where hundreds of poor working mothers like María will struggle again today to provide for their children and themselves.

María's eyes are still heavy and as she pulls herself from sleep the familiar objects of the unilluminated room take shape. Standing out from the bare walls is the small kerosene stove where she cooks for herself and her daughters; there are still some fried potatoes left over from the evening meal. A too familiar meal: the only food she can afford when business is slack. María coughs, feeling her body ache in memory of yesterday's potato sack; too heavy to heft, she had had to drag it along. The sound of Doña Olga's voice—who has peddled different products for 30 years—echoes in her ears:

> Each day you have to struggle, you have to be on your feet running after your customers. When one is a young girl tiredness is not felt because peddling seems like a game, one has a good laugh every now and then and the illusion that everything is going to be fine. When one becomes older and more mature one realizes that there is no hope, that days are all the same; one tires early of sitting and vending, standing, running after customers.

Sometimes we don't even know what time it is, nor the day of the week and the buzzing noise of the people in the market becomes intolerable.

Street selling is the only economic activity María can handle—it is the only occupation that allows the presence of her children at her workplace. She looks tenderly at her sleeping daughters, then hugging the baby, Chabelita, speaks to herself aloud: "No. I'm not going to give this baby away, she isn't going to run the same fate as my baby boy." Having had to give away her son haunts María. The sleepless nights are many as Maria obsessively relives the details of that very bitter time in her life. The boy is now three years old, but for her he is dead. She had to give him up, she could not afford him. The suffering with that last patrona for whom she had been a domestic servant, is still too vivid. She had arrived at that house with Teresita and very soon met a man with whom she developed a *compromiso* (relationship). He deceived her; she did not know he was married. His promises disappeared along with him at the news of María's pregnancy—leaving no hope and no money. Her patrona announced she must leave when the baby was born, she would not have been hired with two children. Then came the hospital and the tearful visit from Teresita—she had wet the bed while mamá was away and the patrona had dragged her from bed, spanked her, and forced her to wash her soiled panties in cold water. It was then, at the edge of despair, that she met a lady who assiduously visited the maternity ward. Hearing María's story, she suggested: "Why don't you give me the child? If you have neither money nor a job how on earth are you going to support him?" And she had given her infant away; there seemed nothing else to do.

María tries to shake the memory as she straightens herself in bed. She touches Teresita gently to wake her. María has decided that today the child will have to miss school, she needs Teresita to help with the acounting while she sells. Her daughter knows how to figure the cost of purchases and is quick at giving change from bills, whereas María is slow and clumsy, often making mistakes: she is illiterate. Chabelita is changed, wrapped in a shawl, asleep. Teresita is awake and coughing badly. María coaxes her into swallowing half a teaspoon of kerosene—the cheapest medicine available. There is no money for a doctor.

Before stepping out of her dwelling she returns to her bed, fixes her eyes on the image of San Martín de Porres, her patron saint:

Take good care of me, dear San Martincito, so that nothing bad may happen to me today at work! Also look after Teresita when

she's working with me or begging for bread when we don't sell.
You are so miraculous, protect us. You are a real father to me.

María makes the sign of the cross, hefts bundled Chabelita against her back, and takes Teresita by the hand. It is already 4:00 a.m. The streets are cold, deserted. A vehicle darts at high speed along the main highway. They walk ten blocks to reach the bus stop where small groups of people stand huddled closely against the chilly dawn air. The majority are ambulantes. Like María they also carry babies and toddlers on their backs and other children in hand for the daily trip to La Parada, the wholesale market. Here the products that must be purchased later will be sold retail through the streets and markets of Lima.

Carmela, a 40-year-old ambulante, mother of seven and already a grandmother, greets María while trying to wake her smallest child who has fallen alseep sitting on the sidewalk.

> Oh! If I were governing this country I would prohibit working mothers from bringing the children along with them to sell and would help them out with a state-run nursery in every neighborhood because children suffer while we sell as they have to endure the cold of the night, the heat of summer, hunger and thirst. Sometimes they are outdoors all day with their little faces exposed to the weather and probably with soiled underwear because we have not been able to change their diapers!

Carmela is a good working companion; María thinks she will sometimes help her sell or do accounts when they get muddled up. But Carmela is always whining and exhausted. She has worked as an ambulante since the age of seven and has gotten nowhere; always the same: tired, gaunt, never energetic, perpetually short of money.

The bus finally arrives and María, together with the other ambulantes, boards. She sits Teresita, who is feeling drowsy and hungry, near an open window, so she will eventually fully wake up.

At 28 María has had relationships with three men; she has given birth to five children—two died in infancy, one was given up. As many other women ambulantes, she faces all the responsibilities as head of the household. María says she will not get involved in a relationship for some time; she has no knowledge of birth control methods and food is too expensive to allow another child.

María is a native of the small village of Combapata, a day's trip from Cusco. The events of her childhood are typical of numerous peasant girls'. Families too poor to feed all of their children or with the naive belief that the options of the city will be better for their daughters than the poverty of the sierra, entrust young girls to town and city families. The expressed, but rarely fulfilled, scenario supposes the development of fluency in Spanish, acquisition of skills as a domestic servant, and a formal education supported by employers.

At ten, María was literally given in trust to a patrona from Cusco. As usual, the understanding was that she would be fed, clothed, and sent to school in exchange for domestic service. None of these promises were honored by the patrona; instead, the child worked a 16-hour day. Childhood and expectations were quickly shattered as María fell victim to both economic and sexual exploitation. She was regularly sexually molested by a frequent visitor to her employer's house. He was never stopped; María continued to be assaulted. One of her older sisters, purely by chance, became aware of the situation and alerted their mother who came to Cusco to fetch her daughter, still illiterate and practically without clothing. This had been María's only opportunity to learn how to read and write. María recalled her mother's words: "I brought you to this patrona thinking she would teach you how to read and write but you didn't learn a thing. If I'd known what was in store for you, I'd have kept you with me in the sierra."

Mother and daughter worked as ambulantes, going deep into the hills of the sierra for wood to sell at the village market. They also peddled chili peppers, sugar, salt, and chicha, an alcoholic beverage her mother taught her to prepare. Rare, wholehearted laughter comes as María recalls the time she prepared a large quantity of chicha and the burro who carried their goods mistook it for water, liked it a great deal, and got totally drunk.

At 13, María again entered domestic service with a family in Cusco, cleaning, washing, and ironing. Here she became involved with a young man, became pregnant, and was deserted. The baby died before its first birthday. Following the death of the baby María was brought to the capital city by a paisana, a woman from her province. She felt encouraged at being told that in Lima she would develop skills, earn a lot of money, and learn how to read and write. Once in Lima this patrona had her working as a maid-of-all-work: she was responsible for cooking, washing clothes, and cleaning for the whole family as well as selling soft drinks from the patrona's small shop. Life was not quite as her patrona had depicted; María was abused verbally and physically. She was forced into sexual relations with the woman's brother-in-law. A pregnancy resulted and, when Teresita was born, the patrona refused both moral and financial support—María was not earning a regular wage but room and board in exchange for her labor. Teresa was not formally acknowledged as the man's child under Peruvian law and to this day remains illegitimate.

Maria served as a domestic in two other Lima households. She remembers one patrona fondly; Maria was paid a wage, she and the child were treated well. The second household was the scene of the birth of her son, still a nightmare for Maria.

Following the loss of her son and her position, Maria was employed as a seasonal agricultural worker—picking and washing onions during harvest season with Teresita at her side. At this time, Maria decided to turn to those skills developed working with her mother as ambulante in the market towns of the sierra. She became a street seller in a proletarian section of Lima, outside the San Juan de Miraflores market.

While at the San Juan de Miraflores market Maria met a man, became his conviviente (consensual wife), and Chabelita was born. He was already married in the sierra, but, like so many *serranos*, had left his wife and five children behind to search for better job opportunities in Lima. Maria remembers how pleasant life was with Chabelita's father; he was always kind, cooperative, concerned for their welfare. He would even take over household duties and see to the children if she became ill. But all changed suddenly; he was run over and killed. His wife in the sierra received compensation from the driver, but never sent Maria that part of the money she had promised her.

After an hour's journey, the bus arrives at La Parada. Maria has Teresita firmly by the hand, Chabelita fastened to her body in a large, faded multicolored wrap. She reaches between her breasts to feel her small bundle of bills—1,000 soles, her only capital. It is wrapped in a handkershief, secured firmly with a large safety pin. Maria, like all the other women ambulantes, believes this to be the safest way to protect her money and herself; thugs and purse snatchers slide daily through the crowds of buyers and sellers dealing at the wholesale market. Maria's bundle will purchase the potatoes she later will resell at the smaller market where she does her ambulatory commerce.

She goes directly to the wholesale potato section and, as she goes about selecting the more expensive potatoes her customers demand, she broods over the fact that she can deal in no other produce for lack of capital. Maria would rather peddle fruit or chickens but cannot afford it. Well, at least potatoes will not rot, and capital is not lost from one day to the next; fruit deteriorates easily, chickens not sold rapidly must be fed, and this requires extra money. Maria buys two sacks of potatoes; today they are 6 soles a kilogram, and she realizes she cannot make much of a profit from her sales this week and, of necessity, will have to steal 100 to 250 grams per kilo of potatoes from each customer. This will require fixing the scales. She has been caught before by a municipal inspector and fined. But what else can she do? She must scrounge to make ends meet.

She summons a *carretero* (a carter who for 10 soles hauls heavy sacks, crates, and baskets in a cart), loads her two sacks of potatoes in his small cart, and wheels her purchase to a trucker whom she pays another 15 soles to take her potatoes from the large wholesale market to her selling area in San Juan de Miraflores.

If she had not put pressure on Teresita to stay away from school today, María would have taken a bus with the baby, returned to her one room dwelling, awakened her daughter for school, and left her 10 soles for breakfast. She would then have taken yet another bus to her regular selling post in the large neighborhood market in the heart of the *pueblos jóvenes* or young towns.

Instead, today she picks up a kilogram of fresh cheese that she will later sell with boiled, peeled potatoes and salt. María will boil 30 to 40 potatoes and place them in a basket with squares of fresh cheese and sell them outside the entrance to a cinema in her own neighborhood. Boiled potatoes with salt and cheese is a delicacy from the sierra and a favorite snack or meal for adults and children.

María and the children board the bus for the Mercado San Juan de Miraflores. Arriving at the market, she claims her two sacks of potatoes from the trucker and starts selling. It is already 6:30 a.m. After an hour's peddling they are feeling hungry. María goes to a breakfast stand inside the market and orders two large cups of dark coffee and two loaves of bread for them to share.

Then back again to sell. Her regular customers come, each buys two to four kilograms of potatoes. One of her good customers brings Teresita a dress which her own daughter has outgrown. This middle-aged customer is kind as are three of María's other regular customers who help María figure out the accounting when she gets stuck. But today Teresita is here; the child is busy both selling and telling her mother how much she should charge and the exact amount of change to give. María is proud of her daughter's skills.

The potatoes sell rapidly today, and María decides to celebrate by buying lunch for herself and the girls. Instead of buying the usual two plates of soup for 10 soles, María purchases two orders of rice and fried eggs for 30 soles.

Then back again to the potatoes. Another ambulante friend approaches María begging her to finish selling her sack of ears of corn.

She is crying. One of her three children is very ill with acute diarrhea and must be taken to the doctor. María acquiesces, though tired, because her friend would always help her out in need. She had sold María's potatoes many times when she had health problems with her own daughter or when she had to run important errands.

It is 3:00 p.m., María has sold enough for the day. Now it is home, and to the laundry. She boards the bus with Chabelita in one arm and a half-full potato sack in the other. She is lucky today to find an empty seat; Teresita stands beside her during the long ride. Teresita has been a great help today. María firmly believes that children should work alongside their mothers, because it is the only way that any money is left over for their other needs. And, after all, she worked as a child with her ambulante mother for years and her mother before her with her grandmother. Somehow, though, she prays her daughter will one day work in a department store selling necklaces; jewelry is more profitable and does not go stale nor rot like vegetables and fruit.

María has set aside the rest of the day to wash and clean her one-room dwelling—the property of a married woman with children. She knows what will greet her. She started paying rent but no longer can afford to, and is living there free. This results in much bickering between the two women. The landlady never misses an opportunity to threaten María with eviction nor to insult her for lack of hygiene: "You filthy, smelly repugnant woman, when are you going to get out of my property?" María would explain once again that it was not her fault Chabelita was constantly wetting and that it was impossible to clean her or change her diapers regularly during market hours. The baby's urine would filter through the shawl that tied her to her mother's back. Lack of time and laundry facilities, a worn and tattered skirt, together with a permanently tired expression gave María a shabby and unkept, dirty looking appearance.

As the bus rattles through countless pueblos jóvenes linked to the main highway by zigzagging lateral streets, María dreads the return home and probable needling from her landlady. María has told her many times that she would leave as soon as she could afford six straw mats and the lumber to build a dwelling on a tiny lot a coambulante worker had given her in the Quebrada de Lurín. She will leave of her own accord and not by force of eviction. She is obsessed with living on her own property, just to look forward to returning home from the marketplace to quiet instead of quarreling. She dreams of heating up the evening meal and crawling into bed with her stomach full and dead tired, but with nobody around to criticize her. For is it not her business and her little girls' only, if she chooses to sleep over her unmade bed when she has no energy to undress or to wash?

The bus continues running through neighborhood squares, past half-lit cinema houses, and busy markets where shoppers engage in their last purchases of food for the day. Another day is drawing to an end, and María worries because she will not have time to do all the laundry nor to prepare the native dish which she usually sells at the entrance of the neighborhood cinema in the evening. Some nights she sells the food from door-to-door. Teresita invariably pleads with her to stay home and not work so hard so that she can rest, so they can be together. As invariably María replies: "If I don't sell food and coffee we cannot make both ends meet."

PERSONAL CHARACTERISTICS OF AMBULANTE MOTHERS

As in María's case, each of the ambulante mothers interviewed comes from the poorest sectors of the rural and urban population. Of the 50 women in our sample 84 percent are migrants, with an average of 17 years in Lima. Of these, the majority—roughly 70 percent—are natives of the Peruvian sierra: Ayacucho, Apurimac, Cusco, and Junín. Only 16 percent were born and reared in Lima.[1]

Most of the women fall into the same age bracket as María: the median age for the group is 31; the remaining members of the sample, about 40 percent, are between 20 and 29. As was the case with María until the death of her compañero, 30 percent of these ambulante mothers live in consensual unions; 8 percent are unwed mothers; 6 percent of the sample are constituted of widowed, divorced or separated women. The remaining 56 percent were legally married at the time of our study. The average number of children supported by each mother in our sample is 3.4. Mercado (1978) has shown that the woman ambulante supports, on average, 3.96 individuals.[2]

María's description of her family history reflects common characteristics of the youth of most women street peddlers. Due to the extreme poverty of their sierra families, most of these women had to begin working at the age of seven or eight. The adult working mothers interviewed, reflecting upon this stage of their lives, describe childhood income-generating activities in terms of survival rather than from a perspective of even constricted options. They say that coming from very poor families, they could not be a burden to their parents, or for those from female-headed households, to their mothers. They engaged in agricultural work and ambulatory commerce. Thirty-two percent were working full-time before age 15; of this group, 14 percent had to generate income before age ten.

⎯⎯⎯⎯⎯⎯ : My father earned very little and could not afford my education. I had to help him, we were many brothers and sisters.

⎯⎯⎯⎯⎯⎯ : Mother demanded me to work out of need, I had to face life as an orphan.

⎯⎯⎯⎯⎯⎯ : There was nothing to grab onto in order to support ourselves and no one to help us. So we started working when our parents got tired.

Many of the ambulante women recall their mother's work in the sierra, cultivating land, tilling other people's soil, tending others' flocks, in return for a meager wage—usually 40 soles a month for their services. Others remember working alongside street-hawking mothers in the small towns of the sierra.

Asked to describe their fathers' work, 22 percent confess they never met their fathers: they are illegitimate, the family had been abandoned, or the father had died. As in María's case, 10 percent of the women remember neither father nor his occupation.

⎯⎯⎯⎯⎯⎯ : I never got to know my father. My mother and myself were abandoned by him when I was an infant.

⎯⎯⎯⎯⎯⎯ : I've been told that my father was a truck driver. He left my mother. Such is life, so I never met him.

⎯⎯⎯⎯⎯⎯ : Father deserted me and my mother when I was small to go and marry another woman. The same thing has happened to me as a married woman. I've been deserted.

Of those women who have some knowledge of their father's economic activities, 54 percent are daughters of men who worked the land as *jornaleros* or day laborers; 18 percent worked as petty retailers; 10 percent were unskilled or semiskilled workers; the remainder, the minority, had worked as barbers and policemen.

The young girl's entrance into the labor market is often triggered by family problems arising from the consensual union formed by the unwed or abandoned mother.

⎯⎯⎯⎯⎯⎯ : My step-father raised domestic animals. He mistreated me, beat me up. That's why I left.

⎯⎯⎯⎯⎯⎯ : Mother battered me physically and, in her ignorance, she would lock me up with my step-father. How I have suffered!

This recurring pattern of family conflict coupled with the poverty faced by young peasant girls precipitates their exodus from the family unit. Most often the mother, or a relative, delivers the child to a family or relatives where she works as a domestic servant and is promised in exchange clothing, food, lodging, and some education. These promises are rarely honored. Giving a young girl in trust to a family is seen by parents as both an alleviation of pressures in providing food for their offspring and an opportunity for the child to meet her own survival needs. Adult ambulante women recollecting this moment of transfer, repeat: "Mamá me entregó a una señora." This literally means, "My mother handed me over to a lady or to the mistress of the house."

There is an implicit understanding that with the transfer of the child the mother's rights and obligations as caretaker of her daughter are ceded to the employer. Terms denoting fictive kinship relationships stemming from the cultural institution of *comadrazgo* are utilized in an attempt to color the transition of the child from family member to worker in an employer's household. The woman employer is often referred to as madrina (godmother) or, in many cases, tía (aunt).

The use of such terms are emblematic of far more than a cushioning of a child's feelings at a very difficult time. Wolf and Hansen (1972, p. 128, pp. 131–135) have documented the importance of godparents in Latin America and the qualitative cultural distinctiveness from godparenting in the United States. In the United States, the bond between child and sponsor, from baptism, has priority whereas in Latin America the most important bond is considered to be between the parents of the child and the sponsor, rather than between godparent and child. The implications are significant in that economic and moral understandings and obligations among the adults involved in the coparenting of a child have priority over any ties between godparent and child.

Under the aegis of the Catholic Church, it is understood that the godparent will take charge of the child in case of family crisis or death—the godparent becomes the surrogate parent. However, in Latin America, this surrogate responsibility is adumbrated by ongoing supportive transactions—be they economic, political, or social in nature—established through the *compadrazgo* and *comadrazgo* ties between parent and godparent. Coparenthood, originating at baptism, is understood as a mutual support pact between participating coparents. Wolf and Hansen show that compadrazgo can cut across social strata; they distinguish between *horizontal* compadrazgo—ties established between socioeconomic equals—and *vertical* compadrazgo—ties between those belonging to different socioeconomic groups. If, for example, a large hacienda owner becomes *compadre* to a favorite worker, this tie does not automatically benefit the worker. There is no question of social mobility, rather, an implicit acknowledgment on the part of the wealthy compadre that the compadre in the inferior social position can count on his protection and help.

When a poor mother entrusts her daughter to an employer with whom she has not established religious ties of comadrazgo—which is almost always the case—she is symbolically invoking the patterned style of the mutual support network with a nonrelative by referring to the employer as godparent. The hope is that in invoking the cultural tradition, the child's well being in her new environment will be guaranteed. In short, the term itself asks the employer for protection, food, clothing, and training in domestic skills, in exchange for services. The contract is between mother and employer —the essence of comadrazgo ties. With this type of economic contract, the powerlessness of the child worker comes into clear relief. Neither mother nor employer consults her as to whether or not she wishes to work as a domestic, to work in this particular household. She has no rights as a worker—her person as well as her labor power are transacted between parent and employer.

Not all of the adult ambulante mothers in our studies worked exclusively as maids throughout their childhood and adolescent years. Many worked alternately as servants for blocks of time, with long stretches as street sellers between domestic jobs. Of the women interviewed, 30 percent describe experiences similar to Maria's: they were socialized into petty retailing work alongside adult vendors. Of these, 18 percent were trained by their mothers, the remaining 12 percent by other relatives.

Despite reporting unhappy, traumatic memories associated with ejection from home into the labor market, the typical ambulante woman always tries to return to her place of origin. The reasons given involve sentimental attachment to relatives left behind. Asked why they had returned at least once to their home, 78 percent say they wanted to visit their mother, both parents if still alive. Many of the women explain that they wanted to meet with their brothers and sisters again, that they could not remember them well as they had been so small when forced to leave the parental household. In our sample, the women average 3.5 siblings still living.

The premature induction of the female child into the work force robs her not only of her childhood but also of her chance for a basic education and, thus, future options. Like Maria, few of the children were sent to school by their employers; they were, at best, sent sporadically, and eventually these too dropped out totally from educational institutions. School work is held subordinate to employers' demands; it becomes impossible to keep up. It therefore hardly comes as a surprise that 16 percent of the ambulantes in our study are illiterate, another 26 percent attended only first and second grade and have become functional illiterates; thus, we see a striking 42 percent of ambulante women who can neither read nor write. The lack of the most meager skills clearly has a detrimental impact upon the women's entrepreneurial activities and options. Of the street vendors, 32 percent report completing third and fourth grade. However, an overall assessment of educational levels attained by the women sellers in the study shows extremely low percentages: 74 percent had not finished primary school; 14 percent completed the 6 primary grades, and less than 12 percent had any secondary education at all. The average number of years of schooling for an ambulante is three. Data from the 1970 census reveal 35 percent illiteracy among women ambulantes in Lima, compared to 16 percent in our sample (Mercado 1978). Österling (1981), in his study of ambulantes in metropolitan Lima, refers to a survey of street sellers (República del Perú 1976) that shows 21 percent of those surveyed never attended school; of this group 94 percent were women.

Almost two-thirds of the migrant women, about 69 percent, had work experience before reaching Lima: 26 percent worked as domestics, 19 percent cultivated or herded domestic animals, another 19 percent had already worked in ambulatory commerce and developed basic skills, and 5 percent had been hired for market work by owners of fixed stalls—these are salaried ambulantes as opposed to the individual hawker-operator.

Based upon previous occupational history, or lack of it, prior to arrival in Lima, ambulante mothers can be grouped into distinct categories. The first category of women vendors is composed of those who worked as hired agricultural hands, shepherds, or domestics. Upon arrival in Lima, with no specific skills to sell in the labor market but with familiarity with domestic work, they either continue as domestics or start work as maids for the first time. Although work site and employer may change, domestic work as the primary mode of economic activity continues for a considerable length of time. The development of a consensual union, marriage, and/or the birth of a child are the causes stated for leaving domestic service. If the domestic servant becomes pregnant and is not married, as we saw in María's case, she is fired by her employer. For the women with children and little or no education, the only viable economic their solution is street peddling. A detailed analysis of the life histories of the women studied showed that street peddling rarely is the first urban economic activity of migrants to the capital city. Our conclusion has been supported by recent research on migration and urban occupations (Österling 1981).

Women who are married and have small children remain exclusively devoted to the care of the household and offspring until the financial situation becomes too tight; then they are forced to start working in ambulatory trade. The majority of husbands or mates are underemployed or jobless.

The women in this group cite two fundamental reasons for their involvement in petty vending: the perception and evaluation of street hawking as an economic activity offering the advantage of allowing children at the peddling site; and the feeling of "independence" and/or greater flexibility than either a factory or domestic situation allows. In both factory and household work the women would be tied to a fixed schedule; they also would be working under the strict eye of a supervisor in an industrial setting, or suffer with a harassing employer during a 16-to-18-hour workday in a household. (A few ambulantes in the study stated they gave up factory jobs because there was no one to care for their children.) In addition to the flexibilities demanded by the fact of offspring, these women are well aware of the fact that their lack of education, training, and skills precluded other economic options.

_____ : My son is very small and I need to keep an eye on him all the time.

_____ : I could not bring my child along with me if I worked as a domestic servant.

_____ : I'm not schooled. What else could I do for a living?

A second group or category of women differ from the first in aspects of their backgrounds: all of them already had experience in petty vending, they worked in their native areas as child ambulantes alongside their mothers. Many of these women migrated to Lima as children, accompanying mothers in search of economic options in the city, who then continued to work at vending in the capital. The occupational profiles of these women show that they represent a link in a generational chain of street peddling—an economic "inheritance" moving from grandmother, to daughter, to daughter's daughter. The majority of these ambulante mothers also make street selling a family enterprise in which close relatives, especially children, become collaborating partners in their small-scale marketing operations. (See Chapter 4.)

A third group consists of those women who have never worked before and venture into ambulatory trade under economic stress. In our sample, 34 percent of the women fit this profile. These individuals never imagined they would have to work outside the home as they relied heavily upon a male provider. Many of the women in this category were abandoned by their mates or widowed. Others were initiated into peddling as assistants to or collaborators with ambulante husbands or consensual mates.

What all of these ambulante mothers share in common is their urgent need to work to help their families survive. As a group they exhibit a consistent lack of basic education, specialized skills, and training that would otherwise facilitate their entrance into the modern sector of the economy. Upward occupational mobility is beyond their reach, except in rare cases. An analysis of the structure of the Peruvian economy shows in recent years a consistent link between rising food prices and the spawning of urban marketers and street hawkers. The situation in Peru is illustrative of economic crises in other Third World countries where economic underdevelopment goes hand-in-hand with an expanding tertiary sector (Babb 1982). Petty commerce absorbs the jobless and underemployed; there women are found in large numbers.

Income earning activities that can be developed alongside childcare often are of the marginal type, and the relationship between a "marginal" female labor force and a woman's economic responsibilities toward her family is not accidental (Buvinić and Youssef with von Elm 1978). Furthermore, women have very restrictive economic options when compared to men and tend to favor vending over other income-generating activities. Ambulante work becomes their preferred survival strategy.

AMBULANTE MOTHERS' REFLECTIONS ON THE TENSIONS ARISING FROM THEIR DOUBLE DAY

Though street peddling and marketing are income-generating activities compatible with reproduction, ambulante mothers handle street vending and domestic work as chain linked; their waking hours are characterized by constant accommodations between two spheres of activities that have to be dealt with simultaneously.

The typical daily load of the average ambulante mother is analogous to María's; she works 18 hours a day without stopping and without rest. Women petty-traders work Monday through Friday as well as Saturdays, Sundays, and holidays when they can earn more. Their work is hard, characterized by tensions produced by obstacles and problems they have to surmount both at their workplace and at home.

Their perceptions of their double day illustrate their frustrations:

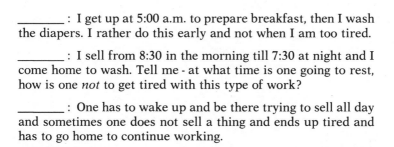

_____ : I get up at 5:00 a.m. to prepare breakfast, then I wash the diapers. I rather do this early and not when I am too tired.

_____ : I sell from 8:30 in the morning till 7:30 at night and I come home to wash. Tell me - at what time is one going to rest, how is one *not* to get tired with this type of work?

_____ : One has to wake up and be there trying to sell all day and sometimes one does not sell a thing and ends up tired and has to go home to continue working.

Complaints abound involving difficulties in commuting from their home to the wholesale market La Parada and from there to their selling places. Working ambulante mothers spend a minimum of two hours traveling from their homes to their selling posts. In order to cut down transportation costs, some ambulantes walk part of the way so as not to have to change buses, or they will teach one of their older children how to buy wholesale. The child travels on a reduced student's fare and the mother can save a little.

Because of the tight connection between daily maintenance of family members through domestic labor and their work in productive activities, ambulante mothers try to carry on their ambulatory trade near their homes or close to their children's school.

As one mother explains:

During the school year I stay up practically all night cooking and doing the laundry so as to start selling in a hurry at 8 a.m. As soon as one of the children comes out of school she/he takes over and I go running home to feed the rest of the family. As soon as they finish eating I run back again and sell till 7 or 8 p.m. Then I go home to wash and finish by 1 a.m.

Working mothers have no access to services and lack institutional supports to ease both their economic and caretaking jobs. One of the biggest problems is their lack of day-care centers. Of the women interviewed, 80 percent declare that if a preschool day-care center existed they would prefer leaving their small children there rather than taking them along to the marketplace, even if that meant paying a minimum amount; 20 percent say that they would rather take them along to the market or leave them with a relative. All ambulantes feel that they would be more relaxed at their vending trade if they knew their children were well cared for. In practice, however, most mothers take their toddlers and children with them to sell because of the anxiety they feel when, of necessity, they have to leave them behind locked up by themselves. Children have been badly hurt while playing unsupervised; others have inadvertently set their dwelling on fire playing with matches or when trying to warm their meals over a kerosene stove.

Ambulante mothers' views on lack of services:

> _____ : The children don't want to leave my side. As long as I see that they won't lack food I take them everywhere with me. One day I locked them up only to find my daughter bleeding. She had fallen from the roof! I'm afraid to leave them by themselves.

> _____ : My children stay home by themselves, I would rather leave them in a day-care center even if I had to pay ten soles because here you can't really work with young children.

Besides the obvious lack of institutional support for caretaking, ambulante mothers cannot really afford medical care when their children become ill because they have no access to workers' health care programs nor health insurance. They usually stop working when their children are sick. As in Maria's case, the ambulante mother's meager earnings decrease even more. Sometimes, when a child gets very sick, the women are forced to pay a private physician who overcharges them, rather than wait long hours to get a ticket for reduced medical attention at a hospital.

> _____ : When my boy gets sick, I first try to cure him with a laxative; this way I clean his stomach. But if he develops a fever I take him to a private doctor rather than to the emergency services in the hospital always crowded with patients. One usually wastes the whole day waiting for one of the doctors instead of selling at the marketplace.

SECURING A SELLING SITE

Ambulante mothers with no experience in hawking as children confront great difficulties upon entering the vending trade. The inexperienced street seller faces two initial problems: she must locate a busy commercial sector in the city, with a heavy traffic flow of prospective customers; she must find a lucrative selling site to which she can return on a daily basis and, eventually claim as her own.

The first obstacle is usually overcome through trial and error. Many ambulante mothers start selling in areas very near their homes, only to discover a want of clients. They then venture, with their goods, to heavily-populated centers of the city: to transportation crossroads where people wait for buses, to stadiums, public squares, parks, markets, and cinema entrances. The ambulante initiate discovers, much to her dismay, that she is one of hundreds, of thousands, struggling for economic survival through street selling. She meets with acute competition for selling space, with rejection and harassment from coambulante workers. Women vendors describe this stage of entry into the market as acutely trying. Before finally locating a strategic selling spot, they must walk up and down the streets offering their wares.

In his insightful analysis of the structure of ambulatory commerce in Lima, Österling (1981, p. 69) presents substantial evidence showing that although Lima street peddlers are known as ambulantes (derived from "ambular"—to wander or stroll) in fact, they do not. For all practical purposes, these ambulantes are permanent vendors—they sell in the same place year round. Through regular utilization of the same selling site, a vendor acquires use rights over a specific territory. This becomes her or his *lugar de ventas* (selling post). Österling points out that the vendor becomes empowered to sell the permanent site, rent it to another vendor, even pass it to descendants in case of death. Details concerning ownership are part of the unwritten ambulantes code, recognized and accepted by all city peddlers. However, the neophyte must learn the hard way:

_____ : (an ambulante mother selling Indian sandals) I have slept here in the street pregnant and with rain falling all over me and holding to this plank of wood that I carry as a portable counter. I've also brought with me my small toddler. All this suffering just to secure a selling spot.

_____ : (an ambulante mother selling prepared food) I have suffered a lot trying to work here in this market and in this place. There were lots of conflicts and quarrels among us at the very beginning because the ambulante who was first in getting here in the morning would grab the best selling spot. I was always late because I had two small children who I'd drag along with me to work at five in the morning. So as I was usually late the other ambulantes would take over my selling place. We would start quarreling and they would shout back at me: "You demand your place here, but we tell you that you only have a place in the cemetery!"

_____ : (an ambulante mother selling vegetables) In my obsession of not giving up my selling place I lost my youngest four-year-old Ricardito. When I was told that Ricardito had disappeared I started trembling all over because I didn't know *where* to look for him nor *where* to find him. So I walked a whole night up and down streets and markets. I did not eat, I didn't sleep thinking a thousand bad things could have happened to my child. I thought I was going crazy. The people of the large wholesale market La Parada suggested that I should go to the police in Breña (a Lima neighborhood) where all lost children found in the city were kept. Fortunately he was happily playing with other children. Recardito had been lost for four days!

PROBLEMS WITH AUTHORITIES

The legal status of street selling creates yet another complex set of problems the ambulantes must face. In their study of hawkers in Southeast Asia, McGee and Yeung (1977, pp. 41–60) discuss at length government policies regarding street vendors. They describe the most negative stance a government may adopt: there is no place and, therefore no right to peddle in cities. Such policy is grounded in the assumption that petty retailing is antidevelopmental, prevents modernization, and obstructs the efficient functioning of a city. When this perspective is adopted, governments interrupt the income-generating activities of street peddlers through removal by force from areas in the city where they operate. The radical eviction of hawkers is rationalized by government bureaucrats as necessary to ease traffic bottlenecks exacerbated by vendors' selling units. Vendors are also cited for allegedly posing hygiene and sanitation problems through the sale of prepared foods on sidewalks and the resulting litter in public spaces.

Österling (1981) documents the massive removal of 5,000 ambulante workers from Lima Cuadrada (downtown Lima) in the first months of 1981. Ambulantes were relocated to another section of the city, Polvos Azules, in the vicinity of the presidential palace.[3] The explanations given by officials for the relocation were traffic obstruction, vendors were not an esthetic sight for tourists, and street sellers placed unfair competitive pressure upon legal merchants with stores in the downtown area. Ironically, many of those ambulantes evicted had, in fact, been hired by established shop owners to provide additional outlets for their merchandise. Other street sellers were dealing in "irregular" goods purchased from large manufacturers who target an elite market; this group pressured for relocation. Österling (1981) in his study of ambulatory commerce shows that in addition to being an economic option for the migrants, street peddling is an important economic activity serving the population at large; in the context of the Peruvian economy it is an error to consider street peddlers as marginals.

Peruvian government policies directed toward workers involved in small-scale commerce are confusing and chaotic. They work against the efforts and interests of all petty vendors, especially against women street vendors and women holding fixed stalls in markets. These vendors constitute the most vulnerable group when targeted for intervention by the bureaucratic machinery of the Ministry of Food, an institution created in the mid 1970s in an effort to monopolize the fixation of prices of basic foodstuffs, whether sold wholesale or retail. Antecedent to this hierarchical intervention in the marketing trade was creation of the Empresa Pública de Servicios Agropecuarios (EPSA), whose basic aim was to control the marketing of basic staple foods. This was the first step toward the state's complete control of production and marketing of all agricultural goods (Fitzgerald 1976; Strasma 1976). Babb (1979; 1980; 1982; 1984), in her exhaustive studies of market sellers in Peru, describes the various mechanisms exerted on petty vendors to regulate, tax, and supervise their economic activities. When marketers, for instance, fail to obey the biweekly summons issued by the Ministry of Food in relation to official prices of foodstuffs, they are heavily fined. Fines are also administered by inspectors of hygiene and weights and measures for violations of rules established by the Ministry. Sellers are ousted from their selling places if they fail to show their identification cards (for which they have to pay) or if they do not come up with the money to pay the different fees required by the regulatory apparatus of the Ministry of Food. This constant institutional harassment restricts and diminishes the profits made by ambulantes and takes the control of the marketing process away from them. Working mothers, whether involved in small-scale ambulatory vending or holding permanent stalls in markets serving the impoverished classes in Lima, have practically lost control over their own work process.

Municipal police regularly interrupt working mothers: chasing them from their customary selling sites; fining them for selling commodities at prices higher than those officially established by the government; penalizing them through confiscation of merchandise.[4] This harassment both in fact and expectation creates yet more tensions for the already overburdened ambulantes. The enforcement of penalities by the *concejo municipal* (municipal council) as well as the open and relentless harassment by uniformed municipal police stems from and is supported by policies authorized by officials of Lima's Chamber of Commerce: they insist that street selling is an illegal economic activity (Österling 1981). Peddlers must, then, be discouraged through on-going implementation of punishment in the forms of restrictively high fees and confiscation of commodities (Mercado 1978).

Since 1977 harassment of small marketers and street vendors in Peru has grown decidedly worse. Babb (1982) attributes the escalation of oppressive measures enforced against petty retailers to increased inflation and an increasingly restrictive political climate. Although inflation and political repression touch all Peruvians, the occupational group formed by marketers, particularly ambulantes, has been singled out for attack. They have become the scapegoats for Peru's government which tries to displace the questioning of its own inadequacy in solving the country's economic crisis by trying to convince the nation's middle class and international agencies that petty vendors are blocking economic development and projecting a false image of an impoverished population.

Of 50 street-hawking mothers studied, 49 had serious complaints concerning municipal inspectors.

_____ : The municipal police drive us like animals, they shout at us, confiscate our merchandise and don't allow us to sell in peace. If we express resentment they tell us to go and complain somewhere else. My fear is that one has to be always on the move, feeling chased all the time and running away.

_____ : These municipal police are mean, they have no heart. You'd think that they have not been born of a woman by the way they treat us. They'll confiscate our merchandise, load it into a truck and one has to run after them. They fined me once that I was selling produce and now that I'm peddling baked goods they come and chase me out of my selling place.

_____ : These municipal police make it difficult for us to sell; one day they took everything I was selling away and I never got it back. So I lost all my money (capital).

CONFLICTS WITH FIXED STALL MARKETERS

Retailers with fixed stalls incessantly harass ambulante mothers peddling within or on the perimeter of established markets. They claim unfair competition, arguing that their customers are taken away from them by vendors who site themselves near fixed stalls where they offer similar commodities at reduced prices, or, encumber pedestrian traffic. There are regular clashes between ambulantes and members of the *cooperativa* of these established markets.

The cooperativa is the governing body of a cooperative market. There are many such cooperative markets in Lima, built by organizations of market sellers—many of whom were street sellers themselves. Cooperative markets are found throughout the poorer districts of Lima (Bunster 1983).

It is common to find municipal councils and cooperativas joining forces to check any increase of street hawkers within their territories. An ambulante mother describes one such conflict:

> _____ : Some years ago the concejo wanted to evict us and they joined forces by going hand-in-hand with the members of the cooperativa of the market where we do our peddling. The marketers of the cooperativa already had their market and didn't welcome our presence because it went against their own interests. So they agreed to our persecution. When attacks on us happen, all of us ambulantes form a common front and at that time we had a leader who told us: Everybody has to stay at their selling place. So we spent the night guarding our selling places!

SUPPLIES: HIGH WHOLESALE, SCANT CAPITAL

Ambulante mothers as a group, and the majority of women marketers selling with fixed stalls, constitute the lowest echelons of their occupational category. They can be seen as a subcategory within the traders' group: operating with the least capital, conducting operations in the most depressed neighborhoods of the city, working under uncomfortable, unsanitary, stressing conditions. With meager financial resources, they are forced into offering those commodities and services requiring the smallest capital investment. Their chief merchandise consists of perishable commodities—fresh fruits, vegetables, fish, prepared foods—as Tables 2.1 and 2.2 show.

TABLE 2.1 Types of Commodities Sold by Ambulante Women According to First Census of Ambulantes in Metropolitan Lima, 1976

Type of Commodity	Total	Women	Percent
(1) Argicultural foodstuffs, vegetables, fruit, garden produce	18,967	13,183	69.5
(2) Cloth, knitted fabrics, clothes, haberdashery	13,062	5,708	43.7
(3) Prepared food	8,809	6,173	70.0
(4) Assorted groceries	4,074	1,806	44.3
(5) Fish and meat	2,326	1,252	53.8

Source: Mercado 1978, Apendice Metodológico, p. 4.

TABLE 2.2 Types of Commodities Sold by Ambulante Mothers in our Study

	Place of interview				
Type of Commodity	Maternidad de Lima	San Juan de Miraflores	Surquillo La Victoria P. Libre Lince	Jirón Union	Total
(1) Fruit and vegetables	7	5	1	2	15
(2) Prepared food	7	1	2	—	10
(3) Clothes, cushions, haberdashery, assorted items of clothing	5	2	5		12
(4) Miscellaneous commodities: cosmetics, spices, flowers, detergents	5	5	—	3	13
Total	24	13	8	5	50

Source: Mercado 1978, Apendice Metodológico, p. 5

Our data show it to be the exception when an ambulante mother is able to increase income and accumulate capital over time. Many of them experiment with a variety of products within the perishable category, but it is rare for one to move through profit to those products allowing a foot up the economic ladder. This is not the case with male vendors. Men in the same occupation operate with more capital, expanding their (entrepreneurial) enterprise; they amass sufficient profit to reinvest in durable goods. Men also tend to secure sites in the best selling locations, the busiest, and most profitable sections of the city.

The economic marginalization of ambulante mothers is strikingly visible to the observer, and acute for the participant, during transactions with wholesale dealers. These economic transactions take place in any of the warehouses of La Parada, the large wholesale market, or with wholesalers in neighborhood markets.

Ambulante mothers are trapped in a cycle of poverty not only because of their meager capital and functional illiteracy, but also because they have no option but to engage in business within a hierarchical and exploitative economic structure. Inefficient buying mechanisms demand that street sellers supply themselves individually. They buy from economically powerful middlemen in the market supply chain. These men can be found selling their wares in La Parada, or from large trucks parked in lots adjacent to neighborhood markets. Most of these suppliers have become major capitalists, investing substantial capital in bulk goods. Wealthy middlemen are able to inflate prices by creating shortages of basic commodities. If, for example, a product seems to be in high demand due to a drop in supply, they move quickly to buy all available supplies and store them until the shortage becomes acute. Ambulante mothers and market women have no choice but to meet the exorbitant prices set. The wholesaler moves to maximize his profit by exploiting these retailers.

The cycle of exploitation and oppression pervades the lives of ambulante mothers. The women speak of being obsessed with worry over scarcity of their product; anxiety and insomnia are common.

_____ : (Seller of vegetables) I go every single day to La Parada. I keep getting up earlier and earlier. I usually step out of the house at 1:00 a.m. Sometimes I see men quarreling on the street and I'm scared. So I hide from their sight while I wait for the bus. I am usually scared and tremble with fear. I used to oversleep and get up at four in the morning and when I go to the wholesale market I would buy in a hurry to find out that what I had purchased was already spoiling. Customers don't buy then and one wastes one's capital.

_____ : (Seller of potatoes) When there's a scarcity of potatoes I leave for La Parada at 4 a.m. At other times we stay there all night hiding in the toilet and we step out when the market is closed. Then we get to the warehouse where the sacks of potatoes are stored. There's a lot of hassle and quarreling over the potatoes

and sometimes it's difficult to get hold of a sack. Finally everybody sleeps over her own sack. Sometimes we have to hide from
the municipal police because they'll throw us out. Some old ambulante women have been found dead in their hiding place.
They're too old and have worked too hard, they can no longer
take it.

There is widespread discontent among women street sellers as
well as an awareness of their exploitation by the wholesale dealers.
They are annoyed that they have to accept, without complaint, the
price the wholesaler imposes upon a specific commodity, disregard-
ing the official prices established by the government on basic products. They must meet the illegal demand without making waves. If
the ambulante mother reports the wholesaler to authorities, he re-
taliates against her by refusing to sell to her in the future or by bar-
ring her access to the product in the market. There is always a
desperate competitor who must buy at the inflated, illegal price.
Sales slips are stamped or written with government established
prices. The ambulante then has two choices—she can pass on the
overcharge to her customers, or she must fix her scales simply to
break even. Such "cheating" inevitably results in further conflict,
both with the public and municipal police.

Findings of our study show that these sellers at no point in the
buying/selling exchange have a precise fix on the amount of their
capital. A vendor of chickens expressed her disorientation in trying
to assess daily gross:

> One never knows how much one earns. For example, sometimes I
> have bought merchandise for 1,240 soles and at the end of the
> day I have recuperated only 1,000 soles which means that I have
> lost 240 soles and haven't earned a sol. I get very discouraged.
> One day I said to myself: "I'll stop selling because I have to work
> so hard, spend on kerosene (to keep a stove burning over which
> chicken vendors pluck the feathers of poultry to be sold), trans-
> portation, carrier and get up at 5:00 a.m. for nothing because I
> lose money. We're overcharged for the chickens by the *polleros*
> (exploitative wholesaler) in La Parada who stamp the official
> price on our sales slip after we've had to pay them a much higher
> price. We first have to give them cash, and if we complain about
> the overcharge they'll say—"You either buy the chickens or
> leave them." We're exploited, taken advantage of by them.

An ambulante mother selling fruit and vegetables in a poor
neighborhood market provides some insight into earning capacity:

_____ : Sometimes I lose track of the initial capital and the money I spend on food will be my profit for the day. There are days in which I only earn enough to buy food, while on other days I'll earn 150 or 250 soles.

In addition to all other constrictions upon the possibility of profit, the majority of ambulantes, like María, lack even the most rudimentary skills in mathematics and accounting which could aid them in an attempt to preserve, reinvest, and augment their capital. Even if such skills were at hand, however, the ambulante mother must draw upon capital to meet unexpected household expenses—such as taking a child to the doctor; or, they may literally have to "eat" their capital after a profitless day, taking it home and preparing it as the day's meal. María is typical, in her tendency to draw from her capital by using potatoes as the basic staple of her family's diet.

Disorientation and confusion over their own business operations make it very difficult to establish the median income of the typical ambulante mother. In an attempt to calculate their daily net income, we had to ask after the value of their stock, daily expenses, gross daily takings, and then calculate and approximate net income. We arrived at a median of 150 soles per day.

Pressures that result from an 18-hour-work day, generating income, and fulfilling domestic responsibilities, create a pervasive, personal sense of despair.

_____ : Sometimes I feel so tired and bored with everything. I work so hard and I do not sell and I'm there trying to sell all day and return home with nothing to feed my children. I go to the store and ask to buy food and pay later but the owner doesn't grant me credit. So I go home and cry aloud in anger and quarrel with my husband. Then he gets out of the house and gets drunk, comes home and shouts at me. For this reason we do not live happily nor is there any tenderness left for the children.

HARASSMENT FROM CUSTOMERS

In spite of the services they do, and must continue to render to the poor, almost all ambulante mothers describe periods of annoyance and irritation with their customers.

_____ : The majority of customers haggle over prices, ask for rebates, and sometimes take merchandise on credit that they never pay back.

_____ : I wish my customers would understand that we have to pay for electricity, water, and food. And that some days we earn and others we don't. I wish they'd be more understanding of our plight and not complain against us at the municipality.

_____ : I keep hoping my customers were more reliable and would pay what they owe me. Some customers owe me money but it embarrasses me to ask them to pay. This is the main reason for our economic downfall: if they don't pay we cannot invest to resell again.

Österling (1981) in his research on ambulatory trade in Lima and McGee and Yeung (1977) in their study of hawkers in southeast Asian cities agree that petty vendors gear their marketing activities to members of the working class. Österling sees the numerous *mercadillos* (ambulatory markets) dispersed throughout proletarian Lima neighborhoods as constituting the working-class functional alternative to the shopping centers targeted and frequented by middle-class shoppers in residential areas of the capital city. Our findings corroborated those of Österling and McGee and Yeung.

Most all of the ambulante mothers interviewed during our research peddle their commodities and services in the markets of San Juan de Miraflores, Surquillo, La Victoria, Puerto Libre, and Lince —low income districts with high rates of unemployment. They supply the urban poor at far lower prices than stores as, unlike storekeepers, they neither have to pay rents nor hire help. Competition among hawkers offering similar wares also keeps their prices low. Due to the perishable nature of their goods, rapid deterioration often forces ambulante mothers to sell quickly and at drastic reductions, thus benefiting customers. Ambulante mothers also provide cheap native dishes to market sellers who are without adequate cooking facilities, to residents in areas adjoining those in which they peddle, and to school children. They clearly serve a positive economic role in meeting the needs of reduced living expenses for the urban proletarian population.

ECONOMIC ASPECTS OF TRADING AND THEIR EFFECTS ON WORKING AMBULANTE MOTHERS' LIVES

In the process of enacting their daily, weekly, and monthly marketing operations, whether they are involved in the petty sale of commodities or services, ambulante mothers like María have to endure tensions, harassment, and problems. There are, first of all, difficulties arising from the close interlocking of tasks related to maintenance and care of offspring that must mesh with their economic activities, difficulties originating from the women's unequal position as workers when compared to men's position within the structure of production. Problems also arise from the illicitness of their trade and their economic vulnerability as petty entrepreneurs and as women workers caught in an oppressive and exploitative trap set for them by prosperous male wholesalers. These men exert power over them from a position of economic strength and authority in a hierarchical entrepreneurial structure. The women's precarious capital position becomes a stumbling block when they try to stock up on merchandise and upgrade their scale of operations, while their lack of education and rudimentary mathematical skills affects their ability to keep track of capital earnings and reinvestment. Finally, there is harassment by customers.

MARKETERS WITH FIXED STALLS

The situation of market women with fixed stalls in the poverty stricken districts of the Peruvian capital does not differ radically from that of ambulante women. Market women, like ambulantes, have maximized their potential in the reproduction of their labor power and social production by combining household and market roles in an intricate process. This group of working mothers superficially appears to provide a link between the formal and informal sectors of the economy. In reality, they do not. On the contrary, the nature of the problems faced by marketers is the same in kind, though larger in magnitude and complexity, as the one that blocks ambulante mothers from participating fully in the entrepreneurial world.[5]

Trading allows market women, as is the case of ambulante women, the necessary flexibility to integrate daily maintenance household activities with income-generating pursuits. From the vantage point of their own perception of the scant economic options available to them—domestic service, petty trade, and factory work for the more skilled—working mothers with fixed stalls in *mercadillos* (small markets) and *mercados* (regular markets) value marketing over other economic activities because they can reduce the conflict stemming from their dual responsibility as workers and mothers.

Market women, like ambulante women, have to surmount a series of recurrent everyday problems in order to fulfill their economic role. Their situational and rational procedure of combining home maintenance activities with marketing as a survival strategy is persistently hindered by the lack of structure in the macroeconomic sphere of Lima's market system. The women marketers in our study are constantly harassed by government officials through the municipal councils that interfere with the women's vending trade.

ORGANIZATIONAL COMPLEXITY OF THE MARKET SYSTEM IN LIMA

The difficult and stress-producing working conditions of mothers in the vending trade originate basically from Lima's market system that is characterized by complexity and lack of structure.

Paraditas and mercadillos are microstructures within the larger vending macrostructures of the market system. A paradita is a trading post, usually erected on a street where aumbulantes park themselves in order to sell. Paraditas are constantly spawning in different districts of the city. Commodities are sold on carts, tables, and on the floor, and these places do not meet minimum hygienic standards. This is one of the reasons accounting for bad relationships between street sellers doing business in paraditas and representatives of the municipalities in which they are inserted territorially. Municipal councils are the only official institutions acting as supervisors of the market trade in Lima and therefore are intervening constantly to stop the proliferation of ambulatory and petty trade; these municipal councils also try to monopolize the administration of fixed markets.

Paraditas represent the first step toward the development of mercadillos, small markets, which develop once municipal authorities have managed to oust hawkers from the streets. These ambulantes are then forced to find an adequate selling spot and temporarily settle themselves in open lots to continue their business. Stalls are built in a haphazard way out of different building materials and with no technical assistance. The aim of these street sellers is to acquire some stability for trading and delimit for themselves a specific selling territory. However, nothing is done about other installations. Under very special circumstances municipalities have been responsible for starting mercadillos which they run with administrative regulations similar to the ones applied to larger municipal markets.

Three basic types of trading centers make up the infrastructure of the marketing processes in the urban set-up. These are mercados municipales, *mercados privados*, and *mercados cooperativos*. The different municipalities in Lima have been responsible for building municipal markets and for renting stalls and shops to market sellers who sell their goods in fixed installations. Municipal markets supposedly have modern facilities such as refrigerated chambers. In practice, however, these facilities do not operate around the clock and are mostly in need of repair so that services rendered to market workers are inefficient or nonexistent. Municipalities are in charge of the administration of these municipal trading centers and responsible for cleaning and supplying guards for markets (Bunster 1983).

Mercados privados or private markets are housed in appropriate buildings constructed for the purpose by private businessmen and companies. These are equipped with refrigerated chambers, storage space, and other services. A concessionaire rents out the right to use these installations. Most of these mercados privados have remained vacant or are sitting half-empty in Lima neighborhoods because the average market seller cannot afford the rental price of shops and stalls.

Cooperative markets are found extensively in the poorer districts of Lima. These have been built by cooperative enterprises made up of the interested market sellers. Cooperatives own stalls and services in a given market and supervise its administration and cleaning. The bureaucratic relationship of cooperative markets with the municipalities in which they are found is conflictive because of the deeply ingrained assumption among municipal civil servants that all markets should be private property and should come under the administrative jurisdiction of municipalities.

Most cooperative markets have urgent problems to solve, such as financing and constructing permanent buildings to house shops, stalls, and the legalization of the land on which these markets now stand, as many of them have proliferated on fiscal property which markets sellers appropriated illegally by way of land invasions.

Most women interviewed for our study had fixed stalls in cooperative markets. It is of interest to point out that 42 percent of the marketing centers in Lima are organized under a cooperative system, 32 percent are private markets, and only 26 percent are municipal markets.

MICROANALYSIS OF WORKING MOTHERS IN TWO COOPERATIVE MARKETS

A selection was made of 36 working mothers involved in small-scale vending and holding permanent stalls in the cooperative markets

Ciudad de Dios and Magdalena del Mar. These markets are centers of trade in poverty stricken districts of Lima with high rates of unemployment, whereas the rest of the women marketers studied are selling in established markets in residential areas of the city. The objective is to present their work-related activities and problems, as well as their views on their conditions, and compare their situation to the ambulante mothers already discussed in this section.

The ages of the marketing mothers interviewed at the time of the study ranged from 20 to 53 years. Twenty-four of the women were living with a husband, two were involved in a consensual union, and ten lived only with their children and were the main providers of their female-headed households. Of the compañeros 7 were unemployed; 21 were working as wage laborers; 3 worked as small-scale vendors, 2 were in the army, and 1 was retired and living on a pension.

The women's level of education is low: 7 are illiterate, 12 are functional illiterates; 10 have over 4 years of schooling or have finished primary school. Only two have finished high school and five have incomplete secondary education. This factor contributes toward their entrapment within restricted economic options and only horizontal mobility is possible within these limitations. (See Tables 2.3 and 2.4.)

The products sold by the market women interviewed are the same as those sold by the majority of ambulante women. Like ambulantes, they operate in areas requiring small capital investment: assorted groceries, vegetables, fruit, prepared foods (native dishes and juices), spices, poultry, and fish. Only 1 woman out of 36 sells meat. They also sell miscellaneous nonalimentary products such as thread, sewing materials, yarn, cloth, and junk jewelry.

COOPERATIVE MARKETS ARE COOPERATIVE IN NAME ONLY

The only concerted action taken by members of cooperative markets is evident during the creation of their marketplace when they join forces to seize land on which to build their market site. Of the women holding permanent stalls, 53 percent acquired their selling place through invasion or land seizure, and the remaining 47 percent obtained their stalls through inheritance and transferences. There are cases of market women who have been hired to run a stall and of others who pay rent to have one.

Cooperative markets have been the result of group action; however, for purposes other than coordinated action on the market site,

TABLE 2.3 Market Sellers with Fixed Stalls and Previous Occupations, Cooperative Market Ciudad de Dios

Informant	Age	Age at first occupation	Years working in market trade	Previous occupations		
				First	Second	Third
1	35	14	10	Domestic	Peasant	Ambulante
2	41	—	6	Peasant	—	—
3	51	15	26	Peasant	Teacher	Ambulante
4	32	12	15	Peasant	Ambulante	Domestic
5	45	8	5	Domestic	Ambulante	Seller bakery
6	23	10	5	Peasant	Domestic	Ambulante
7	45	19	25	Preparing food	Ambulante	—
8	35	13	10	Peasant	Domestic	Ambulante
9	32	14	10	Peasant	Factory worker	—
10	39	14	12	Peasant	Ambulante	Domestic
11	38	12	17	Peasant	Ambulante	Domestic
12	44	12	21	Domestic	Factory worker	Ambulante
13	44	—	—	Peasant	—	—
14	24	19	4	—	—	—
15	34	8	15	Domestic	Ambulante	Preparing food
16	35	12	20	Preparing food	Ambulante	—
17	30	17	10	Domestic	—	—
18	53	40	10	Peasant	—	—
19	21	16	5	—	—	—
20	35	14	10	Factory worker	Ambulante	Ambulante
21	33	13	10	Peasant	Domestic	Ambulante

TABLE 2.4 Market Sellers with Fixed Stalls and Previous Occupations Cooperative Market Magdalena del Mar

Informant	Age	Age at first occupation	Years working in market trade	Previous occupations		
				First	Second	Third
1	53	38	15	—	—	—
2	31	10	—	Peasant	Preparing food	Ambulante
3	50	14	21	Peasant	Domestic	Peasant
4	45	20	15	Peasant	Preparing food	Ambulante
5	32	16	1	—	—	—
6	47	14	20	—	—	—
7	25	25	2 months	—	—	—
8	29	16	14	—	—	—
9	30	7	10	Ambulante	Domestic	Ambulante
10	23	—	15	Ambulante	Ambulante	Ambulante
11	36	19	25	—	—	—
12	49	8	5	Peasant	Domestic	Ambulante
13	34	17	15	Peasant	Ambulante	Ambulante
14	42	18	20	Ambulante	Ambulante	Ambulante
15	32	16	22	—	—	—

Note: Informants 1, 5, 6, 7, 8, 11, and 15 appear with no previous occupation but all of them have relatives already established as small-scale vendors.

they are cooperative in name only. Supposedly under this system the property of the market is social property, that is, members do not hold individual title to their stalls and shops. In practice, however, the conflicts arising among market coworkers indicate that the philosophy sustaining the idea of a cooperative market is not well understood, and speculation is high on rents and transferences. It is of interest to mention here the case of two women who, unable to meet the financial demands placed upon them by coworkers in the transference of a stall they wanted, were forced to hire themselves out as domestic servants in well-to-do homes and leave a relative behind to replace them in the market in order to earn the necessary extra cash for the transferral transaction (Bunster 1983).

The beginning stage of a cooperative market is characterized by provisional wooden stalls; some of the women in our study had built the ramshackle stalls themselves out of assorted materials.

NO ACCESS TO REFRIGERATORS NOR STORAGE SPACE

Cooperative markets do not have refrigerated chambers nor large storehouses. This is one of the many impediments to market womens' economic progress. As in the case of ambulantes, they take perishable stall merchandise home for family consumption, a process that contributes to their decapitalization.

NO COLLABORATIVE EFFORTS FOR PURCHASES

Market cooperatives like Ciudad de Dios and Magdalena del Mar do not utilize the advantages of massive purchase of products directly from the producers. There is no centralized control of commercial operations benefiting average market sellers and they have to supply themselves individually.

Wholesale dealers come to offer their products in trucks and park themselves during the night and early morning in adjacent vacant plots to the markets and paradillas. They bring vegetables, fruit, flowers, and chickens directly from the producers in the rural areas. They constitute the main link in a chain of supplying goods to markets. Small retail dealers, like the women of our study, either buy individually directly from them or go to La Parada, the major wholesale market in metropolitan Lima. However, in either case, they are acquiring products that have already automatically increased in price in the hands of intermediaries.

The amount of time, energy, and cash spent on supplying their stall daily is a constant physical and financial strain on market sellers. As was mentioned previously, when describing the daily routine of ambulante mothers, they have to get up at the crack of dawn, take their children along with them, spend money on bus fares, and pay carriers to load their purchases on buses, trucks, or taxis whose fare they split among other market sellers who are engaged in the same buying process.

The anxiety felt by Marcela, 36 years old and mother of three is indicative of a deep source of aggravation produced by the irrational organization of the marketing process in Lima. This particular market seller, like other mothers involved in small-scale vending, is constantly worrying about next day's purchases the day *before* the operation takes place fully. The following is an account of her reactions after undergoing a lot of harassment to buy a sack of onions during a period of acute shortage of this product.

> Would you like to know what I do in order to make sure that I'm going to have access to a sack of onions? After I close my stall at 3:00 p.m. I go to the wholesale market and go into the onion and potato section as if I were a regular hoodlum! By this I mean that I have to lie to the guards to let me in after convincing them that I'm a wholesale dealer myself and that I'm going in to talk to my sister who's already inside. I go better dressed to impress them. At 5:00 p.m. one of the wholesale dealers arrives in his own truck. 'Will you sell me a sack of onions, señor?" (I beg of him.) He answers, "Yes." But there I have to wait for about three hours till he finally gets around to selling me one. By this time it's already 8:00 p.m. I mark it with my name and go back home to eat supper. Then I return to the wholesale market where I sleep, keeping an eye on my own sack.
>
> Sometimes everything is so hard! Shortages of certain products make it so tough for us! It is then my children practically don't go to school, they are exhausted and go to sleep in class, under the teacher's nose. The school year ends and my children are behind. I *blame* myself because I've had my children stay awake all night helping me out at the wholesale market. When I see them so tired, it breaks my heart and I feel so guilty and so powerless! (Bunster 1983, p. 99)

Within the market scene of Ciudad de Dios and Magdalena del Mar and other markets it is the more prosperous market cosellers, usually men, who become the major capitalists. Because of the wide difference of capital resources available to these large sellers who can invest large sums of money in the purchase of goods and inflate prices to obtain larger profits when a product is scarce (in which case they monopolize it and store it up till the shortage becomes acute), small-scale sellers cannot expand their business.

Working mothers have a very clear understanding of the situation in which they find themselves. They perceive it as one of financial subordination and dependency on these wholesalers who exploit them on a daily basis. For in this way they speculate, compete, and outsell market women with fixed stalls and limited capital. Juanaticilla, mother of seven children and owner of a small grocery stand, formulates the problem and what it means to other working mothers:

> These big sharks, the rich *mayoristas* are the ones responsible for soaring prices. By hoarding products and exerting control by monopolizing them, they make the product more expensive to us and to consumers. The wholesalers are the ones who get enormous profits but we, poor common market sellers, suffer very much . . .(Bunster 1983, p. 99).

In her research on sellers in Bogotá's Plaza San Juan, Moser arrives at conclusions similar to ours and is more precise in defining these two categories of sellers. According to this author, the relationship between large-scale operators and smaller-scale sellers may be simplified into two polar types resulting in the articulation of two differing incentives, with sellers using the market for two very different objectives.

> Large-scale sellers operated *puestos* geared to the maximization of profit and expansion and were upwardly mobile in that the possibility existed of breaking out of the market. Small-scale sellers, who were caught in the vicious circle of small amounts of capital, uneconomic wholesale buying, and very low profit margins, operated below the level at which expansion was possible and operated to maintain the status quo and not become insolvent (Moser 1980, p. 371).

LACK OF COOPERATIVE EFFORTS IN ACCESS TO CREDIT

Cooperative markets are misleading in name because they make no effort to give assistance to their associate members. Women are the most adversely affected because they work with very scant capital. Findings of our study show that market mothers do not have a precise assessment of the amount of their capital. This lack of information is aggravated by the fact that they draw from their reserve quite regularly to attend to urgent family needs. They draw upon their nonperishable goods (infant's clothing, cloth, and yarn) and have also developed a habit of taking home stall foodstuffs when there is no other way to feed their family members or when perishable stall merchandise is about to rot because a refrigerator is not available to them.

When income from the market trade decreases, market women supplement their earnings by preparing hot breakfasts, lunches, or native foods which they sell to their coworkers and the public. Or they may close their stand for the day and go out with a crate of avocados, oranges, fresh fruit, or poultry and compete with the ambulantes selling at paradillas and on the streets.

Added to the constraints blocking the attainment of stability of their small-scale trade is the women's lack of education, basic arithmetic, or rudimentary accounting skills that would help them keep track of the fluctuations of their scant capital. They can never really expand their capital which in the majority of cases either remains stationary or is periodically diminished by withdrawing from it for reasons, already stated above. There is a constant drain leading to impoverishment affecting many of these women sellers and resulting in their financial inability to stock their stalls and obtain higher profits from their retail trade.

Moser uses the term "involuntionary" to define the stunted growth of economic activities of petty retailers unable to expand their trade in Bogotá's Plaza San Juan. This explanation also applies to the situation of the women market sellers in the cooperative markets of Ciudad de Dios and Magdalena de Mar.

> . . . it would appear that the dependent subordinate relationships between this level of petty retailing and the wider capitalist marketing structure, both wholesale and retail, has meant that with decreasing access to resources and the growth of monopolistic practices, the level of economic activity that occurs in the Plaza San Juan has become increasingly involuntionary. It is unable to generate growth but only to reproduce the existing conditions and scale of operations frequently at the expense of its cost of labor (such as the increased use of unpaid family labor) and standard of living (such as working longer hours). The informal sector approach, which categorizes two separate sectors, assumes they each have an autonomous potential for growth and is primarily concerned with the flow of labor between them; it tends to underestimate the importance of the

articulation of subordination/domination relationships within the capitalist system (Moser 1980, p. 383).

This micro-study has analyzed some of the patterned ways in which market women with fixed stalls in the markets Ciudad de Dios and Magdalena del Mar, both located in poverty stricken districts of the Peruvian capital, have managed to develop a present-oriented economic role as retail traders in an effort to adjust their productive work outside the home with the demands placed upon them by their home maintenance activities. This dual role is not easy, and the aspect least valued by society is their on-going engagement with the social production of the work force which exerts constant constraints on their economic production and traps them in the least permanent and lowest-paid or profit-making activities (Beneria 1979). Ambulante mothers and poor women holding stalls in cooperative markets are at the fringes of the capitalist mode of production, but at the same time they are integrated into it, are part of the system, but subordinate to it. (See Moser 1980.)

These market sellers constitute a vital entrepreneurial force providing cheap retail outlets to the constantly expanding low income population of families of wage earners, jobless, and subemployed members of the urban proletariat. Unfortunately they lack institutional support for their difficult daily life: no access to socialized medicine for themselves and their families, no day-care facilities in the marketplace, and no workers' retirement plan. Furthermore, they have to cope with stressful working situations in their already unhealthful occupational environment, produced by the inefficiency of the marketing system in Lima; they have to suffer daily harassment by public officials; they have to accept irrational government policies related to the fixation of prices of commodities by the Ministry of Food, and endure the consequences of unmanageable fluctuations in their scant capital and profits brought about by their exploitation by middlemen.

Taxed by an 18-hour double working day, market women do not have time to develop social or political ties with neighbors or coworkers. Their lack of political clout as a group is due to the fact that they work in isolation and have no time to get involved in unions. Herein lies the reason for the powerlessness they feel as working mothers and their incapacity, so far, to focus jointly on solutions to vexing problems related to their small-scale vending.

The children of market women, like the offspring of ambulantes, collaborate with their mothers at different stages of their double day. Mothers organize and direct their children around household and market activities. They usually start working alongside their mothers at the age of ten, and children selling behind the counter, in total control of the market stand while the mother is away attending to other affairs, is a common sight. However, it is interesting to emphasize that none of the working mothers want their male or female children to follow in their work as petty vendors. Their favorite occupational choices for their daughters, were these to become a reality, are nursing, fashion, and secretarial work, while the desire for their sons is to see them have the opportunity to become skilled in a specialized occupation or profession. They are very vague in pinpointing with accuracy specific types of occupations.

Only four of the market sellers want to continue in small-scale vending, while a third of the women interviewed declare that their highest aspiration would be work as seamstresses. The aspirations of the rest are centered on activities such as nursing, social work, hairdressing, and miscellaneous occupations that would insure them a regular income.

The working mothers of Ciudad de Dios and Magdalena del Mar were asked the following question: "After having lived all these years with all the good, regular, and bad things that life has in store for us, what choice would you make if you had the chance to live over again—would you like to be born as a man or as a woman?" Half of the women interviewed openly confessed that they would have rather been born male. Caught in the subuniverse of the marginally employed and unable to rise because of lack of education and a rigid class system, most of the ambulante and market-women mothers expressed themselves thus:

> I would like to be a man, because if he is educated, he can go in and out of important places and earn more, because men were born to accomplish more.

> I would like to be born again as a man; they only have one thing to worry about—to bring money home—and that's all. Women have to look after the children, cook, wash, and work outside the home.

NOTES

1. The criterion for the selection of the interview group of ambulantes was their workplace. Interviewers of the research team recorded ambulante mothers' perceptions of their work, family relationships, and political participation while they were selling. Interviews were done during slack vending hours. The women were interviewed at the Mercado de San Juan de Miraflores, Mercado de Lince, Surquillo,

Pueblo Libre, and La Victoria as well as in the overcrowded Jirón Union Street in downtown Lima. Ambulante mothers were also interviewed at the Maternidad de Lima (maternity ward of large hospital) where they had time to discuss issues related to their family and workloads while they recuperated from the birth of their last child.

2. We have drawn extensively from the information compiled on ambulantes by Hilda Mercado, a member of our research team, and benefited from insights of her preliminary report on street hawkers.

3. We visited Polvos Azules in 1983 and witnessed the fact that almost all of the ambulante mothers selling fruit and vegetables in downtown Lima had been weeded out during relocation. The majority of street vendors in Polvos Azules sell clothing, textiles, and indigenous arts and crafts for the tourist market, goods requiring large capital investment. Almost all the relocated vendors are men.

4. This is an example of the irrational policies of the Ministry of Food, intent on regulating prices and stripping marketers' control of prices of basic commodities.

5. The criterion for the selection of the interview group of working mothers holding permanent stalls in markets in metropolitan Lima was the workplace. They were interviewed at the following markets inserted in neighborhoods representing different socioeconomic groups: Mercado de Breña, Mercado de Lince, Mercado Modelo, Mercado Ciudad de Dios, and Mercado Magdalena del Mar. The interviews were conducted, as in the case of ambulantes, in pauses during the small retailers' double day. The "Talking-Pictures" album was opened over sacks of potatoes and crates holding live chickens and over counters. Hours of interviewing were recorded in this fashion. (See the Epilogue.)

However, for the purposes of presenting useful data to compare the ambulante and the fixed market-stall vendors, we concentrated our attention on a microanalysis of the working lives of 36 women retailers in cooperative markets.

LIST OF PHOTOGRAPHS AND CAPTIONS

2.1

2.2

2.3

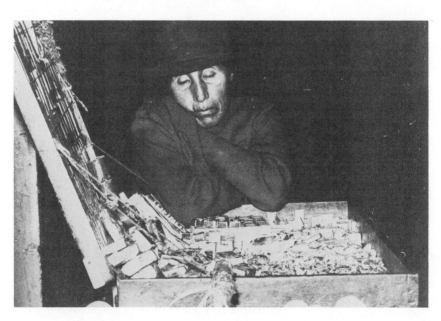

2.4

2.5

2.6

2.7

2.8

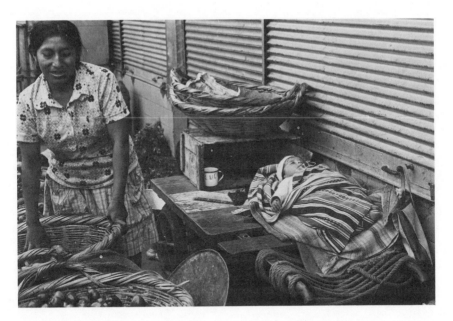

2.9

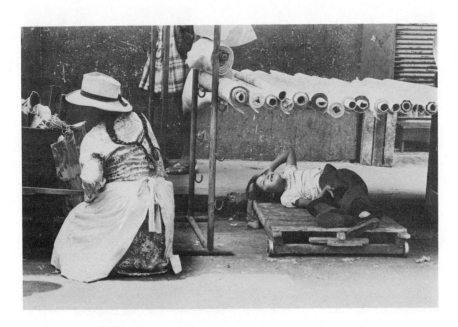

2.10

2.11

2.12

2.13

2.14

2.15

2.16

2.17

2.18

2.19

2.20

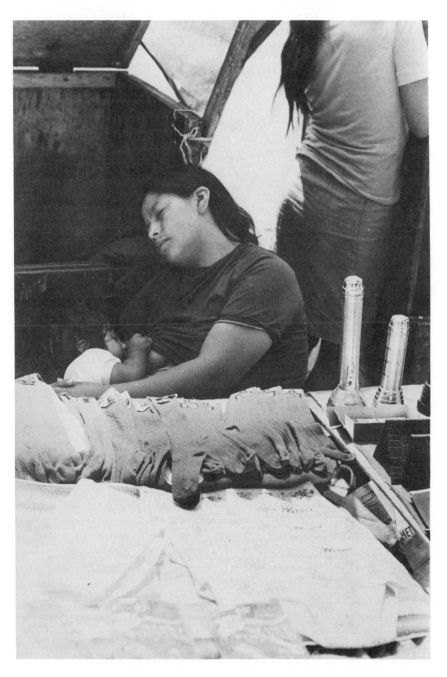

2.21

3 *Motherhood, Family, and Community*

INTRODUCTION

Aside from their long working days, Agripina and her servant colleagues live other lives scarcely imagined by their patronas for whom the maid often becomes simply part of the landscape. Maids look back with nostalgia on their days before the advent of children, when they usually could attend school and could spend their free time with friends and their small earnings on themselves: on clothes, make-up, and jewelry. Their lives were circumscribed by the fact that their one free day occurred only once every two weeks; moreover, because most lived cama adentro when they were single, their personal lives often were absorbed into the life of the patrona and her family. Yet, while their daily routine may have been monotonous, they were not so physically and emotionally burdened as they became with the birth of their first child.

All the women interviewed for this study have, of course, put behind them forever the times when life, at least in retrospect, seemed carefree. For most, their first pregnancy signals the beginning of a life-long struggle, many without a male partner at their sides, when they begin building a second life outside the patronal home. Eventually, the pressures of trying to balance work and their own responsibilities to home and children may force them to leave the servant life altogether, and many will take up selling as the only possible option that combines with their other duties, particularly with childcare. Thus, even though this chapter deals principally with the home life of the domestic servants, the lives of the market sellers and ambulantes in relation to their compañeros, children, and the barrios where they live are remarkably similar, although some market women have better housing and/or live in somewhat better districts.

The two major problems that must be faced immediately are childcare and an alternative arrangement to "living in." Women with one or two children find that to remain in the patrona's house rapidly becomes "insoportable." Many say that the señora doesn't wish the child to emerge from the maid's room at all; unless her room opens onto a courtyard at the back of the house, the child has to stay inside day and night, with the mother running back and forth to feed and change her child in between her other duties.

Thus, pregnancy marks the women's increasing involvement in a set of new, intricate, and often harrowing relationships: first and foremost, with their children; then with their compañeros, and often with relatives (less often with friends). Maids also participate in a network of secondary relationships—to barrio and municipal authorities, school and medical personnel; tradespeople, especially those who sell water, food, and building supplies, the three leading necessities on which women spend their meager salaries.

Because we chose to interview women with at least one child, the trabajadoras del hogar in my group are untypical in that more servants in the total population are single women without children than are married or in consensual unions. The group interviewed for this study might be considered transitional, in that many surely will leave the servant life to become (most probably) street vendors, and those still living cama adentro (21 of the 50 cases) also will find a way to establish a home outside their employer's house, even if they continue to work as domestic servants.[1] If there is one theme that predominates among domestic servants (dwelt upon in the interviews even more than their dislike of their occupation), it is the desire to establish some kind of home life independent of the house where they spend their working hours.

In the following sections, the experience of the women interviewed as they faced their first and subsequent pregnancies will be explored, underscoring in particular their relationships to *enamorados* (men friends) and compañeros. A section following will deal with the important question of childcare, as well as the daily struggle of household workers to combine domestic service with the very similar tasks they must carry out for their own families. A third section details the alternative living arrangements most of the women have established outside the patronal home, as well as the women's somewhat tenuous relationships to their communities. A final section deals with the women's perceptions of themselves and their assessment of their prospects for bettering their lot in life.

MATERNITY AND CHILDREN

The destiny of nearly every young maidservant is, one day, to encounter her first enamorado and begin her family. She does not necessarily view this event negatively: many of the women interviewed, on learning of their first pregnancy, recall their overriding emotion as one of joy that they were going to have a child. Often this joy was intermingled with feelings of desperation as to what family, friends, and patrona would say, and what they would do. There was also, as the women recall their reactions to first pregnancy (an event, for some, many years in the past), often disquiet as to whether the father of the coming child would cooperate: would he be willing to marry (by their own account, all but 1 of the 50 became pregnant before marriage); if not, would he at least be willing to recognize the child legally, and contribute to its support? Table 3.1 shows the reactions to first and subsequent pregnancies of the woman and her compañero; it is important to note that the interviewee is reporting on how she perceived her man's reaction, since the men were not questioned. It appears that the women's fears on at least one score, abandonment, were well founded; 18 of the interviewees were rejected at first pregnancy, and 28 presently are *madres solteras* (single mothers).

Perhaps the most striking pattern in the table below is the fact that so many more of the women register disquiet over how they can support their children (10 with first child, and 19 with their subsequent pregnancies) than the men; none of the men appeared to the women to be worried at the first pregnancies of their compañeras, and only 3 subsequently expressed themselves as concerned. Coupled to the large number of desertions, the conclusion—at least for this group of compañeros—is that the men show an almost total disregard for their progeny and for the women left behind to fend for themselves and their children. It should be noted here that 18 of the 28 who deserted the interviewees at first or subsequent pregnancies either already had other families, or left the interviewee to go off with another woman.[2] In three cases, this was with the concurrence of the interviewee: Hermalinda, whose three children were fathered by the same man, has resigned herself to the fact that he only visits with her—he lives with his "official" wife and their five children. In another case, the interviewee says that she urged her compañero to return to his wife because she did not want "to damage his señora," and in the third case, the rival was a minor and, in the interviewee's judgment, in worse straits than herself.

TABLE 3.1 Reactions to Pregnancy by Interviewees and their Compañeros

Reactions	First pregnancy	
	Woman	Compañero
(1) Happy, joyful	13	6
(2) Sad; with heartache, shame, fear	11	—
(3) Worried: How am I going to support a child?	10	—
(4) Resignation	4	—
(5) Repugnance (because pregnancy was result of rape)	4	3
(6) Mixed: happy, but worried	3	3
(7) No interest, rejected me		18
(8) Anger; didn't say anything		5
(9) Other[a]	4	—
(10) No reply		12

Reactions	Second and subsequent pregnancies	
	Woman	Compañero
(1) Happy	3	3[b]
(2) Worried: how am I going to support this child?	19	3
(3) Resignation	3	7
(4) Had no interest; left her		7
(5) Anger		3
(6) Asked her to get abortion[c]		2
(7) Other[d]		
(8) Not applicable (couple has only one child)	23	23
(9) No reply		2

[a]"Other" reasons include sorrow at having to terminate studies; a psychological reaction in which the interviewee recalls that she went about "as if in a dream," denying she was pregnant, and fear because the interviewee knew nothing about caring for a baby.

[b]One prospective father, reported as happy, nevertheless left home before the baby was born. Thus, No. 4 should actually show 8 men who left. These tables, however, show the *first* reaction reported; many of the women recounted a number of reactions to their pregnancies.

[c]Compañeros requested that their mates secure an abortion, but neither was willing to do so.

[d]"Other" reasons include physical sickness and an overwhelming feeling of fear.

In the first case noted above, the father of Hermalinda's three children has, through the years, always tried to help financially when he could; the interviewee explains that apparently they cannot live without each other. Once her compañero journeyed three days and four nights to the sierra to bring her back to Lima when she left with the children for her own province, trying to break the tie. Three other fathers with second families also contribute at least something to the support of the children borne to them by the interviewees. Edelmira's compañero has a second family, but lives with *her*. In one case, a compañero with two families fell from a scaffold and for some months was not able to contribute to either of his households.

Despite the street wisdom that the maidservant is "easy" and has many enamorados, this is not the case with most of the 50 women studied in depth for this exercise. Fully 34 report that they had their first child with their first boyfriend, including the lone interviewee who married before getting pregnant: "me case sin barriga"-"I married without a belly." Since then, 12 have married legally (1 has since separated). In ten cases, the women did not remain with the father of their first child; yet neither have these women been notably promiscuous, as Table 3.2 shows. There is always the possibility that the low number of unions registered reflects the women's reluctance to admit the extent of their sexual relationships; on the other hand, there was no hesitation either in recounting that they had become pregnant before marriage, or were not in a legal union. Two of the women reporting three or four unions each had only one child, and were the only ones who might be termed "promiscuous" in a technical sense, but further probing would be necessary to determine the real situation.

While many of the interviewees still are very young, and thus the numbers of their unions could change, nevertheless the tendency to form one, or at most, two unions is strikingly similar for each age group, as Table 3.3 shows.

TABLE 3.2 Household Workers by Number of Unions and Whether Compañero is Present or Absent

Number of unions	Compañero present	Compañero absent
1	16	19[a]
2	6	6
3 or 4[b]	—	3

[a]Includes one widow (not legally married), and one separated (who was legally married).

[b]Only one woman had four unions.

TABLE 3.3 Household Workers by Age and Number of Unions

Age	1 union	2 unions	3 or 4 unions
19 and under	6	—	—
20–24	11	3	1
25–29	10	3	1
30–34	4	3	—
35 and over	4	3	1
	35[a]	12[b]	3[c]

[a]Of 35, 16 have compañero present, 19 absent (1 died).
[b]Six with compañero present, six absent.
[c]All three of the third and fourth compañeros have departed.

Age at first union is an important factor in the number of children a woman may produce over her reproductive period. Again, at least with this group of 50 case studies, the ages of the first union and birth of the first child are somewhat older than folk wisdom would suggest; median age of first sexual relations is 17 years of age, and for giving birth to a first child, 19 years. The median number of two children each produced by the interview group is much lower than the interviewees' natal families, where the median number of children is five. Nevertheless, since 85 percent of the interviewees still are in their reproductive years, no firm conclusions can be drawn on their completed family size. Only 16 of the 50 interviewees say they want more children; of these, 9 are presently living with a compañero. Table 3.4 records the numbers of children by age group of the women participating in the study.

TABLE 3.4 Number of Children of Household Workers by Age Group

Age groups	1 child	2 children	3 children	4 children or more
19 and under	6			
20–24	8	6		1
25–29	5	2	5	2
30–34	3	2		2
35–44		2		3
45 and over			2	1
Total	22	12	7	9

Several factors might nevertheless contribute toward larger completed family size for the interviewees—not only the fact that many will move out of domestic service and into employments such as street vending and market selling, but also the very small number of domestics who are practicing any birth control method or even know about one. Only eight of the women have at least some knowledge of a method. Table 3.5 documents the knowledge and practice of interviewees.

As was noted in the previous chapter, offspring are perceived as definite assets by the *ambulante* and market women, while for the servant, children pose a great difficulty in continuing in that occupation: "No se recibe con niño-They don't hire you with a child"

TABLE 3.5 Contraceptive Methods Known or Used by Interviewees

Age	*Compañero Present?*	*Method*	*Results or remarks*	*No. of children*
(1) 42	No	?	Good results	5
(2) 27	No	Pill	Thinks they are bad for the nerves	4
(3) 23	Yes	Injection	Knows about; wants to use later	2
(4) 25	Yes	Rhythm	Also believes that being a laundress—because it is so taxing—prevents her from conceiving	1
(5) 32	No	Spiral	Used for two years; doctor told her her daughter was born without a hand because of pills	6
(6) 20	Yes	Pill	Says that when she takes pills, her stomach aches and therefore she has stopped taking them.	2
(7) 30	No	Prescription (?)	Says that the doctor gave her a perscription.	1
(8) 22	No	Pill	Taking pills	1

Note: Nos. 3, 4, 6, and 8 want more children.

was a constant refrain. Some years ago, a social scientist working on the fertility of women in Peru also noted the small numbers of children produced by maidservants as a group, and speculated very learnedly on what aspects of the occupation might inhibit their fertility, i.e., long hours, hard physical work, inadequate nourishment. What he should have noted, of course, is the fact that women with children simply move out of live-in domestic service, leaving the field mainly to those who still are single, or who have one child. It is important to remember Sara Lafosse's estimate that about 40 percent of single mothers in Peru are domestic servants (1980, p. 315).

Margo Lane Smith (1971) has speculated that one route out of the servant role for younger women is to marry up: a petty bureaucrat, or a member of the police. So far as the present group is concerned, very few male partners (whether present or absent) fall into such job categories. Since so many of the women are young, they still could meet such men. Of the 22 women with compañero present, only 1 man is a white-collar worker. Among those who have rejected their compañeras, on the contrary, are three police/civil guards and two empleados, and two students (one studying business and one at the university). Table 3.6 shows the occupations of spouses, and whether they are present or absent.

TABLE 3.6 Occupation of Spouse of Household Workers and Whether He is Present or Absent

Occupation of spouse	Present	Absent
Manual worker	10[a]	4[c]
Doorkeeper, guard	3	2
Street vendor	3	1
Carpenter	1	2
Police, military	—	3
White-collar employee	1	2
Servant	—	3
Farmer	—	2
Other	4[b]	4[d]

[a]Includes three mechanics, two construction workers, two factory workers, two textile workers, and a casual laborer.

[b]Includes a stevedore, student, and chauffeur.

[c]Includes two construction workers, a factory worker, and an obrero whose specialty was not specified.

[d]Includes two students, a slaughterhouse worker, and baker.

An interesting question in relation to compañero is whether the fact that the women are working gives them any power of decision in the household. Of the 22 women with the spouse present, 21 say that the man should decide, and 1 says that both should exercise power in the household. Of the 28 with the spouse absent, 13 say that the woman should decide, but 3 qualify that it should be the man, if one were present. What is interesting is that, in the case of four households where the man is not present, the woman still defers to him on decision making (in two of these households, the absent father does not contribute toward the support of his children). In one case, the interviewee says that both should decide, and in three others, their own mothers and/or fathers make the family decisions.

The most common response to this question underscores the fact that the women believe that the man should command simply because he is a man:

> —My husband, because he is the man and he contributes more to the support of the house.
> —Always it is the man who commands and decides.
> —My husband—one cannot do just what one pleases.
> —In my house, the husband is the boss.

But in some cases, the women have reasons for saying that the man should be in charge, even in the household:

> —My husband. He leaves me just enough for the daily expenses. At the beginning, I demanded that he give me his salary, but he told me that since I am not married to him, I don't have any right to it.
>
> —The man. He has more character, he was created to command.
>
> —My husband because he is the man of the house (he contributes even though he has another family). Yes, I would like to work because I would like to have my own money and to spend it as I please.
>
> —My husband; he has the greater responsibility as the head of of the house (from a woman abandoned since the birth of her child, and whose compañero never has contributed anything).

COMBINING WORK AND FAMILY

Once a household worker has children, she must make provision for childcare if she keeps on working as a servant. The child-care problem is, without doubt, the most pressing one facing the interviewees, the one they mention most often. Many strategies are followed, as Table 3.7 shows.

TABLE 3.7 Arrangements for Childcare by Household Workers

Living arrangement	Older Sibling	Relatives	Neighbors	Nursery	Keeps with her	Leaves alone
Live-out maids	10[a]	2	4	4	8	1
Live-in maids		7[b]	1		13[c]	

[a]In two cases, older brothers; in eight cases, older sisters.
[b]In two cases, children are with relatives in the home province.
[c]In one case, an older child is with her comadre while the household worker keeps his sister; in another case, the child's grandmother has one twin girl, and the mother keeps the other with her. (Comadrazcio is the relationship set up between a woman and the godmother in baptism of her child.)

In nearly one-half the cases, as Table 3.7 shows, the mother, whether she lives in or not, cares for her own child or children personally. This confirms one of the major conclusions of Anderson, Figueroa Galup, and Mariñez (1979), in a recent study of childcare in Peru, that "the only practical solution to the problem of combining childcare with any other activities is to take the child along with her." Eight live-out maids bring their preschool children with them each day to the patrona's house. In one case, the patrona, who is "very good," takes care of the maid's child; in the other cases, the household worker is under the same strictures as her colleagues who work cama adentro: to keep her children quiet and out of the employers' way. Those mothers who live out but who, nevertheless, must bring children with them face another difficulty the live-ins do not: they must rise even earlier than their live-in colleagues in order to get the rest of the family off to work and school, then face a long bus trip at rush hour with their infant and/or toddler in tow. After the day's work is done, the return journey home must be faced. Of the eight women who bring their children with them to work, seven have only one preschool child. Even if they bring two children with them, as does Regina, they often still must make arrangements for the older children—sometimes for the afternoon and early evening, for those who go to school only in the mornings (because of overcrowded conditions, some Peruvian schools run classes on a split schedule, with morning and afternoon sessions).

For those 13 women who live in with their infants and small children, life as a servant is doubly difficult. They must attend to their children in between their many tasks, often on the sly because otherwise, "the señora says I am too much with my child and not doing my work." Faustina was fired from one post because her child—whom she had tied in her room—screamed too much. "Sometimes I didn't have time to feed her, and she got hungry. Whatever they gave me, I always divided in two, and for that reason my child is thin." Victoria manages by slipping away every little while to look in on her baby in her room, "because the señora doesn't wish the child to come out." Another interviewee sums up one of the major problems in taking one's child to the patrona's house:

> Many patronas don't want to hire a servant with a child because they have their own children, small children at home. Sometimes the little kids fight—my little daughter and the daughter of the patrona. Sometimes, too, my daughter is restless, annoying; sometimes she grabs the ornaments—and the patrona doesn't like that at all.

The fact that many children spend their preschool years tied or shut in the maid's room has serious consequences for their development. Several interviewees mentioned that their children were slow in talking or walking. Carmen Pimentel, the Peruvian psychologist who assisted us in the early stages of our study, tells of one four-year-old she treated who couldn't walk or talk, but only rocked back and forth. His young mother, terrified at losing her job when she became pregnant, agreed to her employer's demand that she could stay only on condition that the señora would never set eyes on the child. Subsequent treatment revealed that the boy was not autistic, and he gradually responded to concerted efforts to stimulate and teach him. But he will never be completely normal.

Relatives and neighbors (the latter usually paid) are next in importance as child-care suppliers, providing this service in 14 cases. Often a woman who works cama adentro still must board a child, and this arrangement has its own problems. Juana, who lives in, works in an isolated district far from Lima and from where her child boards. She recounts that sometimes she cannot go to see him on her day off because she must earn another 50 to 100 soles washing—ironically in order to meet the costs of boarding her son. She is afraid that the woman who takes care of him doesn't feed him properly, and that her son doesn't love her because she sees him so seldom. "You understand that a son is the only thing there is in life," she says. In two cases, younger children are with relatives in the household worker's province of origin; the rest are in Lima. This contradicts, at least for this group, another piece of folk wisdom: that maids always send their children off to their home province to be raised by relatives.

Older siblings also account for a significant percentage of the child-care arrangements. In some cases, the caretakers are very young, but the mothers have no alternative: two nine-year-olds and one seven-year-old are left with their younger brothers and sisters. The mother of the latter says that her daughter "helps me wash, iron, bathe the babies—she can do everything." Clodoalda's ten-year-old lives in with her, and takes care of her three-year-old sister while the mother works. All of these older children attend school only sporadically.

In only one case are infants left on their own (a girl of two and one-half years, and her little brother aged eight months). A visit to Carmen's house revealed that, apart from the danger, the children are growing up like two small animals. The little girl defecates everywhere, and she cannot really respond to the needs of the infant who simply is left unattended until Carmen's return.

Another strategy of those with children is to try to solve their problem by changing specialties, from household worker to ambulantes. Hermalinda and her cousin several years ago decided they would try their hand at selling chicha, a fermented corn drink. But they had to give up after a week. "We didn't have anyone to show us where to sell, or to tell us how," she laments. She considers herself fortunate that her patrona decided to accept her back. Several other women have become laundresses—"the most desperately exploitative work" (Moser 1981, p. 24)—because they had no other option. They either arrange to pick up and deliver the laundry to the various houses, washing in their own homes and often in extremely inadequate facilities, or they try to finish the washing and ironing by 4:00 p.m.—which allows them to leave much earlier than the household worker who must stay through dinner in order to serve the family and clean up afterwards.

Daycare does not appear to be a viable solution for these women. Only rarely can a convenient center be found; if the mother must make a long detour to a nursery or preschool, she often cannot get to work on time. Child-care centers typically have long waiting lists or are too costly, and there are few centers. The Ministry of Education has, by and large, left nursery schools to the private sector, concentrating its attention on preschool education (Anderson, Figueroa Galup, and Mariñez 1979, p. 41). However, both private nurseries and preschool programs concentrate on older children (from 3 years to 5 years and 11 months), since it is more expensive to set up a nursery center for infants. The fact that the regulations for day-care centers are so strict, requiring very high standards in terms of physical infrastructure, furniture, and trained personnel also has inhibited the proliferation of day-care centers (*ibid.*, pp. 41–42). Some less structured, less formal system of *mini-cunas* is needed: that is, dozens of small day-care centers set up for eight to ten children each by women of the neighborhood in their own homes, who would receive small subsidies in the form of food and equipment from the municipal government.

In an ironic twist, Mercedes was offered a job in a day-care center, which she would have liked because it would have solved the problem of what to do with her own three-year-old, as well as her infant granddaughter. Mercedes' daughter of 17, the new mother, would like to work, but she cannot because she must stay home to care for her little sister and her own baby. However, the pay was in milk and food, but no salary, so that Mercedes couldn't accept it; since she is the sole support for her five children and one grandchild, she needs cash. At other times, placement in a day-care center is not the end of a household worker's problems. When Zulema's daughter proved too restless and mischievous for the day-care center, the proprietor asked that she not bring her any more. Now Zulema's mother stays with her daughter on the days Zulema goes to her clients' homes to wash and iron.

A closely related problem is the question of what to do when a child is ill. The employers, by and large, see this as strictly a problem that the domestic worker must solve for herself, although there are some exceptions. One dismaying fact is that women who work fulltime cannot make use of the free medical attention offered in the pueblos jóvenes which function on a system of "tickets," according to the number of doctors who will be available that day. Mothers must arrive very early at the clinic in the hopes of, first, acquiring a ticket, then settling down to wait—sometimes the whole morning. Because domestic servants cannot afford the time or cannot secure permission to be away from work, they must bear the expense of a private physician when their children get sick.

In nine cases, household workers report that their employers take the sick children of their helpers to the hospital or clinic, and in four cases, medicines are paid for by the employer. Three give time off (and one of the three doesn't discount her helper for the days she can't work). Four mention that they receive a salary advance to cover the cost of doctors and medicine for their children; seven receive propinas or tips to help with the purchase of medicine or to pay medical bills; 13, however, report that they never receive tips for this purpose.

What is missing from the women's many strategies is anything but occasional help with their children by their compañeros. As Anderson, Figueroa Galup, and Mariñez (1979) also report, childcare is viewed as strictly a problem for the mothers—both the routine daily minding, or even times when children (ordinarily in school or cared for elsewhere) are ill. This is true even though (in the Anderson, Figueroa Galup, and Mariñez study) many of the men reported that they had taken care of their siblings when they were younger. Both women and men view this as perfectly natural: when a man is grown, his obligation is to provide for his family, and that means that he normally is not around to take on child-care responsibilities. But the reverse is not true; even though most believe that it is equally a woman's responsibility to bring in money, she also is expected to either make arrangements for the children's care or to oversee the children herself—even if the man is out of work and around the house.

When the women were asked directly how they solve their child-care problem when they go out to work, none mention their husbands or compañeros. However, in response to an earlier question (whether the husband or compañero helps in the house), several do mention that they sometimes receive help with childminding. Of the 22 who live with their families, 5 men occasionally take on child-care responsibilities (of these, 2 are husbands and 3 are convivientes). One compañero lives with his other family, but visits and sometimes takes care of his children in the house of his concubine.

One of the ironies of the child-care question is the fact that poor women are engaged to look after affluent women's children, while their own are (as some put it) *botados* or thrown out on the streets. Hermalinda walks her patrona's two children to their *colegios* in the mornings, and then goes to accompany them home at noon. In the afternoon, after giving them their lunch, she spends some time playing with them and entertaining them—in fact, she says, she doesn't have time to sit down because she must always be trailing the children around "because they could suddenly fall, or injure themselves." Yet her own children are left in the barriada, where the 4-year-old runs with the pack of neighborhood children, grabbing onto the backs of the buses and trucks that travel up and down the hilly terrain. When her infant son became ill, Hermalinda's nine-year-old daughter had to remain at home for nearly six months' to care for him and the four-year-old; subsequently, the infant died, and Sonia now is repeating the first grade for the third time. During her son's illness, Hermalinda locked the three children in her reed hut because of the danger to the girl left on her own in a lonely corner of the barriada, where "one never knows what the men may do." Hermalinda often worried about how her daughter would manage with the kerosene stove, which she had to light to heat up the noon meal. "Sometimes, as I am running after the señora's children, I see my own children locked in, and the house going up in flames," she says.

Although childcare is the greatest preoccupation of the women, there are many other household tasks that the domestic servant who lives out must replicate in her own home: at the least, they daily shop for and cook not one, but two principal meals, as well as get their children off to school in the mornings. On weekends, there is no time to rest, because Sunday off provides the only day to do washing and ironing for the worker's own family, plus the heavy cleaning.

The most frequent response to the question of how they manage their heavy double day is "me levantar temprano" and "trabajo rápido"—I get up early, and I work quickly. Since domestic servants customarily arrive at 7:30 or 8:00 a.m. in order to serve breakfast, they must leave for work by 6:00 or 6:30, or sometimes even earlier. This means that they rise at 4:30 or 5:00 a.m. Often they do not return from work until 8:00 p.m. in the evening, or even later. This means that they can only feed their children (and compañero), and do a bit of cleaning and straightening up at night. Eugenia says that she is "always in a hurry." Osoria does her own work rapidly at night; she is now accustomed to the double burden, she says, but it leaves her very tired. Even on her day off, Rosa says, she has to stay in the house of her employers because there is so much to do for her own children, and because it is too difficult to take the children with her in the bus.

Many remark that they could not carry on without the help of their children. "I have to make my children help me get things done," says Fandila. Her two older daughters help with the six younger children. "They clean, wash dishes—it is good for them to help, because before you know it they'll be older, and they'll more or less be able to make it on their own." Less help is available from husbands, although some do assist when their compañeras are particularly burdened or ill. Table 3.8 shows which compañeros help. As long as the man is present, his willingness to help does not appear to be based on whether or not he is legally married to his compañera; convivientes help at almost the same rate as husbands when they live with their spouses.

TABLE 3.8 Helps with Domestic Tasks by Compañeros

Living arrangement	Yes, regularly	Sometimes	Never	No reply
Legally married	4	4	3	
Compañero present	3	2	5	1
Compañero absent	4[a]	2	15	7

[a]One legally married, is separated.
[b]One conviviente, deceased, helped when he was alive.

At the patrona's house, if the maid lives in, there is always her own child to care for in the short free spaces of time. Regina says that when she is serving dinner, her own children often cry from hunger because she does not get around to feeding them at the proper hour. Sometimes she sends her three-year-old son to quiet her eight-month-old daughter; sometimes, too, she still gives the breast to her son when he cries.

Those who live in with their child or children have a continual struggle to attend to their own children's needs without exciting the señora's wrath by devoting too much time to their own affairs. Answers from the survey point to the fact that most patronas wish to see and hear as little as possible of the maid's children: the interviewees talk of the difficulties of keeping small children quiet and, especially when they begin to toddle, out of the way of the mistress.

Dora, who has all three of her children with her at the patrona's house, (her husband is a seaman who rents a room to use with her when he is in port) never gets to bed before 1:00 or 2:00 a.m. "The thing is, when I get finished with the señora's tasks, I have mine to do. I have to wash diapers, clean my room, bathe the children and myself, and wash and iron my uniforms." The three children (aged three years, two and one-half, and eight months) mainly stay in her room, and she feeds them there. The patrona provides noon lunch for all four, but Dora must prepare dinner for her own children, from her own supplies, after the family dinner is over. Maruja, who takes her child with her, says that sometimes she doesn't have time during the day even to bathe her or comb her hair. Clodoalda's ten-year-old attends to her three-year-old, washes, and irons, and cooks easy dishes. Domitila reports that the señora doesn't like her child (a girl of seven) to be out of the house. "Sometimes when the señora seemed annoyed with her, I sent my daughter to lunch with a friend. But the señora didn't like it and said that she preferred her to stay at home and to help me. Sometimes the señora sends her to the store."

No matter how onerous is their "second shift"—either within the patronal house, or in their own domicile—the overwhelming majority of women find the work for their employer more tiring (29 interviewees) or equally so (15 replies). "In my own house, I can rest a moment, but at my job, I cannot"; "Here in my own house, I can sit down awhile"; "At home, one works in peace, but on the job, one has to keep going, even though one is sick because there is an obligation"; "At home, I do what I can, but in my employment, I have to keep going"; "At home, if I want to rest, no one says anything, but at work when one let's up a little, they fire you." What the household worker thinks is most ideal is if the señora goes out to work, and is not at home all the time, supervising the employee and following her around with constant instructions: "Since the señora goes out to work, I do the things in my own way, and in peace."

When they are asked about what type of work might accord better with their own child-care and home responsibilities, the women want to work in a factory (11), as sellers (10), or doing sewing/knitting at home (8). Age does not seem to make a great difference in what a domestic would choose to do if she could, except that those who can't think of an alternative have the youngest average age (22 years). Those who would like to be factory workers average age is 25; those who would like to sell are a little older, 28 years. Those who would prefer to work at home are 30.4 years. What does make a great deal of difference in the replies is whether the servant already lives outside the patrona's house, or whether she still is a live-in maid. All but one of those who live cama adentro, for example, can't think of an alternative occupation, while the great majority of those who would like to do factory work already have a foothold outside the employers' homes. Table 3.9 shows the occupations the interviewees would choose as more congruent with their childcare and other tasks (these replies, it is interesting to note, are quite different from the aspirations of the women when they are asked to think about what they would choose if they could start over in life; these answers are much more realistic and in actual accord with what might be possible options).

TABLE 3.9 Occupations Cited by Household Workers as More Consonant with Childcare and Home Responsibilities

Living arrangement	No change	Change within domestic service	Seller	Sewing at home	Factory	Store	Don't know
Live-in maids	2	3	2	5	2	1	6
Live-out maids	4	2	8	3	9	1	1

LAND AND HOUSES

It would be hard to exaggerate the primordial desire of Peruvian women (and men) of all social classes to acquire their own *terreno* (land) and to erect some kind of habitation on it—as one interviewee states: "even if it is just a *choza de esteras* (reed hut)." Indeed, the Martínez, Prado, and Quintanilla study (1973, p. 44) of rural out-migration records that one-quarter of the women said their major reason for migrating to Lima was to have a better house.

In this section, the emphasis is on the living arrangements of the household workers. Much of the analysis also applies to the market sellers and ambulantes, many of whom began their work life as domestic servants and went through a process similar to that described here in gradually achieving a home of their own. The difference between servants and sellers in relation to home and community is one of degree: many of the market women have advanced beyond both the ambulantes and the servants in the kind of houses they occupy. While they sometimes have better housing, they are, however, for the most part living in the same districts as the other women, or in the lower-middle class barrios.

There have been numerous studies of the pueblos jóvenes of Lima. These "spontaneous" settlements actually are carefully planned invasions of vacant land on the periphery of the city. As time passes, the government is pressured into paving the roads and bringing in services. In many cases, however, instead of waiting for long years, and residents themselves collect *cuotas* for water and electricity through their block associations. These settlements have grown from small nuclei to very large agglomerations of people.

What is interesting is the fact that so many of the 50 household workers interviewed for this study have taken concrete steps toward realizing their dream of an independent living arrangement; 40 of the 50 have a domicile outside their patrona's residence. It is true that such an alternative often is a condition of continued employment; because they become pregnant or already have children, they are not allowed to work cama adentro. For many, however, the arrangement is not forced on them entirely by circumstances; indeed, 11 of the 40 continue to work cama adentro even though they have another living arrangement. The principal reason given is that the travel time and costs are too great to go and return to their own homes each day, but they do go on their days off. In several cases, the women still are building their houses on their terreno.

One-half of the 50 domestic workers have a stake in land and a house (usually in a pueblo jóven): 9 women without compañeros hold their land and house on their own, 20 live on land held by their spouses, and 5 share a house with relatives (and thus their stake in the house and land is unclear). One woman is allowed to live free with her husband in a choza erected on land belonging to her employer. Even though they have a house and land, 6 of the 25 still work cama adentro, as noted above.[2]

Of the ten women who have a terreno with a spouse, eight are legally married. They and the nine women who hold land on their own (with compañero or relative) are somewhat older than those who rent or still live exclusively cama adentro (ages average out at 30.9 years old and 26.6 years old, respectively). This indicates that some years of work are needed to achieve a stable living arrangement outside the patronal home.

Of the remaining 25 household workers, 15 rent: 1 rents a choza on the land of a friend; 5 rent small houses with their compañeros, and 9 rent rooms (in 7 cases, they rent rooms on their own, and in 2 cases they share a rented room with their compañeros). Of the 15 renters, 5 still work cama adentro and go to their rented house or room on their days off.

Table 3.10 shows the districts where the 40 household workers who have an outside living arrangement own land or rent. Table 3.11 shows how those who have land acquired it. In most cases, the women either took part in a mass invasion of unoccupied land or received land through a government program; in only two cases was land purchased. The housing arrangements of the market women and ambulantes are less complex: the majority live in a pueblo jóven.

In Lima, after land is acquired, people usually build a reed hut, sometimes of two or three rooms, with at least one room eventually roofed over when the galvanized tin can be afforded. From there, they graduate to an adobe brick house, first built on one floor, to

TABLE 3.10. Districts where the Domestic Workers Live (N = 40)

	Pueblo jóven	Lima (Centro, Barrios Altos, La Victoria, Rimac)	Other district
Have stake in land and house	19[a]	2	4
Rent	1	9	5

[a]Includes one interviewee living on land of employer; status unclear

TABLE 3.11 How Domestic Workers Acquired their Land (N = 25)

Alone or with others	Purchased	Invasion[a]	Government[b]	Other and no information[c]
With husband or relatives	1	4	8	3
Alone	1	4	3	1

[a]Includes insecure title in four cases.
[b]Includes insecure title in two cases.
[c]Includes three unknown and one interviewee living on the land of her employer.

which they often add a second floor. Sometimes they are able to build with what they call *material noble*, either adobe reinforced with concrete, or concrete blocks—and to insert the steel rods necessary to keep the structure standing in case of earthquake. If they are fortunate, they may eventually move to a *chalet* (a small tract type, modern house, usually one floor) in a housing project. One domestic worker, for example, moved to a chalet in a housing project sponsored by the Peruvian air force when her compañero got a job with the air force as a civilian employee.

Seventeen of the live-out maids occupy adobe houses or chalets. In only two of these cases has a household worker managed to build an adobe house on her own, without the help of a spouse or without sharing with relatives. This is not surprising—building a house is a costly business, accomplished little by little as building materials can be bought, and requiring the financial and physical collaboration of more than one family member. Table 3.12 shows the type of habitation of the 40 household workers who have a domicile apart from their employer's house. Sellers are better off compared to domestics.

TABLE 3.12 Type of Own Housing Household Workers Occupy (or Would Like to Occupy in the Future)

Rented	Choza	One-story brick adobe	Two-story brick adobe	Chalet	Residencial	Don't know
9 (0)[a]	14 (1)	13 (6)	2 (20)	2 (15)	0 (3)	0 (5)

[a]Numbers in parentheses refer to the type of housing domestics would like to occupy in the future. Don't know includes one who would like to go abroad, and two who want to get back to their province.

So far as their barrio of residence is concerned, 24 of the 40 who maintain a house or room apart from their employer's domicile unequivocally declare that they like where they live (or go on their days off); 6 are somewhat ambivalent, and 10 actively dislike their barrio. Highest on the list of desirable attributes mentioned by those who are content is "tranquility"; also important (in order according to the number of times mentioned) are electricity, piped water,[3] sewage, schools, markets, and medical posts. Not many residential areas where household workers live boast all of these amenities, but the women appear satisfied if there are some improvements, either underway or promised. Another important aspect mentioned by the contented is that their barrio is close to where they work, so that they need only take one *collectivo* (jitney cab) or bus.

Those who express dissatisfaction with their barrios point to the lack of electricity and running water (one woman has passed 20 years in the same two-room house without either); the dust and dirt, and lack of parks, plants, and trees; the fact that children have no place to play, and the *gente mala*—the bad people, by which they mean principally thieves and drunkards. One woman recalls that several times men of her barrio, when inebriated, have come after her with knives; another that someone who robbed her "carried away everything, even my little hen."

It appears to make a difference in the women's level of contentment with their barrio of residence if they have a stake in the land. Of the 24 expressing satisfaction, two-thirds have land, but only one-half the renters are satisfied with their barrio. The satisfied do not necessarily live in the best districts; dividing residential areas into five strata, we find that 16 of the 24 who are satisfied with their barrio live in a pueblo jóven, while only 4 of the 16 unsatisfied or ambivalent do so. Those who are dissatisfied are not, however, all hoping to move eventually to a better district: three want to go back to their province or abroad, and six don't know where they would like to move if they could. Four would go two steps up to a better area, and three would go one step up if they had the opportunity. Table 3.13 shows where the women live in terms of satisfaction/dissatisfaction with their residential communities.

Thus, aspirations of upward mobility, at least insofar as this particular group of women is concerned, are not very great, paralleling the realism of their aspirations in relation to work. It is interesting that only one specifies a move to any of the more fashionable barrios such as Monterrico, the Planicie, Santa Cruz, or San Antonio (where eight of the women work), and three who aspire to live in an upper-middle class neighborhood specify Miraflores and San

TABLE 3.13 Satisfaction/dissatisfaction with Barrio of Residence

Barrios	Districts according to class[a]				
	Upper-upper	Upper-middle	Middle	Upper lower	Lower
Satisfied (N = 24)					
Present barrio of residence			5	3	16
Unsatisfied (N = 16)					
Present barrio of residence			4	8	4
				Own province or abroad	Ambivalent or don't know
Want to live in	1	3	3	3	6

[a]Districts in which the interviewees live or would like to live were classified as: upper-middle: Miraflores, San Isidro, and Santa Cruz; middle-middle: Chaclacayo, Surco, Surquillo, Breña, Barranco, Chorillos, Jesús-María, and Lince; upper-lower: Barrios Altos, Lima Centro, La Victoria, La Molina, and Collique; lower-lower: Pamplona, Ciudad de Dios, Comas, Caja de Aguas, San Gabriel Alto, Villa El Salvador, Villa María de Triunfo, Chacra Puente, El Agustino, Huerta Perdida, Santa Isabel de Villa, Canto Grande, and San Juan de Miraflores.

Isidro. Household workers certainly are not insensitive to the contrast between the barrio or barriada where they live, and the barrio where they work, both in terms of the physical environment and in the attitudes and behavior of the people. "It's another system of life," several said. They are realists.

So far as the type of house they would like to occupy is concerned, the women appear also to be realistic about the home they someday want to construct. While only one interviewee (who has yet to move from her patrona's house) says that she would be happy to have even a choza, nearly all want either an adobe brick house or a chalet. (Table 3.12 shows the type of house in which the interviewees presently live, as well as the type they some day aspire to, "God willing.") Three say they would like to live in a residencial, the local name for a large, luxurious house in a good district, but in the main they aspire to what may be more possible: an adobe brick house in a pueblo jóven, which they will build themselves, or the type of chalet found in a government housing project. One woman remarks that the residencial is "not in keeping with my condition."

When they are asked about what features they would like in their homes, the women want, above everything else, sufficient room for themselves and their children to have privacy. Seventeen mention that what they most would like in their house would be sufficient bedrooms for each family member. Fourteen want a *sala* or *sala-comedor* (livingroom or living-diningroom combination), and seven mention a garden. When describing the barrio where they work, many women mention that what they like most is the green grass and flowers. In most places where they live, there is no possibility of cultivating any living thing—the barriadas often are built on the hilly sand dunes surrounding Lima; the houses are too close together, and water is too scarce and costly to plant flowers and trees. Most barriadas are dusty, arid places with not a single green leaf to be seen anywhere.

In the face of so many who say they are satisfied with their district (16 who hold land and 8 who rent), it is interesting that only 1 person has anything positive to say about the municipal authorities. Another thinks that "the authorities try to help, but they aren't able to because there are no funds." Of the rest, the vast majority either did not know if the authorities were doing anything (12 women) or said that they are not helping the people (18 interviewees): "no hacen nada"; "nada todavia"; "no quieren hacer nada"—they're not doing anything; nothing yet; they don't want to do anything. Eight interviewees mention that there are *asembleas*, that cuotas are being collected for electricity and water, or for street repairs. The women have definite desires as to what they want the authorities to do: Electricity: 10; Running water: 9; Better transport, roads: 6; Sewer system: 4; Schools: 4; Title to land: 4; General renovation: 3; Markets: 3; Parks: 2; Police: 2; Medical clinic: 2. Mentioned once each were: church, help for the poor, cheap rent, fiestas, pharmacy, bookstore (by an illiterate woman), and work for the men. The total adds up to more than 40 because some interviewees mentioned more than 1 improvement they wished the municipal authorities to undertake.

THE HOUSEHOLD WORKER AND HER COMMUNITY

Apart from their stake in land, which doesn't involve them in much community activity, domestic servants in the survey have very few links to their barrio of residence. This is not surprising, in view of the fact that they are home only on their days off and very late in the evening. Time off does not mean time to go to meetings or to participate in the life of the barrio, but to catch up on washing, ironing, and heavy cleaning. Nor is it surprising when one recalls that very few of the household workers like to work with others, or even associate with other servants in their employers' neighborhoods—not to mention the almost complete rejection of any organizational or trade union activity.

Only Juana ever belonged to a women's association in her barrio, and she is not able to go any more. Eugenia intends to start going to a club that was recently organized in Caja de Aguas. The most common women's organization in the barriadas is the *club de madres* (mother's club); however, these usually hold their meetings in the daytime, making it impossible for mothers who work away from home to attend. Nor do many women participate in their block associations, which have been formed in most pueblos jóvenes to oversee the daily life and development of the community—only 3 of the 25 having access to land and house ever participate in such meetings (although such meetings usually are held on weekends or at night to accommodate the men). Block associations, in any case, are considered to be more the business of the menfolk than of the women, although those women who head their households are welcomed and even expected to attend. Women most commonly say they do not have time for meetings: "siempre estoy trabajando," they say—I am always working.

Public meetings and manifestations also are not attended by domestic household workers. Several had gone to July 28 (Independence Day) parades, and Faustina recalls that she once went on a bus to a high school "to hear about the progress of the Peruvian woman." Several say they have watched demonstrations on television or from a distance, but they do not participate actively "for fear that something might happen" or because "they break heads, throwing rocks." Sabina says that she would like to go, but her husband doesn't wish her to do so—"He says 'foolishness'." The most common reaction to the question of whether the interviewees participate in public meetings and manifestations is "No, no I have never gone."

More formal links to community and nation are provided by the various legal papers that are necessary to carry on one's personal and work life. By far the most important is the voter registration card, used as a general identity card for transacting most official activities: applying for a job, going on a journey (even within the country),[4] buying on credit, cashing a check, applying for social security (this card is important because it also admits one to the public health clinics); enrollment in school, marrying—in short, for performing any legal act.

Of the 50 interviewees, 17 say they presently have their electoral registration card; 3 have lost theirs, and 5 say they are in the process of applying. Most women have at least one paper which they sometimes use as an identification in lieu of the electoral card — their tax payment record, for example, or their birth certificate, police certificate of good conduct, or health card (the latter two sometimes required by a prospective employer). Curiously, only 1 of the 50 has ever used her electoral card to vote.[5] Thirteen have no official paper of any kind, even their birth certificate, necessary to secure all other documents. If a woman's birth is not recorded, the person must journey to her province and appear before a judge with witnesses in order to obtain her certificate. Men, most of whom are called up for military service, have an easier time since their military papers serve as an identification.

At the time of the survey, all young women aged 18 were being registered for universal military service for the first time (without, however, any provisions for actually calling them up for training). This measure did appear to waken a latent patriotism in many of the women, and there is almost unanimous and enthusiastic approbation among the interviewees about the idea. Only four said that they would not like to serve. Aside from patriotism, many believe that military service would provide an opportunity for young women (as it does for young men) "to learn many things"; "to come out with a profession"; "to learn technical skills." If she were 18 years old, says Paulina, "I should like to learn a little more; I like the uniform and to leave the army trained and ready like a man. One learns many things, for example, auto mechanics and industrial machinery."

Several others say they would like to serve, but not to bear arms. Manuela asserts that she would not like to kill, but would go to the laundry or cooking section. Felipa observes that service in the armed forces is good "because one comes out with all your papers and is able to obtain employment anywhere." But most are not thinking primarily of what military service would do for them in terms of their own betterment. Emilia echoes most of the interviewees in their love of country: "It would be beautiful to defend our country with the same courage as a man."

So far as putting their confidence in other women to manage local and national affairs, most of the household workers think that women could be good public officials, and that all women should enjoy equal rights and responsibilities with men. The positive attitudes toward women participating in public affairs cut across all age groups and do not depend on marital status or on whether the woman is living outside the patronal home: roughly equal numbers are in the positive and negative columns on these questions, as Table 3.14 shows.

TABLE 3.14 Household Workers' Attitudes toward Equal Rights for Women, and Women as Government Officials

Living arrangement	Women and men have equal rights and responsibilities			Women can govern as well as men		
	Yes	No	Don't know	Yes	No	Don't know
Live-in maids	13	7	1	12	6	3
Live-out maids	19	5	5	17	6	6
Compañero present	15	4	3	13	6	3
Compañero absent	17	8	3	16	6	6

The women are hard put to name any women leaders, either in Peru, in Latin America, or in the world at large. Of the interviewees, 24 say that they cannot recall anyone—one remarks "There are bound to have been very many, but I hardly know them." Consuelo de Velasco, the wife of Peru's military leader at the time of the study, is mentioned 11 times; the women seem to know of her work in the pueblos jóvenes, particularly in Villa el Salvador. María Delgado de Odría, wife of a former military dictator, is mentioned twice, and Irene Silva de Santolalla, Peru's first woman senator, once. Several historical figures are recalled. María Pardo de Bellido, Joan of Arc, and Rosa de Lima each get one mention, and the Virgin Mary, three. Peru's Miss Universe is named twice. Other contemporary women mentioned once include "the princess of France" (?), "la Reina Isabel" (Queen Elizabeth II), a recently convicted murderess, and a local barrio leader.

SATISFACTION IN LIFE; PROSPECTS FOR THE FUTURE

What kind of feelings do the women have when they view their lives—positive or negative? In whom do they confide? What do they think the future holds for them and their children?

One of the most revealing questions asked the women in relation to their personal lives was whether they would choose—if it were possible to live over again—to be a man or a woman. Only 6 of the 50 interviewees say they are satisfied with being women; 1 says that it makes no difference. All the rest would, if they could, live their lives over again as men.

Most of the women envy what they believe to be the greater freedom to come and go that men enjoy, and their lesser responsibility toward their children. Many say, "Wherever the man goes, he lands on his feet" (an application of a Peruvian proverb). "I would rather have been a man," they say because:

> *Maruja*: I would have studied more, and would have been responsible in everything. A man, in order to defend my brothers and sisters and my mamá. My mother always wanted a little boy, but I don't complain, no, I don't complain.

> *Carmen*: Sometimes it seems to me better to be a man because when he goes to work, he earns his money, no? Then he comes home irritable, angry, and the dinner has to be ready, the baby changed, the house clean. But the man only works, nothing more. On the other hand, the mother of the family has to take care of a mountain of things, no?

> *Hermalinda*: The man even though he has children always is on his own, no? He has his work, he has a higher salary than the woman, to support his children. But a women does not have the same wages, or the same energy for working and caring for the house. Men are always, how does the saying go? The man once he leaves the house is a bachelor, he is always single in the street.

> *Zulema*: The man can do many more things than the woman, things that require strength. A man can get water out of a stone, he can go to the street, and come back home at whatever hour he wants, while the woman cannot do any of these things.

Of the few who say they are happy to be women, several mention that "at least I am a mother. I have my children."

To whom do the women turn when they have problems? This question already has been touched upon in relation to friends in the working environment (Chapter 1, pp. 60–61). While only one interviewee says she confides in a friend at work, five have friends in their barrio whom they turn to in time of need. Others turn to female relatives as their chief confidantes (13 interviewees). Eight go to other persons, including two who confide in their patronas, one in her eldest daughter, one in her unmarried sister-in-law, and the others in male relatives. Only 6 of the interviewees turn first to their husbands in time of trouble, and 16 of the women confide in "nadies" (nobody). Table 3.15 shows the persons in whom the interview group confides and whether or not they currently are living with a compañero:

TABLE 3.15 Household Workers and Persons in Whom They Confide

Living arrangement	Nobody	Compañero	Sister	Mother	Friend	Other	Don't know
Compañero present	7	5	3	2	1	4	
Compañero absent	9	1	3	5	5	4	1

So far as religion is concerned, do the women turn to the church, and do they find support and solace in worship? Three-fifths of the interviewees do not participate regularly in any church activity except for the feasts of Santa Rosa de Lima, San Martín de Porres, or El Señor de los Milagros, when 4 of the 30 nonparticipants sometimes go to the processions, or for baptisms and weddings, when 9 have gone. Many mention that the church is too far away, they don't have time, or the señora does not give permission. Several say that they did go to church as girls in the sierra.

Of the 19 who do participate, 11 go to mass regularly, and 8 occasionally; of these, 2 are members of fundamentalist sects. It is interesting that when Hermalinda's son died, during two days of the wake, making the burial arrangements at the municipality, receiving neighbors and relatives, building the coffin, and making the burial robe, no one thought of calling on the church, even for the burial itself, although there was a parish nearby.

Will the future be better? And what part can the women themselves play in improving their lot in life and in making a better future for their children? Considering their circumstances, the women as a group are remarkably optimistic: one-half unequivocally believe that their future will be brighter, and another eight say that "perhaps" things will improve. Almost all believe that life will get better through no other means than their own efforts: "Depends on me"; "Through my own efforts"; "If I work hard." Several believe that life in the future will be better because their children are studying and will be able to take care of them. Others think the future depends on acquiring their own terrenito (little building lot) and house. Three would depend on God as the major force in a better future, but only one thought that fate would play the principal part in her ability to better her situation.

In Chapter 4, the women's relationship to their children is discussed. The early socialization of female children to work roles and how children collaborate in their mother's work is examined.

NOTES

1. Of these 21 women, 11 already are "in transition": 6 have a stake in a piece of land in a barriada (3 alone and 3 with their compañeros), and 5 have rented a room or a small house (1 alone and 4 with compañeros).

2. In three cases, the women's compañero occupies the land and house. Otherwise, this can be a risky business. One interviewee recounts that she almost lost her land because she could not live in her house and only came to the barriada on her day off. The block leaders had agreed to evict her in favor of a family that would continuously occupy the land, and it took many anxious days of importuning the authorities to regain her rights.

3. What is referred to here is water piped to general use spigots, in contrast to buying water from delivery trucks. Most pueblos jóvenes provide little possibility of running water to individual homes.

4. The public cars that travel between cities require the person's registration number as identification in case of accident.

5. Because of military governments that had ruled Peru from 1968 onward, only older women would have had an opportunity to vote in the elections of 1956, 1962, and 1963, plus the municipal elections.

LIST OF PHOTOGRAPHS AND CAPTIONS

3.1

3.2

3.3

3.4

3.5

3.6

3.7

3.8

3.9

3.10

3.11

3.12

3.13

3.14

3.15

3.16

4   Working Children

In an underdeveloped Third World country like Peru, urban working children contribute both to the dependent capitalist system and to the social reproduction of the labor force. They can be seen everywhere in Lima, involved in domestic and nondomestic income-generating activities.[1] They share, in this respect, their mother's double day—a day that must be devoted to both domestic work/family maintenance and to economic activities involving petty trade and services. Many participate with their mothers fully in both.[2]

Morice (1981, pp. 133–34) has observed that children become engaged in economic activities when their work is needed because of unemployment in the family, the threat of future unemployment, and/or an inadequate collective income. De la Luz Silva (1981, p. 163) also notes the connections between poverty and child labor: in families of the very poor, children are perceived as an asset; they can contribute to the family pool of resources, constituting a reserve workforce to be tapped when—as is usually the case—adults cannot provide adequately. Survival needs of the nuclear family unit take priority over the child's needs—education and recreation.[3]

From infancy, children adapt to the environment of the street sellers' workplace. Infants and toddlers are seen everywhere, bundled comfortably against their mothers' backs, leaving their arms free to carry and peddle goods while, often, two or more offspring clutch onto their skirts. From their perched perspective, babies observe the colorful, chaotic street scene that they will one day claim as their own. The generational cycle of economic activity will inescapably absorb them as they approach their sixth or seventh year; they then will be formally incorporated into income-generating activities to supplement their parents' income. They will work with their mothers, forming an early economic collaboration as "natural" working partners. Bundled babies are already, in a sense, sharing their mothers' full work day. Sleepy baby faces, smiling baby faces, impatient baby faces, serious baby faces peek over their mothers' shoulders watching as the women coax undecided customers into commercial transactions.

The comfort of this closeness to their mothers provides the child with a security that allows them to observe and explore the bustling urban street environment. The child learns to distinguish the noise and lights of the city, from dawn to dusk, sometimes well into the night, as he or she accompanies mother through her daily work routine. If the mother is a fruit or vegetable seller, the day will begin with a trip to La Parada, the large wholesale market, where they will wait for the warehouse doors to open; if the mother sells fresh fish, together they will endure the chill of Terminal Pesquero where fishermen arrive with their catch. Child as well as mother face the rigors of weather, long waits for buses or collective trucks which shuttle them from warehouse to workplace, and the pressures and hassles of congested streets and walkways in the overcrowded arteries of the city.

The great majority of working children grow up in the mercados, mercadillos, and paraditas [4] in the streets of downtown Lima and on the heavily populated streets of the depressed neighborhoods—it is here their mothers can find buyers for their wares. Children are found accompanying mothers at the entrance of cinema houses, stadiums, outdoor fairs, bus terminals, railroad stations, and *plazas* (city squares).

The street is the home and locus of socialization. The children of working mothers become accustomed to sleeping in the midst of deafening noise—in cartons and empty fruit crates, over roughly assembled push carts displaying shoes, knitted *chompas*, and assorted produce. Babies, toddlers, and older children are often seen sound asleep beneath makeshift tables; just overhead are offered herbal remedies for curing a variety of diseases, woven baskets, fabric remnants, cosmetics, brushes, hair curlers, or cheap jewelry.

Meals are taken on the street. Mother shares a warm plate of food with the children, brought from home by an older sibling or purchased from another ambulante mother. The small child is washed, groomed, and dressed in the presence of coworkers and passers-by. Bodily functions are performed on the street, in front of everyone—there is nowhere else to go. Adults, also, have no choice but to eliminate in the dark streets and lots adjacent to their working areas. Urination and defecation in the streets, common throughout underdeveloped Latin American cities, inevitably results in a stench which becomes close to unbearable from mid-day on, especially during the hot southern winters.

Familiarization with the urban set-up and strategies for adapting to this complex physical, social, and economic environment are the childhood tasks for the working boy and girl. The child's ability to perceive and comprehend the dynamics of the street will determine whether or not the family unit will have the resources to move from the world of malnutrition to that of mere poverty. Adaptation to the urban environment requires the development of specific social skills that will facilitate her or his incorporation into the commercial world of the streets. The working child learns to interact with adults and children from different social classes as well as her or his own peer group. Learning to handle oneself socially and economically means survival; the street is the arena for education and vocational training.

The formative years of children of domestic servants provide a stark contrast with ambulante children. Although they, too, share the territorial and social environment of the mother's workplace—a private home—they are rarely permitted to explore the employer's house, but rather are strictly confined to the mother's bedroom. Chaney's in-depth interviews with 50 domestic servants for this volume reveal 13 with children confined to their cuarto (maid's quarters) during the daily work routine; 8, who live cama afuera (on their own, rather than at the employer's), bring children to their workplace; 10 report leaving youngsters in the charge of older siblings who share family chores so that the mothers can go out to work (of these, 8 are daughters, 2 are sons); 9 leave children in the care of relatives—the domestic's grandmother, mother, father, or sister; 1 is forced to leave children locked up in the home; 5 count on neighbors, and 4 are sending their infants to nursery school. Two maids state they are unable to find work as employers often refuse positions to women who have children.

Many of the maids interviewed describe the negative impact on their children's physical and emotional well-being because the rigid monitoring of the daily routine by employers. One of the women lamented that her son was growing up casi mudo (almost dumb) as he was literally imprisoned in her quarters the entire day—no one talked nor paid attention to him as she went about her chores.

Regina, employed cama adentro with a three-year-old son and an eight-month-old daughter, complains that her employer's family treats her children poorly. She has little time to devote to them and can hear them crying with hunger as she serves dinner to the family. In order to quiet her older child, she gives him the breast.

Seven-year-old boys and girls develop skills appropriate for street sellers through observation and imitation of their mothers and other street sellers, testing out acquired knowledge on the spot. Some ambulante mothers work with two or three children at the same time: they find a strategic site in a plaza, a downtown street, or a supermarket entrance in a residential area and direct the children's economic activity. The children learn to hawk their goods, to collect money and make change, and to handle themselves with speed and efficiency in this world of the small entrepreneur.[5]

Frequently two siblings can be seen working together. Such is the case of Lala and Lola, eight and nine, who peddle woven plastic bags up and down the Jirón Unión in metropolitan Lima. They are instructed to signal their mother each time they complete the walking-selling circuit so she can keep track of them, since it is difficult to distinguish children in the swarming crowds that invade the Jirón Unión during the evening rush hours.[6] The experienced working child, in an eagerness to show off her or his expertise and style, often offers comments and suggestions to the neophyte:

> One has to shout the merchandise at the top of your lungs!

> One has to walk up and down offering what one is selling because otherwise we small ambulantes are not seen by adult customers unless we approach them and talk to them.

> One has to try to go out to meet and sometimes confront women customers and offer them a rebate.

Although the children usually learn their skills from their mothers or a relative, frequently a woman ambulante of goodwill or a neighbor will offer to teach intricate selling skills in exchange for the child's services. This is often the case when neither parent is a street seller. It sometimes happens that children themselves take the initiative to start working. This is particularly prevalent among boys who will only ask the parent's authorization to work when they have already become involved in the business of selling or providing services, often surprising their family with gifts of food.

In some instances, a son or daughter is put to work by an authoritarian father who decides, because of desperate economic needs, that his offspring should go out to earn. The father is the official decision maker within the traditional Peruvian family; his *machista* authority is never questioned, and his wife and children must accept and execute his orders. The forced induction of children into income-generating activities by surly and harsh parents often results in a traumatic experience for the child.

Ana María

I'm twelve years old and I started working in this market two years ago. My papá works as a plumber and as a bricklayer but the money he gets isn't enough to feed us all. I have six other younger brothers and sisters. My mamá has to stay home with the little ones and can't go out to work.

So I get up at six o'clock every morning and sell here till midday. Mamá cooks some food and brings it to me so that I can eat before going to school in the afternoon.

When I started coming to this market I was very lucky because I didn't have to run after buyers—many señoras (older women shoppers) approached me without my having to chase them.

It was my dad who came with me for the first time and urged me to work to help feed the family. He's also the one who goes four to five times a week to the large wholesale market and buys what I'm supposed to offer at my selling place. In summer I sell vegetables or fruit, and during winter I peddle spices. In winter I have less time to study or play because when my papá brings home those assorted spices bought in bulk—cinnamon, oregano, black pepper, bay leaves, and basil—I have to sit down for hours in the evening and pack them in hundreds of little packages. Sometimes I eat my evening soup while I'm working and then go straight to bed. I'm so tired by then!

My parents pocket all the money I earn but they give me a little on Sundays so that I can go to the movies with my little brothers and sisters.

I'm worried because I don't have much time to study and I'm afraid to get stuck and fail to be promoted to sixth grade. I'm sad because things are difficult at home. Papá quarrels a lot with my mamá. How I wish the whole family to be happy without quarreling!

I like to sell because I feel I'm really working to help my parents and the little ones. Right now I'm on vacation so I've brought my little sister to be with me while I sell. I carry her on my back and she loves it!

Many children describe how their father or father surrogate had ordered them to get out of the house and sell merchandise that he would bring home. A large number of these children did not have a family tradition of street peddling, so it had been the father who explained to them what to do in order to sell. The economic collaboration of the child under these circumstances creates a major conflict for them; they must face a foreign and completely unstructured situation.

Some of these cases reflect the extreme economic duress of parents who have no alternative but to forcibly recruit their children as cheap, available labor power to both the emotional and physical detriment of the youngster. The children are obliged to work long hours besides going to school; they sometimes must drop out of school for long periods of time.

Saul, a junk jewelry child peddler, explains what happened to him one day:

> I was eight years old when I started working. My father taught me how to sell. The first time I went out by myself I was very worried. My father said to me, "Come on sell." He took a piece of paper and pencil and drew a map. "You go this way, turn that way and behind the Santa Rosa bridge you turn again. There are lots of people there."
>
> I tried to sell all day; then it got dark and I was afraid I would not be able to get back home. I didn't know where to take the bus. Then I started thinking that someone could rob me. An older woman, a grandmother went by, and I asked her, "Where do you catch that bus going to Ermitano?" "Here at this corner," the old woman said.
>
> I got home and mother was back from fetching water. Mother said to me, "Your father was about to go and find you."

The working child has to go through a rite of passage whereby she or he graduates from the category of "apprentice" to that of street seller. This transition, in the form of a functional test, is made when the mother, or some other adult who has retained the services of the child, decides that the working boy or girl can be trusted to sell without any supervision. Children await this opportunity with a great deal of anxiety until they prove they are able to approach a customer, sell an item, package it, and return the exact amount of change. Working children with many years of experience as well as those just starting out speak of the tensions and worries they had felt that unforgettable day. They also express their fears that some adult will rob them of the merchandise entrusted to them by their mothers, or that some older delinquent bully will mug them and rob them of their goods.

Luisa

I come from a family of six sisters and we all help our mamita in her *tamal* business. When I was about six years old my mamá taught me how to prepare the meal of the tamales and how to tie them up in three different sizes: small, medium, and large.

We all started selling on the streets around the age of eight. At first we always went with someone older and after a few times we've been left by ourselves. My oldest sister Chabela, for example, started off with my grandmother. Abuelita used to sell tamales in the basement of a market in San Roque. It was like a wide corridor, where all the customers walked to and from the marketplace. Granny had a burrito on which whe would load the tamales. Sometimes she and Chabela would go selling on the street from door to door.

Unfortunately, I didn't have a chance to sell tamales with my abuelita and her burrito nor play with it the way Chabela did when she went with her. When abuelita was too old to work she found a fixed selling post for Chabela at that same market where she had offered tamales in the basement. My sister has grown up selling in that same place.

In my case it was mamá who taught me how to sell. I can remember the first time she left me on my own and I did very well! It was six thirty in the morning and my mamá left me at the entrance of the Panadería Italiana (Italian Bakery). I was very scared for fear of not selling at all or not giving change back correctly. But everything went well, and I got home with the money of my sale for the day. I have kept that same selling post, at the entrance to the bakery, for three years. I go there Saturdays and Sundays and sometimes on weekdays.

I work for my mother, but she's kind and will let me take money from the profit of the sale to buy ice cream or cookies if I get hungry.

A really scary thing happened to me about a year ago. A man came up to me and asked me, "What's the price of the tamales?"

"I have some for five soles and others for ten soles," I answered.

"Wrap me five tamales at ten soles each, but have you change for a 100 soles bill?" the man said.

"No señor," I replied. "I have little change, a few coins and I also have a 100 soles bill."

"Don't worry," he replied. "Give me your 100 soles bill and I shall have the cashier at the bakery change it for me so I'll meet you there." He talked all the time in a nice way so I trusted him.

I sold two more tamales, left the business unattended and headed towards the bakery. When I started asking after the man, no one had seen him, he'd just disappeared. Later on the package of tamales were found inside the shoe store. Probably he'd thrown them inside as he was walking and he'd fled, robbing me of a hundred soles and five large tamales. I was very upset and sad that day and cried all day. . . But the man was never found!

EXPLOITATION OF THE WORKING CHILD IN THE CONTEXT OF AN UNDERDEVELOPED STRATIFIED SOCIETY

Working children perceive the world around them from the vantage point of their family's position within the social structure. In Peru, income distribution by social class is devastatingly unequal and unfair, the product of the control of the resources and wealth of the country by the ruling classes, who also monopolize political power. Within such a stratified social context, the relationships of the members of the upper and middle classes with the bulk of the members of the working class are characterized by attitudes of authoritarian paternalism and benevolent disdain intended to disguise the endemic and implacable exploitation of the proletariat, an inexhaustible source of cheap labor.

Viewed from this macrostructural perspective the exploitation of working children is less visible. Most of them work for their parents, but as members of families belonging to the labor force, they are as exploited as the adult members of the workforce. Morice (1981, pp. 147–48) notes in his concluding remarks on children in the informal sector: " . . . in summary we strongly maintain that, in our view, child labour is, in general, characterized by the convergence of inherited social relations and an exploitation, of which the ultimate gains—whatever the intermediate processes—serve the dominant capitalist mode of production."

When working children get themselves involved in economic activities as a survival strategy shared with other family members—as when they go into the street by themselves or alongside their mothers to sell, or when they are hired in service occupations—they realize that the income level of their families and their life style are worlds apart from that of the bourgeois families they service. Working children note their own clothing: the shoes, a size or two too large, hand-me-downs from siblings; they keenly realize that they must wear the same clothing in summer and winter as opposed to children from middle and upper-class families.

It is, however, in the condescending arrogance of the adults with whom they deal economically that children learn that they are discriminated against because they are poor and cholo.

Adult customers and employers expect submissive and subordinate behavior from the working child. An outside observer is shocked to witness the ill-treatment of working children by many adult petite bourgeoisie and bourgeois customers. It is common to see young street sellers exploited by customers who start haggling over prices, ordering the children to sell their merchandise more cheaply and threatening them, saying if they do not bring down the price they will not buy from them at all. Sometimes the children, in desperation at not having sold at all during the day, are forced to reduce prices. At other times old matrons and young homemakers insist they do not have the price of the shopping bag included in the cost of the item purchased; they, too, pressure young street sellers to lower prices. When small ambulante boys and girls insist upon a minimum price, women customers shout down at them arguing that the product they are about to buy is too expensive anyway.

Children who sell services and semispecialized skills are constantly humiliated and abused by adult customers who bully them. When a child washes a car in a parking lot or on the street, there is usually a fixed rate for the work; when the adult enters into such an agreement, the child assumes the contract will be honored. Unfortunately for the working child, it is common to see the customer return, approve of his clean car, and then offer the child a much lower fee, commenting in a paternalistic and indifferent voice: "You're too small to be earning so much money, this is the reason I'm paying you less." Children try in vain to argue with the adult, but to no avail. They explain that the cost of living has gone up and that, in turn, so have charges for their services. Nevertheless, the rights of children as workers are ignored, they are made to feel powerless and demeaned, their self-esteem is shaken, and their trust in the adult world is lost.

The defenselessness of the child who works in the street becomes more pathetic still when they are abused by people within their own social class. Many small ambulantes confess that they live in permanent fear that some adult man, generally unemployed or alcoholic, or delinquent teen-agers will rob them of their day's sale, or try to cheat them or distract them in order to steal their wares. Working children realize that they are victims of abuse, deceit, and exploitation from adults and recognize their impotence in taking any corrective measure. (Luisa's and Angelita's cases illustrate the economic harassment of working children by adults.)

María de la Luz Silva (1981, pp. 1975–76) corroborates many of our findings in the concluding remarks of her study of urban poverty and child labor in Chile. She shows that working children's physical well-being suffers when they have to earn a living or look after themselves in whole or in part. The mere fact that working conditions are bad, de la Luz Silva emphasizes, gives children an image of the world and of human relations in which solidarity and love are virtually unknown. Only the most cunning children or, "those most able to strike fear into would-be competitors" are able to make it in this world.

The most dramatic cases of exploitation of working children are found in countless, pitiful situations of female child workers—generally under 12 years of age who serve as maids in households of the upper-lower, lower-middle, and middle classes. They are victims of exploitation in a situation where their employer and employer's family members simply appropriate the child as a servant with no compensation whatsoever. These small servants have usually come from the countryside, the sierra, from very large peasant Indian families. Their mothers have either given them away or placed them as apprentices of domestic skills in the hope that their daughters will learn the urban style of life, learn to speak fluent Spanish, and become literate. As noted in the case of María, the promise of sending the child to school often is not kept, working hours are beyond the child's stamina, and they are expected to fulfill the obligations of an adult maid: cleaning, cooking, washing, preparing breakfast and sometimes larger meals, and looking after the children of the family. It is part of the traditional cultural mores that these female children are also there to be approached by the sons of the employer or sometimes the employer's husband himself, to fulfill their sexual needs. The small servants sometimes are sexually abused, and often beaten as well. Evidence from several studies reveals that some child servants are subjected to severe beatings when they happen to break a plate, forget to run an errand, or act in ways which at the moment displease the employers.

What allows for this extreme exploitation of child labor is the defenselessness of the child as a minor and as a worker with no legal rights. Morice (1981, pp. 146–47) terms this mode of exploitation "quasi-feudal," due to its grounding in a dependent personal relationship between child and employer whereby the child supplies labor within a *paternalistic relationship* (italics ours) for which he or she gets protection, lodging, and food. Morice shows that the employer may be a parent, or the owner of a small craft workshop or business where the child is retained as an apprentice. Small-scale urban enterprises can only run at a profit through the utilization of lowpaid or unpaid labor. But, herein is the contradiction in this form of exploitation. The creation of a commodity involves appropriation of a child's surplus value, and as children's work is not socially recognized, it cannot be sold freely on the labor market. At this point Morice talks of "superexploitation": the juvenile labor force is not paid at the same rate as adults doing the same work, thanks to the maintenance of quasi-feudal dependency. In this category of superexploitation, child-created value is essentially extracted from the absolute surplus, that is, through protracted working hours (Morice 1981 p. 147).

In the specific case of the child domestic servants, the dependent paternalistic or maternalistic personal relationship is established on the basis of fictive relations of kinship and through the institutions of comadrazgo and compadrazgo (see Chapter 2) whereby the poor mother entrusts her child to an employer who adopts the child within the context of godparenting. Through this complex social network, the small maid is literally owned by the madrina or the padrino, and the employer has absolute rights of ownership over the child and an obligation to look after her or his welfare. Within this institution is the origin for the quasi-feudal abuse perpetrated upon the working servant child. The superexploitation of the child working as a domestic servant, in a home or in small restaurants, is extracted through long working hours, no pay, or a meager wage at the most.

The problems of child labor can only be understood in the overall context of pervasive poverty. Challis and Elliman (1979, pp. 78–90) believe that in Central and South America, the very existence of a small minority of extremely wealthy people not only does nothing to alleviate the suffering of the poor but, in fact, this very wealthy class is the real cause of the suffering and socioeconomic level in which the poor are locked. According to these authors, children are part of the large mass of people who suffer owing to deprivation, and thus they must be put to work at a very early age in order to contribute to the family's struggle for survival. Challis and Elliman's (1979, p. 89) final assessment of the situation for these working children is very grim indeed: "We can conclude that child labour in Latin America occurs on a large scale, and in some very unpleasant forms; also that it is a symptom of a generally deeply disturbing situation of poverty and disease, of stark contrast between the very rich and the desperately poor, of suppression and dispossession of the indigenous population. Probably in no other part of the world will it be harder to eradicate."

CHILDREN'S VIEWS OF WHY THEY WORK

Working children in Peru find themselves contributing to the communal family economic enterprise, the cultural survival strategy that allows families to subsist in a society characterized by the economic processes of underdevelopment. Urban children's work is participatory in the sense that they work for their parents, in most cases for the mother, or by themselves to supplement the joint family income. Work itself is the training ground for learning economic survival skills.

The adult conversing with working children in order to understand what motivates them to work to supplement the earnings of their mother, or of both parents if she or he has them, is overwhelmed by the deep affection that these children feel toward their mothers, and by the strong feelings of solidarity they profess toward their families. They explain at length that they work because they love their mothers and they want to help them. "Children who don't work are bums who don't love their mothers enough to help them," or, "I work for my mother, to help her, otherwise we wouldn't have any food to put in our mouths," are the patterned responses of the children, illustrating a sentimental and moral attachment. They are quick to add that they work for their family and to "cooperate" with their meager earnings toward the family's economic pool. A 12-year-old girl sums up her situation: "I give my mother all the money I earn; I'd like to give her more because I have so many small brothers and sisters, and my father and I are the only ones who work."

Working children manifest a great sense of obligation and fondness toward most members of their families, especially toward their mothers and siblings. These children appear to have been socialized to make themselves responsibile for the welfare of others and to subordinate their own desires and actions to the well-being of the family group. Many express the desperation usually associated with an adult provider at their inability to earn sufficient money to buy food and clothing for their mothers and small siblings.

To have a secure job, regardless of the type of work required, as long as it generated money; to have the certainty that there is never going to be lack of food—and, if possible, good food for themselves and their families; to sleep in their own beds, and upgrade the dwelling in which they are living, are the pervasive wishes of the working children. When these statements are considered in depth, it is the inevitable conclusion that working children are deeply preoccupied with the family's well-being. It is significant that the only item the children want for themselves is a bed—the only luxury they dream of having some day. The rest of their wishes are strictly family oriented in nature, further underscoring the depth of commitment to mother, father, and younger siblings. Their constant worries concern helping to provide the very minimum for sheer survival: food, a roof over their heads, and a place to sleep and rest. Another very important wish reported by working children with fathers present was for the father to obtain a stable job as a worker if at the time he was unemployed—a situation that affects most unskilled urban workers. If the father had abandoned them, their wish was for their mother to maintain her earning capacity and for her always to have some fixed type of work.

Angelita typifies the commitment of working children toward their family's well-being. She was observed and interviewed during after hours of her work scaling fish in Chorrillos.

Angelita

I was very proud of myself one day and almost feeling like a grown-up while going around scaling fish, when all of a sudden the sea got very rough and a big wave came over my working bench and swept away three *pejesapos* (goosefish) that I was cleaning for a lady customer! Fortunately the lady didn't scold me, as it really wasn't my fault but the sea's, and she had to wait longer for me to start all over again.

My mamita started bringing me along when she came to work here in Chorrillos. I only played with the other kids when I was very small—we'd all play by the ocean—but when I turned seven she started showing me how to handle fish and clean them carefully. That's how I started working for my mother who also sells fish.

Dad has a cleaning job in one of the large ministry buildings downtown. But what papá, mamá, and myself earn isn't enough because we are a big family. I'm the oldest of seven children and the only one who works. The sister who comes after me stays at home taking care of our little brothers and sisters while mamá and myself work.

At first I was very shy but gradually I got used to this job of dealing with adult customers. I like to work, I like it much more than going to school because I got used to it when I was quite small. I like to sell, to clean fish and give it to the buyer all neatly arranged in a bundle. I'm usually hired by a vendor who pays me ten *libras** a day for scaling fish. Sometimes I earn from 30 to 40

---

*A libra is worth ten soles

libras net a day and more when I buy fish here and sell it down the streets or pueblos jóvenes like Ciudad de Dios.

For a couple of years I worked doing just that. I'd get up at 4 or 5:00 a.m. in the long summer vacation from school, and I'd come to Chorrillos to buy fish directly from the fishermen when they arrive with their boats loaded after a night's catch. Fishermen are very good to kids; sometimes they'll give us one or two handfuls of fish for free, as a present. This way we kids earn a little bit more. Then I'd board a bus to Ciudad de Dios and shout my merchandise on the streets. By 9:30 a.m. I was through with selling.

Not too long ago I got very scared when I was robbed of my day's earnings after a hard day's work. It happened like this. I had come here to Pescadores and had cleaned *pejerreyes* (a variety of mackerel) all day. My purse was full of money and it was stolen from me! Working children like ourselves are many times the victims of evil grown-up people who rob us of our day's pay. Fortunately it's been the only time it's happened to me.

I believe children have to work in order to help their mothers buy them food and clothes! 'Cause one is just not going to go off and steal from somebody else when in need! We are too many children in the family and money is always scarce.

Children who don't work are like bums and don't love their mother enough to help her. I'll always help my mamá both at home and in her business. When I grow up and have children I'd like to have four. I'd also want them all to be girls because I've noticed that women work harder than men.

The permanent lack of money so characteristic in poor families of Latin American cities, where the father and/or the mother are underemployed or jobless, is further aggravated during periods of statewide economic or family crises. During these crises of acute need, the working children are the only economic providers; for them a decent and regular family income becomes both an impossibility and an obsession.

The absence of a minimal income means hunger for all family members, the fear of eviction from their dwelling, and having to suffer the degrading and depressing experience of looking at the few family possessions. Beds, stove, pots, pans, and a variety of broken cooking utensils, and dilapidated furniture are piled up on the street by the police, once the landlord accuses the family in crisis of failing to pay the rent.

SOCIALIZATION IN SEXUAL INEQUALITY OF MALE AND FEMALE CHILDREN: THE TRIPLE OPPRESSION OF YOUNG FEMALE WORKERS

Although male children may sporadically share their mother's double commitment to family maintenance and work outside the home by caring for younger siblings while she peddles, buying wholesale for the store she runs in the house, or working cama afuera as a domestic servant, the burden of surrogate mothering and domestic activities falls on the shoulders of her female children, usually the oldest.

Anderson, Figueroa Galup, and Mariñez (1979), in their study of childcare in urban and rural Peru, conclude that childcare is exclusively a woman's responsibility. Women devote their energies single-handedly to seeing to the everyday routine of feeding, cleaning, dressing, and entertaining their children. The authors also found that when mothers want to free themselves for full-time work or for participation in community affairs, they tend to rely on their older children, and that they prefer the girls to take over or the oldest child (even though it may be an older male child if there are no older female children in the family). Contrary to the stereotyped view that when children grow up in an extended family the mother is relieved in part of her total responsibility for childcare, the study points to the fact that although relatives are present, their contribution to care is sporadic and not in any real sense available to ease the mother's child-rearing role. Fathers in families of rural areas divorce themselves completely from responsibilities related to childcare, while in the urban squatter settlements fathers perceive their concern in relation to children limited exclusively to economic maintenance—a responsibility that they are already sharing with their working wife or compañera in a consensual union.

> Very few fathers mention playing with their children or taking them anywhere. The norm that eliminates attention to children from the adult male role is very strong. Men by no means lack knowledge or skills for child care, however, since most of them cared for younger siblings during their school years and teens. Ironically, child care seems to drop out of a man's set of acceptable activities the moment he establishes a household of his own, fathers his first child, and undoubtedly the most crucial factor—acquires rights to the labor of a woman in managing the household and rearing the child (Anderson, Figueroa Galup, and Mariñez 1979, p. 2).

Benería (1979) contends that male domination develops around the need to control reproduction in its different aspects. She also argues that sex-related differentiation is one of the most pervasive forms of human exploitation. She sees this exploitation rooted in the personal interaction between the sexes, in basic social institutions such as the family, and as supported by economic and political structures. Taken together, these factors constitute a "complex system of power relationships between the sexes which typifies the subordination of women at different levels of society" (Benería 1979, p. 205).

Socialization in sexual inequality between male and female children starts very early. In order to understand its specific cultural characteristics and functions we must analyze the nature and functions of traditional sex roles in Peruvian society and probe into their historical roots.

The dependent capitalist economic ideology and social structure of a developing country like Peru is supported by the traditional Catholic family system and by the Spanish cultural heritage which spawned the ideology of machismo. Machismo involves a system of beliefs and attitudes that espouse the superiority and social and economic value of one gender over another: masculine over feminine. Capitalism, sexism, and age-grading become inextricably intertwined and perpetuate one another through family and society at large in the posture of cultural patterns, values, and attitudes that regiment relationships between the sexes and, at the same time, establish and extoll the dominance of the husband over the wife. She as well as her children are completely subordinate to the authoritarian male head of the family. Under these cultural pressures the socialization of working-class boys and girls is markedly different.

Carlos Castillo Ríos (1974), a Peruvian educator and writer and an authority on the problems of Peruvian children, explains the cultural frame of reference of the gender system in present day society:

> The life of the marginal family develops within the framework of "machismo," a set of patriarchal values that lay the foundation for the predominance of the male over the female. Because of "machismo" the wife must obey her husband and he is the one who makes decisions in the family where he exerts his dominance from every angle. There is no such thing as the "tamed male" in working class families.
>
> "Machismo" is a phenomenon which is inextricably tied to the oppression of women and which has deep, historical roots in

Peru. The legend goes that Manco Capac, founder of the Inca Empire, was ordered by the Sun his father to teach men masculine arts and his wife Mama Ocllo to teach women the "proper" activities of their sex. This difference between men and women led to the establishment of masculine and feminine roles that became accentuated during the Spanish Conquest and were later to negatively influence the behavior and socialization of the Peruvian child from the moment of its birth.

Principally in the upper and middle classes, but also in bourgeois and proletarian homes the newborn female is dressed in pink, the infant male in blue. From that moment on the world of the girl is made up of dolls, small stores and gadgets for the home in an obvious preparation for their future destiny—the submissive caretaking of the male. Young boys are instead surrounded by cars, trains, pistols, and planes, and they have to learn how to behave "like men"; they must not cry and they must be strong and tough to later on assume their roles as heads of their families and as the owners and protectors of the home.

These stereotypes—whose unfortunate results are not well understood—are accepted by the members of the proletariat and cultivated by the family, the worker's union and the population at large. Young girls in school take cooking lessons, decoration, sewing and home economics courses not deemed "appropriate" for men (Castillo Ríos 1974, p. 108).

There is a popular saying which is part and parcel of machista ideology: "the man belongs in the street and the woman belongs in the house." This distinction is readily accepted by working children who start behaving accordingly. The small boy has ample liberty to roam the streets by himself or in the company of his friends with whom he forms nomadic gangs shifting from one place to another in the neighborhoods. He enjoys running small risks and fabricating adventures as well as inventing formulas to earn a little money—looking after parked cars, serving as messenger and carrier of bundles and small packages, and peddling goods alongside mother or on his own.

Working male children contribute mainly to the mother's economic activities by participating in their small business and helping them sell, by engaging in economic activities on their own, and giving them roughly 75 to 80 percent of their earnings. They collaborate with their mothers in tasks related to some stage of the process of economic production. Augusto's case is typical. He is ten years old, the youngest child of an ambulante, who, at the time of the study, was working in Jirón Unión, one of the busiest streets in downtown Lima. Augusto participated with his mother in petty trading, but did not help her in household tasks. When business was slack he became impatient because his sick mother slowed him down when peddling. These are segments from a long conversation with him:

> I don't earn money for myself but to help my mamita because she loves me a lot and lately she has been sick with asthma. When she gets those asthma attacks she cannot work, so I take over.
>
> I get up very early in the morning, most of the time at 5:00 a.m., and go to the *terminal frutero* (wholesale fruit market) where I get one or two large crates of avocados that I sell here in downtown Lima. This we do in summer; in winter we sell chocolates.
>
> When business is slow we have to pick up our merchandise and try our luck in some other part of the city. We try to sell quickly somewhere else before the fruit ripens. When this happens I usually go myself and leave my mamita back home. I seem to move around faster when I go alone.

Working mothers described the many ways in which their male children help them in business. Perhaps the outstanding characteristic or pattern that emerged—as opposed to the working female children—is that boys learn how to buy products and raw materials wholesale for their mothers' businesses. Boys are entrusted with capital to invest and establish the same commercial networks as their mothers. While still in school, they make use of their student's bus pass to go back and forth from home to the wholesale market and return to their mother's workplace with the products she needs.

The working female child, by contrast works twice as hard as her male counterpart. As well as working outside the home in income generating activities, she is expected to contribute to the maintenance of the family by assisting her mother and, in many cases, replacing her in the draining domestic tasks which must be performed on a daily basis: keeping all family members fed, clean, and looked after.

Viewed from this perspective, the female working child suffers a triple oppression and exploitation as a minor in the labor force, as a member of the exploited working class, and as a female child in the sex-related exploitation within the family, the forced sharing of her mother's adult caretaker role.

Through the mother, her role model in the culturally prescribed gender-related division of labor, she learns of the constraints placed on the woman due to her role in reproduction, and, how mothering will affect the extent and nature of her participation in productive activities. Through her socialization process, the female child becomes aware that the focal point of the work of women is the ambit of the household; the home is the territorial basis for all activities related to physical reproduction. According to Benería (1979), the household

> is the basis for the traditional division of labour by which domestic activities are seen exclusively as a woman's domain. In this sense, the household becomes the very root of patriarchy and the traditional domestic division of labour becomes its most immediate manifestation. The second consequence is the restriction of women's mobility which is prevalent in most societies though in different degrees of intensity (Benería 1979, p. 209).

Female children, therefore, share with their mother the reproductive sphere of the household. There is no discontinuity between the early nurturing domestic activities and their adult women's activities centered around the social reproduction of the labor force. Following are four typical cases of how young working girls juggle domestic activities, economic participation with their working mothers, and school:

> *Carmencita*, ten years old and one of seven children in her family was interviewed outside the Lince market, in a middle-class neighborhood, where she worked selling fruit behind her family's pushcart. Hers was an interesting case because she started selling as an ambulante, working for a "señora ambulante" who hired her as an assistant, selling for five soles a day, and used to leave her completely in charge of the stall. Carmencita's mother developed an interest in street selling and became a fruit vendor on her own. Carmencita was working every morning in the family business, going to school in the afternoon, and contributing in the evening to the daily maintenance of the family. She said with pride:"I help my mamá around the house. As she's so busy, I cook for the whole family. I prepare everything at night, leaving all vegetables and meat chopped. Then I get up early next day and cook the large family meal, leaving it ready. I know how to do everything a grown-up woman has to know: I can cook, look after my younger brothers and sisters, and shop."

> *Margarita*, nine years old, is the eldest child in a large family where the father worked as a bricklayer and her mother stayed home looking after the young toddlers and the baby. Margarita

used to get up at five o'clock in the morning to serve her father breakfast. She and her mother would take turns cooking the family's meals and caring for the young. She would go to school in the mornings and had a job scaling fish at the fisherman's wharf. On Sundays she would work as a child ambulante on her own, perched behind an enormous basket of sweet potatoes.

Sonia, age nine, is the daughter of a domestic servant who was working cama afuera, at the time of the study. She was staying at home in the mornings to care for her two younger brothers. She made the beds, cleaned the house, cooked lunch, and took out the garbage. She had missed so many school days taking care of her infant brother when he became ill, that she had to repeat first grade.

Aurelita at seven years old, had already taken over family maintenance activities so that her mother could leave the house everyday to work as a domestic servant, cama afuera. Aurelita looked after her younger brothers, entertained them and put them to bed, cleaned the house, and chopped vegetables so as to have everything ready for her mother to prepare dinner on her return from her daily work in the evening.

Due to the nature of her chores related to family maintenance, the working female child is more house bound with the exception of her contribution as a breadwinner outside the home. Although the small ambulante girl moves within the boundaries of the street scene peddling her goods, she is always beside her mother or under her protective supervision and that of her close relatives. They try to shield her and advise her of the constant danger that lurks over every working female child and adolescent—constant harassment by men on the street who may rape her or seduce her, eventually exposing her to a promiscuous sexual life that may well lead into prostitution.

Female working children share their mother's double day in different ways: the majority of working girls interviewed participate equally with their mothers in activities dealing with family maintenance and income generation. On many occasions older female children replace their mother's presence in the household by devoting their energies exclusively to chores basic to the social reproduction of the labor force: cooking, cleaning the house, washing clothes, and looking after younger siblings, father, and impaired older relatives. Thus they free their mother as completely as possible from the constraints of domestic tasks, allowing her to devote most of her time to economic activities. Family obligations quite often interfere with the girls' opportunity for even the most basic education.[7]

The female working child may take over completely as the main breadwinner of the family. In a crisis situation, Julia is such a case. Let us hear what she has to say as she became a full-fledged ambulante due to a family crisis:

Julia

I think that the rich children, who go from school to home to study and watch television, have a much better life than I do.

I started selling when I was seven years old. Nobody taught me how to sell. I learned all by myself. I started selling corn, lemons, avocados, and eggs.

One day while my mother was selling eggs she became ill. She fainted in the market. Before she was taken to the hospital, she told me, "Go, sell all these eggs, get rid of them, even though you will have to sell them cheap."

So I walked up and down the streets, up and down, till I had sold them all! I sold about fifteen kilos of eggs—there are around sixteen large brown eggs in a kilo.

When I finished selling, I went to the hospital and asked the guard at the door where my mamita was. He took me to room number 705 and there I found her. I gave her the money from my sale and she started to cry. She was in that hospital over a month and a half. That was when I started to sell together with my brothers and sisters.

Everyday I go with my mamita to La Parada. My father gets up at 3:00 a.m. He works cleaning apartment buildings in the city. Mother gets up much later, at 5:00 a.m. She then wakes me up. Sometimes when I wake up my eyes are glued together with sleep. I feel like going back to bed. My mother washes my face with water and then my eyes open; I feel much better then, I put on my school uniform.

We go to La Parada and buy a hundred avocados, it all depends on their quality. There are some trucks which carry vegetables and fruit and ambulantes back to their selling posts. For two and a half soles they bring us here, to the market in Miraflores. It is already 6:30 a.m. We have breakfast in Señora Juanita's shop—the eating place where there is a big clock which doesn't work. From there I go to school till 1:00 p.m.

From school I come back to the market and sell till night time. I am the one who helps mother the most of her seven children. My oldest sister, Consuelo, who has a little baby, also helps my mother.

I don't like working that much now. When I carry a lot of weight, my hands get tired. When you carry around something that weighs an awful lot, your fingers get sore and red and calloused. I don't enjoy selling nowadays because my hands hurt.

I don't like it either when the men from the city government come in a station wagon and chase the ambulantes and take away the goods they are selling. They also chase children, street vendors like myself. We have nicknamed one of the men Gorila and the other one Blind Duck. Gorila and Blind Duck get off the wagon in their uniforms and if they get hold of us we lose all of our merchandise because it is taken to the municipality.

When they arrive and start chasing us, I hide behind those trees outside the market. Gorila confiscated all the avocados that Consuelo was selling. She defended herself by kicking and scratching him.

The money I earn is for my mamita. Out of the money that I give her, she gives some to me. I put that money in a little stewpan with a lid that I have at home. I save it; I already have saved up eight libras. You know, all of a sudden I may become ill, and who's going to pay for the doctor? I can use that money to pay for the doctor and for my other small needs.

I do not have much time to do my homework because I work all week long and also Saturdays and Sundays. I try to do my school chores at night, whenever I can.

When I grow up I'd like to work in a circus, with clowns, music, animals, and acrobats. Perhaps I will continue working as a street vendor like my mamita.

SOLIDARITY AND CLASS CONSCIOUSNESS IN WORKING CHILDREN

The economic responsibility that working children assume at a tender age accounts for their realistic assessment of the world around them; it also generates feelings of solidarity towards other working children and an incipient awareness of class consciousness and loyalty to their working peers.

Manifestations of class solidarity and empathy toward other working children can be found in the reasons that children give for preferring to buy from a child like themselves rather than from an adult peddler. They explain that they purposely approach a working child because they feel that children have to sacrifice themselves a lot by walking up and down the streets and by "shouting" their merchandise—hawking sometimes in vain if they have not succeeded in calling the attention of customers. Children mature very early in their daily struggle for survival and become committed to helping out the workers of their own generation who may be having difficulties with their daily work. They will often lend a hand, trying to ease the responsibility of their peers as providers for the families by buying from them or by sharing in their income-generating activities, helping them sell to get rid of their goods, or by an offer of help in cleaning cars.

Manolo, eight years old, sells *butifarras* (sandwich made of a roll with pork or fried egg and spicy onion dressing) outside the entrance of a cinema:

> I like to do business with other children because they make good customers. When they come to see a movie their parents buy them lots of sandwiches. When I buy something I prefer to buy it from a working child like myself because I know how hard they have to work.

Urban working children distinguish three different categories of children: the children like themselves who work because "they love their mothers," vagrant children "who do not love their mothers and therefore do not work alongside them nor collaborate economically with them and who have free time to raise hell in the streets because they do not go to school either," and the wealthy children whose "parents do not want their children to work and who lead privileged lives."

Children from the middle and upper classes are always in the company of their parents and surrounded by relatives and domestic servants, and they play inside their homes and with children of their same social class. They only venture into the world outside their homes under the supervision of an adult. Poor children in a society where class differences are so marked, do not have a very precise picture of the lifestyle of children from a social class so different from their own and with whom they dare not compare themselves. The bourgeois child is generally seen from a distance, never alone, and always closely chaperoned. The poor child rarely has access to mansions of the upper classes which she or he often mistakes for hospitals, hotels, and other public buildings because of their size and splendor. Wealthy children are idealized by working children who believe that, as opposed to themselves, they do not have to work, "eat good things," and go from school to their homes to watch television.

By contrast, working children have a tremendous disdain for children of their own social class whom they look upon as bums if they roam the streets, beg, and do nothing because "they do not help their mothers in their work and they don't go to school."

Therefore all types of street peddlers, auto washers, shoe shiners, and child domestic servants have a positive perception of themselves as family providers that enhances their self-esteem. One of the preferred themes of conversation of working children is their constant criticism of the idle and vagrant child.

Their overall appraisal of idle children is confirmed by Castillo Rios (1974) who made a study of 143 child beggars in the city of Lima. He reached the following conclusions: 63 vagrant children were six to ten years old and 84 percent of those who were included in the sample were boys; 64 percent were registered in primary schools. However, they were children who had no supervision from their families or their schools, and therefore both the parents and the teachers ignored their street activities because they were begging in a district that was not their own: The money collected from begging was used to provide themselves with things that were independent of their basic needs; 56 percent of the child beggars had a father or both a father and a mother (Castillo Rios 1974, p. 140).

PERCEPTION OF MARRIAGE AND FERTILITY BY YOUNG WORKERS

Working boys and girls express the view that they want to get married—this is true more so with working girls interviewed than with working boys. Boys candidly explained that they want to become fathers even though they would never marry, thus manifesting the already sexist or machista values internalized during the process of acculturation. Both working boys and girls declare that they do not want to have more than two children, three at the most, because they feel that parents need a lot of money to start a family and that children are too expensive to rear. This realistic assessment of their hard experience as members of families in poverty comes up in their conversations over and over again, as does their understanding of the socioeconomic environment in which they are entrapped. These small, tenacious workers know that they have to work very hard in order to merely subsist; they are also aware that they have to help their poor families who are rigidly locked into an economic system that does not allow its members any substantial economic or social mobility. The children are also cognizant of the fact that the members of their families can only survive if they pool their labor power and income and make survival a joint family effort. They also show a clear acquaintance with the bleak fact the total family income will never increase in proportion to the inflationary cost of living.

In addition to thinking that they want only two children as an ideal family size and of not being too sure whether they want to get married, many children worry about not being able to continue helping their mothers were they to channel their energies into supporting a family of their own.

There are many other value laden clusters of opinions related to economic participation that are voiced consistently by the working children interviewed. These clusters can be grouped under three basic cultural themes. The first theme would be that of work as an expression of love for sacrifice, the working child offering her or his income-generating activities as a gift of love to the mother and to the rest of the members of the family. The second cultural theme would be the self-perception of working children as necessary and readily available laboring hands within the household, vital to the economic survival of the family, a cultural belief and attitude that strengthens the working child's self-esteem and which insures that the child does its best in the performance of its economic activity. The third cultural theme is a consequence of the first two and can be summed up in the desire of the working children to repeat the cycle of socialization and participation in economic activities of their family of origin by in turn socializing their own children in the prescribed cultural style that will guarantee the transmission of the elaborate network of economic aid among members of the household. Thus they will assure that their own children in turn respond in the same way as they (working for their mother) when they become old and are forced to retire from hard work because of illness or old age.

There are only a few isolated cases of children who categorically exteriorized the fact that they want to have children so "that they'll work for me." They view the parent-offspring relationship as one of open exploitation. These children are physically abused if they fail to be adequate economic providers. One of the most dramatic cases is that of an eight-year-old whose Indian mother from the sierra was the head of a household of seven children, and who—out of economic anxiety—mistreated all of her children, forcing them to work all day until midnight, selling candy at the entrance of a cinema in downtown Lima. She would not allow her children to play or talk to other working children. This particular child, as well as others in similar circumstances, state outright that they want to have children exclusively to make them work for them. Thus the cycle of socialization in work, economic exploitation of one generation by the antecedent one, and child abuse was most likely to repeat itself.

A few of the female working children interviewed admit that they often think of differences in economic responsibility between adult women and men when it comes to providing for their children—as so many fathers deserted their children; and of the double load of the working mother whose energies are divided between economic activities as the family's economic provider and domestic activities as mother. Three little working girls were interviewed separately; they all agreed that if they were to become mothers themselves, they would rather be mothers of female children because "women work harder than men."

LACK OF HEALTH CARE AND THE CHILD WORKER

Working children feel anxious and worried about the possibility of becoming ill and of not having the means to pay a doctor for his services, let alone having the money to purchase expensive prescriptions. The bulk of the population lives in the so called pueblos jóvenes. Dwellings here vary from those consisting of one or two rooms with thatched walls and no roof to the more comfortable ones that have been built out of brick, mortar, and wood, but which nonetheless have an unfinished quality about them—it takes an owner an average of 20 to 30 years to earn the money necessary to finish these houses. Malnutrition, subhuman sanitary conditions of the depressed neighborhoods, as well as the lack of unpolluted drinking water because there is no sewage system, contribute to the development of all kinds of diseases. Working children are seen with chronic colds, with running noses and eyes, and chronic coughs. They constantly complain of headaches, earaches, and upset stomachs, and they also cry themselves to sleep when afflicted by toothaches that cannot be treated because of lack of financial resources.

The working child suffers from all of these health problems, and boys and girls become anxious about getting sick; they are aware that if a person cannot afford the specialized services of a health practitioner they run the risk of dying. Children understand the causality between illness and death; with adults they attend wakes of babies who have died in just a few days of dysentery, and the funerals of toddlers who have died of sicknesses provoked by acute malnourishment. The children participate in funeral processions carrying paper flowers and walking long kilometers over sand dunes on their way to the cemetery over which squatters later will build their flimsy dwellings. Death with its ceremonial ritual, especially in the case of the demise of adults whom children have known as neighbors or as members of their families or as working partners, leaves them with a permanent vivid impression that life and death go hand in hand; that the definitive difference between one state and the other is produced by the presence or absence of health—health that they think can only be bought from a doctor provided they have the means. One of the most frequently voiced wishes of working children, ranging from eight to ten years of age, is the desire to make enough money to take care for their health problems as well as of those of family members.

There is no adequate socialized medicine program to answer the need of poor urban dwellers. The most poignant illustration of the abandonment in which the inhabitants of the pueblos jóvenes find themselves is garnered through the uneasiness and vulnerability felt by a working child of eight. Julia, at the time of the study, sold avocados, lemons, and eggs along with her ambulante mother. She was constantly worrying about her future as a worker and was already saving a meager sum which she would hide in a secret place in case she felt the need of consulting a physician. (See Julia, pp. 190–91.)

CONFLICT BETWEEN SCHOOL AND WORK

Working children are in constant conflict between their need to work and contribute toward the family's economic pool and their desire to attend school regularly. All of the working children interviewed complain of the obstacles they must surmount in order to do their homework, difficulties created by the demands of their street peddling, and by the fact that work and school schedules overlap. Many children drop out of school altogether when there is a vital urgency to solve a family crisis. Saul, a nine-year-old peddling junk jewelry in downtown Lima explains with bitterness:

> I do not enjoy selling. If I didn't have to stand here working I would like to go to school or go home and study.
>
> I work because father gets drunk, especially on All Saints Day. How are we going to eat? That's what I wonder. So there are many times that I say to my mother, "Mamita, I'm going to work 'cause how are we going to eat if I don't?"
>
> When father gets drunk I sell all day and miss school. Today I'm not there because I'm selling.

I only work for my father. He works selling necklaces, chains, and bracelets on Jirón Unión. He works at this only. He's lost his papers and cannot work at anything else.

My father sometimes doesn't sell a thing all day. Who's going to help him when he doesn't? Sometimes when I'm leaving for school after lunch, he comes home upset and without money. He tells me, "It's because I haven't sold anything, so let's go together and buy merchandise, lots of it and go out and sell." On those days I don't go to school. . . .

I make 30, 40, or 50 libras every day. On Sundays my mother gives me 10 or 15 soles. I ask her to save this money for me. When I have enough I can get myself a sweater and other things.

I like to earn money. There are some ambulantes who sell a lot. I would like to sell as much as they do. That's why I walk up and down the streets. People buy from me this way. I would like to be able to afford all of my mamita's clothing and suits for my little brothers.

Fernando, an 11-year-old boy is having a hard time trying to meet the requirements of his school work while contributing toward the survival of his family by working alongside his mother:

I'm eleven years old and I hold two jobs at the same time. I work for my mamita here in the market and also washing cars of customers who park in front of the supermarket.

We are ten brothers and sisters of the same mother and the same father. I'm the oldest boy and the only one who helps mamá. I get up at 4:30 or 5:00 a.m. every morning to accompany her to the wholesale fruit market where she buys one or two crates of avocados or any other fruit of the season that she'll peddle during the day.

I work for mamita during the morning, and I try to get extra tips by carrying packages for the lady customers who come in their cars. I also wash cars when my mother doesn't need me in her business.

But I don't have time to do my homework. I'm in fifth grade and my favorite subject is math. Sometimes I have to stay up until 1:00 a.m. to finish my school work for next day. The thing is that I always want to play, but there's no time. You have to work and study so hard to end up being someone important when you grow up.

Absenteeism from school is directly related to the work cycles of children during the year. These work cycles can be permanent in which case the child is forced to work all year round, including weekends, with the exception of Sundays. Or they are semipermanent and seasonal which is the case for the child who works only during weekends and winter and summer holidays, and the child who migrates from the rural areas to the city and works there during the long summer holidays to earn money to put himself through school during the year in the sierra. Generally, this situation is typical of male children who work as shoe shiners in frequented city plazas. Herminio typifies this kind of situation.

> I work in the city of Lima during the summer months. But I come from Huancayo, a large town in the sierra. I work to put myself through school. Many kids like myself do the same. It is very hard to get jobs in the sierra. They are scarce and very badly paid.
>
> I have a father and a mother and seven brothers and sisters. My father comes to work here in Lima because he gets higher wages in the city than in the sierra. But my mamita and all the other children stay in the country while we work here. I am the fourth oldest of the children and my mother is glad that I can work as a shoe shiner so that I can finish school.
>
> I have already saved 2,000 soles. With this money I'll buy my uniform, shoes, and books. I need more money to pay for my room and board at a family's home near the school which is in the sierra.
>
> When I become a man I'd like to be a professional, probably a school teacher. For this dream of mine I'm willing to put up with anything and make sacrifices.

The majority of working children were going to school at the time of the study. However, almost all of them were behind in their studies and enrolled in the first, second, third, and fourth grades of primary school with 9 to 12-year-old working children still only in second and third grades. Very few had managed to get to sixth grade.

Working children's daily economic activities produce feelings of anxiety and frustration due to the conflict with school attendance. Their schooling is sporadic; they fall behind in their work and have little time for homework; as a consequence, they feel insecure and inferior in front of their classmates. Many children become depressed and decide to quit school altogether; others resort to extreme individual solutions such as the case of Jośe Luis. A ten-year-old shoeshine boy, Jośe Luis works every morning at the entrance of an elegant cafe in Lima. He became very worried about the poor grades he was receiving at the school he attended in the afternoons, so he enrolled himself in a night school. As a result, his homework doubled. He cannot meet deadlines at the two educational institutions. Let us listen to Jośe Luis's conflict in his own words:

> I'm ten years old. I live in Salaverry which is in the district of Surquillo, but I come every day in the early morning and Saturdays and Sundays to polish the shoes of my customers who sit at this sidewalk cafe here in Miraflores. I shine their shoes while they eat sandwiches and cake and at night when they come for drinks.
>
> I work very hard. Lately I haven't been able to come because I don't feel good. I have chest pains and can't breathe. But I don't have the money to go to the doctor. I don't enjoy working right now because I get tired very easily. But I cannot stop working because I support my papá who's very old, he's over seventy years of age.
>
> Papá was a truck driver and had a terrible accident. So he now sits home and can no longer work. He made the shoe-shine box for me. So I live with my dad and an older brother who is loquito (a little crazy) and who doesn't do anything for a living and with my brother Pedro. This brother is not sickly like me nor crazy like the older one, so he works very hard polishing shoes and shining cars for the rich. There's only Pedro and myself to bring money home for papá, loquito, and ourselves.
>
> After work in the morning at the Café Miraflores, I go to school. I'm enrolled in two schools: I'm in second grade at the San Augustín where I go from 1:00 to 6:00 p.m.' and in third grade at the San Vicente where we go at night with my brother Pedro. I do all my homework but I'm not a very good student. There are so many things I lack like notebooks, crayons, and an eraser. When I try to borrow crayons from the other kids they beat me up . . . And when the teacher has me come in front of the class and write something on the blackboard, the same boys start yelling: "How much? How much?" They make fun of me because I work!

CHILDREN'S REALISTIC ASSESSMENT OF THEIR OCCUPATIONAL FUTURES

Working children perceive school as a pleasant place with an environment in which they can study, read, and play. With the exception of one small girl, who works scaling and cleaning fish and derived great satisfaction from her work and boredom from school, the child workers characterize school as a very attractive institution because of the activities it offers. The most attractive activity cited is the possibility of playing; working children have neither time to play nor to socialize with other children in a climate of camaraderie and of physical and emotional relaxation. Working children tend, then, to equate school with fun and play.

All of the children point out that their preferred subject in school is mathematics and that their second choice is social science. They find math instrumental for their work and enjoy showing off their skills with the four basic operations in front of school mates and teachers. Social science is perceived as a window to the world—probably because of the working child's fascination with the urban environment and their curiosity to explore a world beyond the boundaries of their city. A case in point is the request made by a girl who sells tamales and who wanted a calendar with photos from different countries, which she hung up on the dilapidated walls of her shabby dwelling.

When it comes to educational and professional options, the working child does not deceive himself or herself with adult job possibilities that are structurally out of reach. On the contrary, she or he knows that higher education is expensive, that specialized studies take too much of the time alloted to work. Boys opt for occupations that are feasible because of the short training required. All of them agree on wanting to become policemen, sailors, auto-mechanics, carpenters, primary school teachers, and professional soccer players. The female working children are also very realistic and select secretarial work, nursing, and hairdressing as their favorite choices. However, a group of working girls expresses low expectations, stating they would probably end up being street sellers like their mothers, or domestic servants.

There are a few exceptions to these patterns, since male children express the hope of becoming doctors, engineers, or lawyers —careers demanding time and money. These boys are working with relatives or for market sellers with fixed stalls in the main city markets. Their employers are established entrepreneurs belonging to the upper or lower-middle classes and optimistically upper-mobile. They are the exception rather than the rule; most of them had been ambulantes or had come from a generational line of ambulantes who had finally "made it" through petty vending into the larger markets. They accumulated sufficient capital to invest in a fixed stall, license, and merchandise. These employers represent the link between the informal and the formal sector of the economy, and the working children with higher aspirations looked up to them as role models. Mario, whose father was temporarily jobless and came from a poor family, illustrates this point very well.

Mario and his Godmother Aunt

I have been helping my aunt for a year; she doesn't pay me for my work at her food store but she buys my clothes instead. I have to obey my aunt because she is my godmother which means that she is like a second mother to me. If I disobeyed her it would be a sin.

I like working for her everyday, from 7:00 a.m. to noon. Then I'm off to school from 1:00 to 6:00 p.m. Sometimes, when there's no school, I stay in the marketplace and help her through the evening until night comes. I help her unpack and wrap the merchandise into small packages for next day's sale. I enjoy weighing and packing sugar, rice, spaghetti, dried fruits, and nuts.

I like everything about my work. I especially enjoy selling to my aunt's customers, wrapping their purchases, and helping them into their cars with their bags. They always tip me and I feel good.

As a salesboy I try to be honest and I do not cheat buyers. I give them their money's worth. If people sense this in you, that you're honest, all doors will open and you won't fail in life.

I'm in fourth grade. When I grow up I'd like to become a doctor, an engineer, anything that I really like. I'm the second best student in school, the one that comes right after the first. On my report card I don't have a single failing grade. I have a very good average. My teacher knows that I work. When I get good grades he congratulates me and sets me up as an example for the rest of the kids.

Some of the children in my school are very poor, their clothes are badly mended, they can't even afford to buy shoe polish. My heart goes out to them and I start wondering why they do not get a job like me and make a little money if their parents don't earn enough to support them.

VIEW OF WORKING MOTHERS TOWARD THE WORK OF THEIR CHILDREN

In their analysis of child work, Rodgers and Standing (1981, pp. 23–15) suggest the importance of researching and understanding the social and cultural framework in which the economic activities of children are embedded, as well as the nature of decision making at the household or other microunit level in addition to structural economic factors.

Although we do not intend an exhaustive analysis of this complex problem, it is critical to examine, even briefly the relevant cultural patterns that emerge when interviewing working mothers concerning their view of child labor.

Sellers regard their children as important members of the family's productive unit. The child's participation in domestic work and economic activities is considered inherent to the process of socialization. Child labor in the household and on the streets of Lima is described by adult men and women as something of an introduction and preparation for adult life. As one mother explains simply:

> Children have to start working early in life. It's the only way in which they can learn their obligations as members of a family. When children suffer young they make better adults.

Therefore, early suffering is considered good for the child, as it will temper character and arm them with courage, resignation, patience, and skills required to survive in a difficult socioeconomic environment.

Another mother ambulante comments,

> I have a high opinion of children who work because they are very, very valuable human beings and have a lot of merit because they start looking at economic activities they can perform in order to help their parents.

A third mother adds:

> I believe that children should never be brought up lazy but should grow up working and collaborating economically with their parents or their mother. In case the child's mother dies, or the father, he or she won't be left in a defenseless situation but will already know how to face adversity. Children will have less problems if they are trained in work from an early age for then they can fight off exploitation completely or be less exploited.

Decision making in the family regarding when a child should begin working rests mainly with the mother, if she is the head of the household. The responsibility for transmitting the attitudes attached to the economic value of children within the family's productive unit, the culturally accepted gender division of work in the household, and the teaching of family maintenance skills is perceived as her working mother's role by societal standards. We encountered three cases of fathers who had abruptly decided that their children should work and literally forced them into the street without any previous apprenticeship in street vending. In some exceptional cases the children themselves have gone off to try their hand at economic activities. Hermalinda, a domestic servant described how her mother, who had worked as an ambulante all her life, had one day been caught by her own mother, Hermalinda's grandmother, preparing and selling tea at a market. She had seen some vendors doing this and had gone off by herself without telling her mother!

From over 100 similar cases, we have selected the following testimonies of Lupe and her mother Nena to illustrate the natural participatory working relationship between children and their mothers, the offspring's early socialization in work, and their mother's ambivalent feelings. The overwhelming majority of mothers interviewed are torn between the need to resort to the use of their own children as economic assets and the realization that struggling for economic survival is harsh on children, robbing them of their childhood and a full-time education.

Lupe, a small eight-year-old girl and her mother are always seen busily selling prepared food behind their push-cart; they are ambulantes outside the Lince market in metropolitan Lima. This is what Lupe had to say:

Lupe

I'm eight years old and I've been working for my mamá for the last half year. I like working for her because there are so many things to learn. We get to the market early each morning. I help her till mid-day, when I'm off to school in the afternoon.

There are many things that I can handle here already. For instance, when mamá sells her prepared food on dishes to her regular customers who are people who work inside the market, I go to fetch the empty dishes and they pay me. I also know how to give back change. Sometimes mamá walks around the market voicing the type of dish she's prepared for the day. I'm left in charge of the push-cart with food. And I know how to wait on customers while she's gone because she's shown me the amount of food to give for the money.

In return for my help mamá gives me pocket money that I take to school where I buy my notebooks, books, and pencils, chewing gum, and chocolate cookies.

I love school and I've already learned how to read. I'm in second grade and I like math more than anything else that they teach me.

Nena

A child ought to learn to know life from an early age and, most important of all, he or she has to learn how to struggle and to accept the fact that life is full of misery and wretchedness. In this life a child has to be taught how to cope with all kinds of different situations especially so in our case, which is the case of the poor. We don't have the economic means to enjoy very many things; we want our children to be exposed to suffering from the beginning, so that they'll get used to it. Though I must confess that it is extremely difficult and painful for me as a mother to express these feelings because my daughter had to start struggling so soon. (She started sobbing at this point.)

It makes me, however, very proud that Lupe already knows how to cook and also understands the value of money at the age of eight. She's not a demanding girl, and she tries to understand me and to accept her father's absence (he abandoned us). There are other children like my Lupe who are understanding of their parents. Take Carmencita, our neighbor here in the market who also works alongside her father and mother as an *ambulante.* Carmencita shares every moment of her life with her parents, both the good and the bad ones, and she knows that the day that they don't sell is a tough one because they'll scarcely have enough for a meal.

Most street sellers are almost illiterate. Fortunately and thanks to God's blessing I was able to finish primary school. At night I've tried to follow beginning courses to become a nurse's aide. But this year I had to drop them because I've had many problems with my second attachment to a man. It's all been a failure. Therefore, there's nothing else for me to do but face difficulties alone. People say that life for a woman is a burden and a cross, and if Christ suffered so much carrying that cross, what's then left for a woman except more suffering?

Life for an *ambulante* is very harsh. For example, let's talk about today. It's already past 2:00 p.m., and I haven't gone home to cook lunch for the children. While they are still eating I have to leave the house and go to La Parada where I buy all the stuff that I need to prepare food for tomorrow's business: *bofe* (lungs of cattle), *mote* (stewed corn), and potatoes. When I return it's already time to feed the children again and put them to bed. Then I sit down and start cooking what I'll sell the next day.

I'm a mother who wants her children to share life with her and experience its ups and downs together. Lupe is already familiar with my trade, and she helps me a lot both at home and at the market place. Every morning she gets up early and goes to the bakery to buy all the bread we shall need for our business. In the meantime I have arranged the push-cart with prepared food to sell that day. After Lupe returns home with the bread, she wakes her small brother up, washes and dresses him, gives him breakfast, and walks him to school. By this time I have left for the market-place and she joins me there and works with me all morning.

It saddens me to realize that Lupe is not really leading the life of a child because she doesn't have time to play and enjoy herself more. It makes me unhappy that I don't have the time nor the money to take her to a park, to the movies, or to a place where she'd have lots of fun. Her only entertainment is to go to church on Sundays and then she rushes home to help me.

I have worked in factories long enough to realize that the worker is very exploited, especially women. On top of it all you have to be well-dressed and stick to a fixed schedule, and you can't take your children along. They scarcely give you a few minutes to eat. If you want to make a bit more money you have to work extra hours, skip your meals, and abandon your children. This is the reason I decided to give up my work in a factory for street selling. Street selling enables me to be with my children and take better care of them. All children need to have their mothers with them. Children are something so delicate and fragile and everything they experience registers inside them. Children are like photo cameras, they take everything in. And if they see others suffering they adapt themselves to the situation. As a consequence of all this, many children have been harmed.

As part of the basic training to become a nurse's aide, I had to get practical experience at the Children's Hospital. There I learned that 89 percent of the children hospitalized suffer from nervous disorders and have a variety of learning problems as a result of maternal desertion. This is the reason why I don't ever want to abandon my children or leave them helpless under somebody else's care.

I felt very offended one day when an ignorant woman insulted me by crying out. "How can you be a *placera* (market woman)? Aren't you ashamed? It's almost like being a beggar, dragging your children with you." I calmed myself by thinking that this was the only occupation in which I could keep an eye on my children.

Other women with whom I worked at the factory have seen me selling prepared food on the streets and they have exclaimed, "But Nena, for heaven's sake, why did you exchange factory work for street selling?"

I think that many of those women factory workers feel that I have climbed down socially and that they belong to a higher social class because they are working at a textile industry. I always respond to their remarks by saying, "When it comes to social class we are in the same boat, for you as factory workers are part of the proletariat and I'm also a proletarian as an ambulante. Things would be different for you if you were at the managerial level, but that's not your case."

NOTES

1. Our interest in studying urban working children stemmed from the broader study of 200 working mothers. We saw them working alongside their mothers, supervised by their mothers, fathers, or older relatives, hired by an adult, or working alone.

We observed and interviewed in depth 50 children of each sex, combining the traditional ethnographic approach of participant observation with a structured interview made up of 32 open-ended questions. Interviews were recorded.

Observation of working children engaged in economic activities in the informal sector of the economy was relatively easy because of their accessibility while working in markets, streets, and public squares. We observed them systematically at various times of day on weekdays and holidays while they worked. We also had access to many of them at home and watched them performing domestic tasks. Patterns of daily routine emerged.

In trying to understand the processes of the work of children we also utilized indirect approaches to complete the picture of the life-cycle pattern and its impact upon childhood years through interviews with key adult informants who had been child workers themselves—adult women and a few men who had worked as child servants and street vendors. Thus, we were better able to understand the generational cycle of socialization in work.

The questions in the questionnaire for our group of working children were directed at comprehending a series of themes related to children's work. The following are the basic sociocultural topics on which we concentrated: (1) The role of work in the socialization of children (apprenticeship, positive and negative impacts on children's physical and emotional welfare); (2) children's perceptions and explanations of their economic roles; (3) children's perception (assessment) of the world around them in relation to their economic activities, schooling, free time, and awareness of class differences with nonworking children; (4) working children's views on family, marriage, and fertility; (5) children's aspiration level in terms of their occupational future; (6) patterns of exploitation of working children; (7) gender-related inequalities between male and female working children and the female child's excessive contribution to production and the social reproduction of the labor force.

2. This chapter aims at an understanding of the role of working children in the context of the family's productive unit and the overall economy of a poor country like Peru. It is by no means exhaustive but rather an invitation for other researchers to do similar comparative, yet more complete, research on this issue.

3. A consistent effort has been made by international organizations to assess the number of working children in the world. This is a difficult task as children are not usually registered in statistical surveys of the labor force and the official estimates cover only full-time child workers. Cordell McHale, McHale, and Streatfield (1979, pp. 62–65) quote an ILO source that estimates that in 1975 there were 54.7 million children under 15 years of age working in the world, and that 3.3 million were found working in Latin America. Rodgers and Standing (1981) refer to 56 million children working in the world in 1976, and probably that the number was much larger at the time of the survey.

4. Mercados are established municipal or private markets housed in appropriate buildings constructed for the purpose. Mercadillos are small markets which have originated haphazardly when municipal authorities oust vendors from the streets and ambulantes are forced to find adequate selling spots. They temporarily settle in open spots in order to continue their business, while some have built stalls with no technical assistance. A paradita is a trading post usually erected on a street where ambulantes park themselves in order to sell.

5. Figures on the number of working children in Peru at the time of our study are contradictory. Rodríguez Heredia (1979) points to discrepancies in the statistics released by national Peruvian institutions. He notes, for example, that the National Statistics Institute maintained that in 1972 in the whole of Peru there were some 80,000 children from 6 to 14 years of age employed, while the Ministry of Education stated that 114,000 young people were working in Greater Lima alone (Rodríguez Heredia 1979, p. 129).

6. At the time our research was undertaken for this study, Jirón Unión was one of the streets in downtown Lima where sidewalks were jammed with vendors obstructing the transit of pedestrians. City officials have now banned street selling in Lima cuadrada (downtown Lima) and have relocated some of these ambulantes in another section of the city called Polvos Azules.

7. Chilean psychologists Maria Angélica Kotliarenco and Soledad Rodríguez have done an in-depth study of 60 proletarian boys and girls aged 6 to 11 attending school in a poverty stricken neighborhood in Santiago, Chile. The psychologists tested the male and female children's intellectual, verbal, and manual skills. Marked differences were found between boys and girls. Boys had a richer vocabulary and were aware of current events and scored higher than girls on I.Q. tests. This striking difference became most evident when the children reached 11 years of age. The psychologists attribute their findings to the fact that the female child is pressured into the traditional female caretaker role at an early age, her homework hours are constantly interrupted, and her school duties not respected—as opposed to the boy's—if she has to look after younger siblings and engage in domestic skills. Psychologists found that girls rated higher in manual dexterity than the boys. Girls, as opposed to boys in the study, repeated grades more often and were absent from school for longer periods of time. (See Kotliarenco, and Rodríguez 1982.)

LIST OF PHOTOGRAPHS AND CAPTIONS

4.1   Ana María, 12, peddles spices in winter, fruit and vegetables in summer.

4.2   Junk jewelry peddler Saul started working when he was eight years old.

4.3   *Tamaleras* Luisa and her five sisters, along with their mother, peddle tamales; they each began selling around the age of eight.

4.4   When Angelita was seven, her mother taught her how to scale fish; before then, she played with the other children in the waves.

4.5   Augusto, ten years old, says: "I don't work for myself, but to help my mamita."

4.6   Julia, here selling lemons, saves her money in a little stewpan at home "in case I become ill" and needs to pay for a doctor.

4.7   Herminio comes from Huancayo in the summer to earn money for school; there are no jobs in the sierra, and he has seven brothers and sisters.

4.8   José Luis, concerned about his grades in afternoon school, enrolled at night. He is in second grade and is ten years old.

4.9   Mario works for his madrina (godmother) every morning, and goes to school in the afternoon. She does not pay him, but buys his clothes.

4.10 Lupe, eight years old, helps her mother until noon, then goes off to school. Her little brother watches.

4.11 Nieves comes everyday to the beach to sell plastic bags to people who buy fish; her sisters, who are older, scale fish.

4.12 The mother's workplace is where she socializes her children; this child is growing up in La Parada, the wholesale market.

4.13 Lupe at eight years old is caught up in a three-generational cycle of street vending.

4.14 Future ambulante looks out on the passing scene from his mother's broom cart.

4.15 Time to pack up and go home; young ambulante helps her mother arrange the stall for the night.

4.16 This ten-year-old *tamalera* child takes over her mother's domestic activities, and prepares dinner for a family of eight.

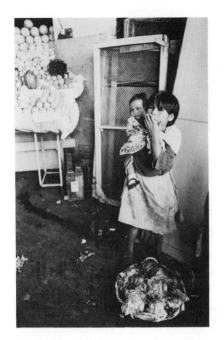

4.1

4.2

4.3

4.4

4.5

4.6

4.7

4.8

4.9

4.10

4.11

4.12

4.13

4.14

4.15

4.16

Epilogue
Talking Pictures:
A New
Methodology

The use of still photography, or "talking pictures," combined with open-ended interviewing, as a research strategy will be discussed in this epilogue. Using it, the interdisciplinary team of which I was a part studied 200 working mothers in Lima, Peru.[1] Some were illiterate, but bilingual (Quechua and Spanish). Others, who had resided in the city all their lives, had a rudimentary education equivalent to the completion of the first three grades of primary education. They were street vendors, factory workers, domestic servants, and market sellers with fixed stalls in the main markets.

One of our principal goals was to analyze the adjustments that these women, marginal to the occupational structure, had made in order to survive within an underdeveloped, dependent capitalist structure. Such a "mode of production has enormous repercussions in shaping the ways in which the marginally employed view and experience their many worlds. Ultimately consciousness reflects existence."[2] Because of this, we wanted the women to formulate their conventional, explicit, and conscious rules of behavior as workers, mothers, and members of unions, to state their values, objectives in life, and aspirations. We also desired to tap an inner world of feelings, values, and significance. Relying solely on verbal communication, through interviewing, is not the best way of understanding the subjectivity of informants who may have difficulty with language. Using photography in the social sciences is, of course, not new. We were influenced by Margaret Mead, among others; by her courses at Columbia University on methods and problems in anthropology; and by her pioneering publications. (See especially Mead 1963.) She has stressed that the best camera recording is made by the individual who combines training in photography or filmmaking and anthropology (1975). Though we share her general views, our approach, as we evolved the talking-pictures technique, was inter-disciplinary and collaborative, which entailed its own methods.

DEVELOPMENT OF THE PHOTO-INTERVIEW

We first investigated to see whether the subjects of the study were familiar with photographs, a luxury for the bulk of the popula-tion of countries in the process of development. But in spite of its high costs, poor people in Latin America try to record the important events of their life cycle, of that of their family, and sometimes of that of the neighborhood or community to which they belong. In towns and cities photos of first communion, baptism, or marriage may protrude, extravagantly framed, from otherwise bare walls in slum dwellings, and carefully packed photographs of a child's wake and funeral may be kept under key with such other important documents as a marriage license.

Proletarian families are also familiar with movies and television. Sets were found operating in the most dilapidated houses, a phenomenon common to large cities of Latin America. Families may lack the bare essentials of food and clothing, but will become in-debted for years to buy a television. The most watched programs are soap operas produced in Mexico, Venezuela, Argentina, and Peru. The plots often deal with a female heroine of the working class, typically a domestic servant, who achieves upward mobility through sex. She is usually seduced by an upper-middle-class student or an upper-class man and gives birth to a child. Through self-denial, hard work, and refusal to settle down with a man from her class, she wins the child's father over and eventually marries him. This is the happy ending, though getting him to the altar sometimes takes a life time.

Working-class women also devour foto novelas, the equivalent of the "true confessions" story or the dime novel for the English-speaking public. The novels are presented through the photographic arrangement of scenes illustrating different chapters or sequences. Technically, there is no readable literature in the magazine, with the exception of very short captions printed in large white letters over the corners of the photographs to interpret what is going on, in case the photo is ambiguous. The dialogue of the main characters and the conversation of the minor actors are also printed in this fashion.

However, for women and their families who had recently migrated into the city from the highlands or from jungle areas, photographs were a novelty. Their inclusion in the photo-interview posed added problems and introduced added variables within the expected range of cultural and idiosyncratic interpretations. This was especially true of some of the street vendors, or *ambulantes*, who peddle their goods inside and outside the markets and on the main streets of Lima, often attired in Indian dress. For example, we took a Polaroid picture of an *ambulante* who was selling prepared food outside a market. The photo portrayed her leaning against a wheel cart and evading the strong sun by wearing a beautiful wide-rimmed straw hat. We handed her the photograph and told her she could keep it as a *recuerdo*, or souvenir. She thanked us but politely refused to accept the fact that she was the woman in the photograph. She crossed the street to a friend of hers, another street vendor, who reinforced our statement. Matching her sense of self with the image of the straw-hatted woman staring back at her from the picture was such a forceful revelation that she burst out with manifestations of childish glee. For about half an hour she abandoned her selling post at her cart and did the rounds in the market place, showing her coworkers the photograph and giggling uncontrollably.

In general, we utilized a Polaroid camera to catch the interest of the female workers in our study, to engage fully the ones who were more knowledgeable of their environment and willing to help us, and to open communications and to assure trust in us. Latin American Indians and the rest of the mixed urban population are wary of tourists snapping shots of them; they feel cheated and used because they never see the end result of the action of the prowler with the camera. For this reason we offered Polaroid photographs as gifts in exchange for their collaboration. The film is developed in a matter of minutes in front of the interested party, who could then take the photo of self home as a token of reciprocity. As Collier (1967: 13) has said, "The feedback opportunity of photography, the only kind of ethnographic note-making that can reasonably be returned to the native, provides a situation which often gratifies and feeds the ego enthusiasm of informants to still further involvement in the study."

During the first phase of photographing, we followed Collier's recommendations closely. We shot pictures of the total environment of our four basic occupational roles—street vendors, market women with fixed stalls, domestic servants, factory workers (see Figs. 1–3). We recorded overviews of markets, factories, and private homes belonging to the city's different social classes. The team's photographer/psychologist combed the streets of Lima for three

Fig. 1—Credit for all photographs, Ellan Young

Fig. 2

weeks in order to choose salient aspects of the panoramic vistas and to become familiar with the complexity of the specific places we would select for study. To interest women, we explained that we were investigating working mothers in the city to commemorate International Women's Year, whose celebration in 1975 coincided with the Peruvian Woman's Year officially proclaimed by the military government.

Fig. 3

During the second phase of photographing, we had the full collaboration of key informants, about 25 women from the 4 occupational groups under study. They allowed the photographer and the anthropologist to follow them around during daily, weekly, and monthly work, and domestic routines. Ideally, we would have taught the key informants how to use the camera and then made their shots part of the photo-interview kit. Sol Worth and John Adair, in a pioneer experiment, instructed seven chosen native collaborators.[3] We gave up the idea for many reasons. The Navajo, though living on reservations, form part of a large national culture which exposes them to the technology of film, whereas our working mothers belong to a developing society in which cameras are luxuries and the process of picture taking is surrounded by the aura of high complexity, if not magic. On-going communication between researcher and informant will, because of the informant's knowledge of her or his culture, keep the researcher "from being carried away." Informants not only help to determine the emic dimension of a phenomenon, but they check, correct, and modify the components in a set of photographs that will later serve to illustrate a whole category of events.

When the photographs were developed, we took them back to our key informants for the first elicitation meetings. During them we chose the most appropriate pictures to be included in the final photo-interview kit. We kept in mind Collier's assessment of the photograph as a focus on which the interviewee may center her or his attention. As such, it promotes empathy between interviewer and interviewee and provides a fluid and fruitful context for understanding and data gathering. We also asked our informants to aid us in a tentative arrangement of scenes under researcher-defined categories. For example, which photographs would an informant pick to show the kinds of machines operated by men and by women in a factory?

The photo-interview kit was assembled with 120 photographs chosen from over the 3,000 that were shot. They were pasted in a large album, designed for the study. The format, though bulky, was a versatile interviewing tool. It could be opened on the grass; we talked to many maids while they were taking care of children in parks. It could also be accommodated over crates and piles of vegetables in markets. The pictures were then combined with a structured, but open-ended questionnaire.

The whole photo-interview was then given to a group of key informants who had not collaborated in the previous stages of its construction. They were asked to read the photographs, to respond to the questions, and to react by criticizing the interview. Only after testing did we go to the groups of working mothers selected for the study. During the first experimental photo-interview sessions with informants, we became aware of the fact that, not only did they enjoy talking pictures, but they were eager to do well during the two-to-three-hour structured dialogue. They asked such questions as, "How did I do?" or made such statements as, "I liked our conversation very much; it is the first time that I talked about my life as a worker and as a mother."

A decision was then made to focus on these extraprogrammatic segments of conversation to aid in assessing both the informant's evaluation of the photo-interview and the interviewer's experience. Questions were appended to each long interview. The informant was asked: (1) What did you think of our talking pictures? Do you think these photographs illustrate accurately the everyday life of a worker like you? (2) Would you add other photographs to the album? Which ones? (3) Which photos in the album did you like the most and why? Not like and why? (4) What did you think of me (the interviewer)? The researcher also observed the subject and general reactions to the event. (See the organization of the photo-interview below.)

Patterned statements about the world of the subjects of our study emerged as we pulled together the responses of the 200 women. Of the pictures included in the family set, all the informants selected the same one as their favorite: a scene portraying a working woman at home, sitting at the table with her husband and her five

Fig. 4

daughters (Fig. 4). She is laughing and looking fondly across the table at her toddler. Empty dishes and cups are scattered on the table. The recurrent evaluation of the family scene by all the informants was: "It is a beautiful photograph because the family is together"; "They are having fun together"; or "They have time to share each other's company." Most working mothers almost never have the chance nor the time to enjoy their families; factory workers have to comply with work shifts stipulated by the management, which contribute to atomizing further their already fragmented family interactions. Market women—street vendors and those with fixed stalls—have to get up at 3:00 a.m. to start their day buying wholesale, usually taking infants with them and leaving toddlers and older children at home to fend for themselves. Domestic servants are the most alienated of all. When hired young—sometimes at the age of ten—they are cut off from their family orientation. When they grow older and become mothers themselves, their slave-like seclusion in the homes of their employers impoverishes the nature, the quality, and the frequency of healthy and happy family relationships.

Two other photographs in the family set were chosen unanimously. One shows another family, a pregnant mother, her husband, and four children. The mother is putting the baby to bed and the father is supervising the homework of the older one (Fig. 5). This family scence was praised because "the family was together

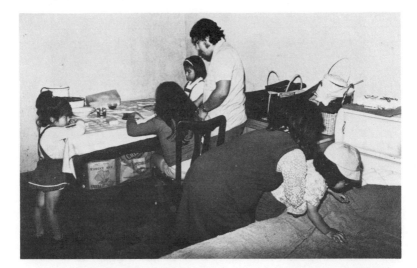

Fig. 5

Fig. 6

and everybody was doing something in the company of other members of the family." The other photo portrays a young couple strolling in a park with their small son (Fig. 6). The bodies of the parents are harmoniously linked to the child's. The activity of the parents with the young son was perceived as an unattainable ideal situation, for most women never had the time to go on an outing solely for relaxation, and all of them would like their husbands or compañeros to share more of their free time with their sons and daughters, something they seldom do, as the men go off by themselves. The members of the research team naively yet purposely included with the rest of the family interaction scenes one of a man sitting in a comfortable sofa, all by himself, watching television. We expected the informants to read the photograph as one of an "uncooperative father" (watching news and film while his wife continued working around the house). However, the replies carried the connotation that it was wonderful to have something (the television) at home to pass the time.

Both manifestations of upward mobility and conflict-laden attitudes were brought forth by the photographs of the different types of dwellings in which the bulk of the working mothers live in urban Lima: (1) the typical one- or two-room thatched house without a roof which is a common sight in the shanty towns, or pueblos jóvenes, that encircle Lima; and (2) the one-story brick house and the half-finished two-story home of the more prosperous families (see Fig. 7). Though around two-thirds of the women in the sample would instantaneously relate to the photographs and talk about their living conditions and their migration into the capital city as they pointed to the different types of houses in the barriadas where they had first arrived, the upwardly mobile women would set theselves apart from the scenes. These women, most with fixed stalls in the markets of the more affluent neighborhoods and a step away from the rest of the still trapped population within the context of the marginal pole of the national economic system, came up with patterned "market-

Fig. 7

stall occupational responses" opposed to the ones of domestic servants, market peddlers, and factory workers. They felt that their
houses, compared to the one in the album, were so much more
decente, decent, of good quality; "certainly their neighborhoods
were so much nicer," as some had managed to buy homes in
urbanizaciones, middle-class houses in residential areas. In spite of
such differences in outlook, it was possible to conclude that the one
material thing that all the poor working mothers dream of is to own
a house, no matter how small. The majority of them were going
through great financial stress at the time of the study to attain this
generalized and strongly felt need.

The value attached to the economic role of children emerged
from the pictorial analysis of working mothers photographed
alongside their working children (Figs. 8 and 9). Child labor is not
perceived as parental exploitation, but necessary for the survival of
the whole family. Eight- to twelve-year-olds of either sex become so
skillful at selling, handling money, preparing and marketing food,
and performing domestic services that their income or salary
becomes an essential part of the whole family's financial pool.
Sometimes they make more than their mothers—usually the ones
selling in markets. In many of the cases the women interviewed had
children who had sporadically assumed the role of worker and family provider, transforming the mother (when ill or giving birth to
another child) or both parents into their dependents. The economic

Fig. 8

Fig. 9

roles of children were also looked upon as part of the socialization process in the urban context. "Children have to start working early in life; it's the only way in which they can learn their obligations as members of a family." "Boys and girls have to keep their minds engaged in something otherwise they roam free on the street; work keeps them out of mischief." "When our children work we all eat better and lead a better life."

The most revealing photographs, for all of the working women studied, were the ones illustrating the most significant events in a woman's reproductive cycle: pregnancy, childbirth, and motherhood (see Figs. 10 and 11). Scenes depicting a dating couple on a bench in the park were the most evocative in bringing forth their remembrances and past love experiences. Marriage and raising a family were clearly perceived as manifestations of love and sacrifice. Photos portraying pregnant women extracted detailed accounts of the way in which they viewed their bodies and themselves, and a picture representing a factory woman breastfeeding her child was rated the most beautiful of all. These photographs were able to stir up their hidden emotions better than any others. For nearly all working mothers, the experience of childbirth and motherhood—in spite of their economic situation—is the most meaningful experience of their lives, and the only one they can really claim as their own. It brings them, apparently, the only real feeling of fulfillment, a sense of sheer being, tenderness, and joy.

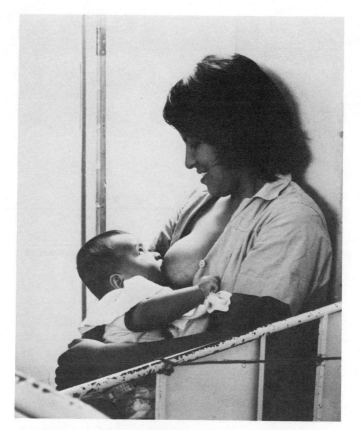

Fig. 10

Fig. 11

The data also indicate a lack of political awareness and of proletarian consciousness. Working mothers do not have the institutional framework that would help them develop a sense of class consciousness and solidarity with the lot of their coworkers. They participate neither in unions nor in political parties—banned by the military government at the time of the study. They understand mobility in terms of their own life and occupational history instead of in terms of their socioeconomic position in the society at large.

We tried to understand the patterned ways in which working women—in our case the Peruvian—saw, felt, labeled, and experienced their many worlds: work, private domain of the family, and those institutions in their society to which they have no access, "including those sectors which produce the symbols and values that endow activity with cultural meaning."[4] We doubt the existence of a better means—for the purposes of a study such as ours—than the talking-pictures technique for establishing communication. Meaningful photographs had a cathartic effect on the women of our sample. They were often moved to tears and strong outbursts of emotion. Again and again, we heard such statements as, "I have seen my life before my eyes and I cry for my sorrows and for the hard life of the working mother like myself." This was especially true of maids and ambulantes who lead an extremely tough existence. Experiencing the photographs, they released and discovered hidden dimensions of the ways in which they structure and conceptualize their life cycle. As researchers, we were invariably overwhelmed by their suffering. The constant reaching out to them during critical moments of the interview gave us added insights into their lives and exposed us to hitherto stifled dimensions of their battered existence.

We strongly recommend the use of a photo-interview technique for other studies in Latin America as well as other nations in the process of development. It is adaptable for the study of working women in any region—rural or urban—and in any nation. However, any study of the specific problems of women in the labor force must be done within an analytic context of the socioeconomic structure of the nation to which they belong.

THE ORGANIZATION OF THE PHOTO-INTERVIEW

The talking pictures kit consists of three general sets. Though overlapping, they can be used independently.

Labor Set

This sequence of photographs is intended to help the working mother focus her attention on a pictorial exhibit of her work environment. It serves as a stimulus for interviewing, a tool for projection, and a means of establishing rapport at the beginning of the interview. Its subsets include:

Panoramic vistas The outside physical culture, surroundings, and personnel of markets, factories, and private homes, as well as the complexity of their interior and relevant aspects of their material inventories.

Types of work Different aspects or activities within an occupation with detailed photographs portraying maids hiring themselves for a job, cooking, cleaning, laundering, and looking after children; street vendors engaged in the sale of assorted merchandise, with the visually explicit difference in ranking by economic capacity.

Daily routine A detailed photographic arrangement, with a different set for each occupational group, displaying a typical daily work routine. Factory workers start the day at the entrance of the factory, punch the clock, work, and put an end to their routine while eating prepared food on the street, bought from local vendors. Market women open their stalls, unload trucks with foodstuffs, snatch a bite while selling to their customers, and doze exhausted during the early afternoon over piles of vegetables while nursing their babies behind the counter.

Services A sequence of photographs illustrating the kinds of services offered to working mothers in an ideal factory set-up, such as medical care and daycare. These photographs are designed to find out if they are part of women's life and to probe into their perception and evaluation of them. For the ambulante women, to whom the majority of these services are not available, scenes showing the lack of these facilities, such as a toddler sleeping in a cardboard box on the street with toys scattered around.

Political participation through unions Scenes of women marching with flags, factory women on strike, belligerent women arguing against two men in uniform wearing helmets during a public demonstration, and a full view of the building of the Ministry of Labor where workers file their complaints against their employers —basic for the sifting of the women's views on the nature and frequency of their union participation.

Interpersonal relationships in work The work milieu of the factory worker, the market woman, and the domestic servant, intended as stimuli for the projection of the working mother's preferential attitudes to different styles of interpersonal relations in work. For example, ambulantes were exposed to photographs representing a vendor working alone selling fruit in one of the main streets of Lima, two ambulante women working together, a woman selling yarn from a bicycle cart with her husband and children, and a prepared-food ambulatory vendor peddling her goods and chatting with another male ambulante. Other photographs render occupational situations in which women were in a position of authority, such as supervisor at a factory, or were under an authority figure male or female.

Socialization A cluster of photos of children of both sexes working alongside adults—included only in the photo-interview of the market women. Designed in this context to investigate attitudes about children working and the value of their economic roles. Photos feature a woman selling inside her market stall aided by a young boy; three generations of female artisans—a grandmother, daughter, and young grandchild carving gourds in their shop; mothers being helped by their children in uniform at their work post in the market; and street vendors shouting their goods while aided by their offspring. Sequence also utilized to flash back and focus on the interviewee's childhood.

Evaluation of occupations and level of aspirations Pictures of 12 different occupations embodied by women of all ages and ethnic groups aimed at investigating how informants rank them and which seem suited for daughters. They include: a market woman with a fixed stall, a peasant woman handling a hoe, artisan, schoolteacher, seamstress, nurse, salesgirl, secretary, and hairdresser.

Family Set

These photographs are designed to illustrate the average working mother's family life and to help us learn about the significance and meaning that the women place on the family. Among its subsets are:

House styles A careful photographic record of the different types of dwellings and neighborhoods in the urban context, the aim to generate data on the housing situation, the value, if any, placed on home ownership, and information relevant to the Peruvian setting, such as whether they had been involved in land invasions to secure a plot of land on which to build their home.

Attitudes, values, and feelings on critical stages of the woman's reproductive cycle and ideas about their bodies and about themselves. Intended to probe into the feelings of the working mothers about male-female interpersonal relationships, sex, pregnancy, childbirth, and motherhood. Shots of young single women, couples on park benches (the patterned style of dating), a pregnant woman alone, a pregnant woman with a child, and a nursing mother.

The typical domestic routine To discover the perception and evaluation of the dual role as mothers and marginally employed workers. Photos of mothers putting children to bed, cooking for them, and washing on the street.

Working mother's interpersonal relationships with husband or "compañero" (mate in consensual union) and children Revolving around the activities of family members, the man in the house helping the working mother in house chores or else not collaborating. To elicit attitudes and feeling relevant to the way mothers structure family relations and roles and their rationale for the allotment of responsibilities within the terrritory of the home, decision making about children's activities, punishments, and rewards (which one of the parents does it under what circumstances), the husband's ideas about the mother working outside the home, and the mother's perception of the same problem. Pictures here include a father playing with a child in a park, and a father alone.

Sequence of children alone at home while mother is away at work Photographs emphasize the loneliness of a little girl in a house, children playing by themselves, and scene of a large group of male children tampering with an old bicycle in a slum.

Activities of children in collaborative work with mother at home and at work Snapshots of young female children cooking with adult utensils, and of a child studying alone, to inquire into beliefs sustained by working mothers about child domestic help.

Participation Set

Under this third broad category of observation and analysis are grouped photos aimed at learning whether the women had been exposed to political institutions and processes at the national and union level, whether they are aware of what political participation entails, whether they are familiar with the voter registration card, to elicit their views on military service for women, and to get their ideas about women's groups and associations and their attitudes about women in key positions in the power structure. For example, the photos include a female judge at a professional meeting addressing a group of men. Two particular subsets are:

Religious behavior Pictures designed to help understand when, how, and why working women would resort to the sacred world for the solution to their problems. For example, a woman kneeling and praying before the entrance of an easily recognizable Lima church, and a portrait of San Martín de Porres, a favorite patron saint.

Migration Three photos—an Indian woman tending a flock of sheep amidst the scenery of the Peruvian highlands, young women buying bus tickets at the station, and a young mother on the street with a toddler and suitcases—presented to learn about attitudes, feelings, and experiences on migrating to the city.

NOTES

1. In addition to the research team of Bunster, Chaney, Villalobos and Mercado, and our photographer, Ellan Young, we are greatly indebted to Jeanine Anderson, anthropologist and research assistant for our study, who tested the interview kit critically and contributed creatively toward its standardization as a research tool.

2. Heleieth Iara B. Saffioti, personal communication with the author. For an important theoretical contribution to women's studies, see Saffioti 1969.

3. Worth and Adair 1975. Worth's 1976 paper (see bibliography) also is relevant to the methods we used in Peru.

4. For an elucidating article on the subject, see Sutton 1977.

Bibliography

Aguiar, Neuma
1976   *The Impact of Industrialization of Women's Work Roles in Northeast Brazil.* New York: Praeger.

Anderson, Jeanine, Blanca Figueroa Galup, and Ana Mariñez
1979   Child care in urban Peru. A report presented to the Overseas Education Fund. Washington, D.C.: OEF.

Ariès, Philippe
1962   *Centuries of Childhood: A Social History of Family Life.* Translated from the French by Robert Baldick. New York: Vintage Books.

Arizpe, Lourdes
1975   *Indígenas en la ciudad de México: el caso de las "Marías."* México: SepSetentas.
1977   Women in the informal sector: the case of Mexico City. *Signs* 3, no. 1 (Autumn): 25–37.

Ary Farias, Zaíra
1983   *Domesticidade: "cativeiro" femenino?* Rio de Janeiro: Achiamé CMB Editores.

Babb, Florence E.
1979   Market women and Peruvian underdevelopment. Paper presented at the symposium on Markets, Marketing and Marketers, American Anthropological Association meeting, Cincinnati, Ohio.
1980   Women in the service sector: petty commerce in Peru. Paper presented at the panel on Women, Work and Inequality: New Theoretical Insights, American Anthropological Association meeting, Washington, D.C.
1981   Women and Marketing in Huaráz, Peru: The Political Economy of Petty Commerce. Ph.D. dissertation, State University of New York at Buffalo.
1982   Economic Crisis and the Assault on Marketers in Peru. *Women in International Development Working Paper* No. 6. East Lansing: Michigan State University.
1984   Andean marketwomen in transition. *Cultural Survival Quarterly* 8, no. 2 (Summer): 34–35.

Baxandall, Roslyn, Linda Gordon, and Susan Reverby
1976   *America's Working Women: A Documentary History, 1600 to the Present.* New York: Vintage Books.

Benería, Lourdes
1979   Reproduction, production and the sexual division of

labour. *Cambridge Journal of Economics* 3, no. 33 (September): 203–25.

Bolles, Lynn
1981   Household economic strategies in Kingston, Jamaica. In *Women and World Change: Equity Issues in Development*, edited by Naomi Black and Ann Baker Cottrell, pp. 83–96. Beverly Hills: Sage Publications.

Boserup, Ester
1970   *Women's Role in Economic Development.* New York: St. Martin's Press.

Bourque, Susan C., and Kay B. Warren
1976   Campesinas y comuneras: subordinación en la sierra peruana. *Estudios Andinos* 5, no. 1: 77–97.
1982   *Women of the Andes: Patriarchy and Social Change in Two Peruvian Towns.* Ann Arbor: University of Michigan Press.

Brown, Susan E.
1977   Love unites them and hunger separates them: poor women in the Dominican Republic. In *Toward An Anthropology of Women*, edited by Rayna R. Reiter, pp. 322–32. New York: Monthly Review Press.

Bunster B., Ximena
1983   Market sellers in Lima, Peru: talking about work. In *Women and Poverty in the Third World*, edited by Mayra Buvinić, Margaret A. Lycette, and William Paul McGreevey, pp. 93–102. Baltimore: Johns Hopkins University Press.

Burkett, Elinor C.
1975   Early Colonial Peru: The Urban Experience. Ph.D. dissertation, University of Pittsburgh.

Butler Flora, Cornelia
1983   Domestic service in the Latin American fotonovela. Paper presented at the Latin American Studies Association conference, Mexico City.

Buvinić, Mayra and Nadia H. Youssef, with Barbara Von Elm
1978   Women-headed households: the ignored factor in development planning. Washington, D.C.: International Center for Research on Women for the Office of Women in Development, U.S. Agency for International Development.

Buvinić, Mayra, and Jennefer Sebstad
1980   Women's issues in the design of progress indicators of rural development. In *Priorities in the Design of Development Programs: Women's Issues*, edited by Mayra Buvinić and Nadia H. Youssef, pp. 31–53. Washington, D.C.: International Center for Research on Women. Mimeographed.

Buvinić, Mayra, Margaret A. Lycette, and William Paul McGreevey, editors
1983   *Women and Poverty in the Third World.* Baltimore: Johns Hopkins University Press.

Castillo Ríos, Carlos
1974   *Los niños del Perú: Classes sociales, ideología y política.*
               Lima: Ediciones Realidad Nacional.
Challis, James, and David Elliman
1979   *Child Workers Today.* Middlesex, United Kingdom: Quar-
               termaine House, Ltd.
Chaney, Elsa M.
1980   Women in international migration: issues in development
               planning. Washington, D.C.: Office of Women in Develop-
               ment, U.S. Agency for International Development.
1984   *Women of the world: Latin America and the Caribbean.*
               Washington, D.C.: U.S. Bureau of the Census, and Office of
               Women in Development, U.S. Agency for International De-
               velopment. WID 1. Available from the U.S. Government
               Printing Office.
Chaney, Elsa M., and Marianne Schmink
1976   Women and modernization: access to tools. In *Sex and
               Class in Latin America* edited by June Nash and Helen
               Icken Safa, pp. 160–82. New York: Praeger.
Chaney, Elsa M., and Mary García Castro, editors
forthcoming   *El trabajo de la cuarta parte: servicio doméstico en América
               Latina y El Caribe.*
Chaplin, David
1969   Domestic service and the rationalization of household
               economy: outline for a comparative study. Paper presented
               at the American Sociological Association meeting, San
               Francisco.
1970   Domestic service as a family activity and as an occupation
               during industrialization. Paper presented at the Interna-
               tional Sociological Association meeting, Varna, Bulgaria.
Collier, John, Jr.
1967   *Visual Anthropology: Photography as a Research Method.*
               New York: Holt, Rinehart and Winston.
Coser, Lewis A.
1973   Servants, the obsolescence of an occupational role. *Social
               Forces* 52, no. 1 (September): 31–40.
COTREM (Comité Técnico Multisectorial de Revaloración de la Mujer)
1974   Política de revaloración de la mujer. Lima: Dirección
               General de Extensión Educativa, Ministerio de Educación.
Croll, Elizabeth J.
1981   Women in rural production and reproduction in the Soviet
               Union, China, Cuba and Tanzania: Socialist development
               experiences. *Signs* 7, no. 2 (Winter): 361–99.
d'Ajuda Almeida e Silva, María, Lilibeth María Cardozo, and
Mary García Castro
1979   As empregadas domésticas na região metropolitana do Rio
               de Janeiro: uma análise através de dados do ENDEF. Rio

de Janeiro: Fundação Instituto Brasileiro de Geografia e Estadística (IBGE). Mimeographed.

Deere, Carmen Diana
1977   Changing social relations of production and Peruvian peasant women's work. *Latin American Perspectives* 4, no. 1 and 2 (Winter and Spring): 48–69.

de la Luz Silva, María
1981   Urban poverty and child work: elements for the analysis of child work in Chile. In *Child Work, Poverty and Underdevelopment*, edited by Gerry Rodgers and Guy Standing. Geneva: International Labour Office.

Del Valle, Delma
1976   Factores determinantes de la participación de la mujer en el mercado de trabajo. Lima: Dirección General de Empleo, Ministerio de Trabajo.

Duarte, Isis
1983   Condiciones de vida, ideología y socialización de los niños de las trabajadoras de hogar en Santo Domingo, R.D.: notas preliminares. Paper presented at the Latin American Studies Association conference, Mexico City.

Duarte, Isis, E. Hernández, A. Garden, and F. Pou.
1976   Condiciones sociales del servicio doméstico en la República Dominicana. *Realidad Contemporánea*: 3–4. (Octubre-diciembre): 79–104.

FEM (Mexico)
1980–81   El servicio doméstico. *Número Especial* 4, no. 16 (September 1980–January 1981).

Fernández-Kelly, María Patricia
1983   Mexican border industrialization, female labor force participation and migration. In *Women, Men, and the International Division of Labor*, edited by June Nash and María Patricia Fernández-Kelly, pp. 205–23. Albany: State University Press of New York.

Ferrándo de Velásquez, Delicia
1984   Perú: participación de la mujer en actividad económica. Lima: Instituto Nacional de Estadística y Censos.

Figueroa Galup, Blanca
1976   La trabajadora doméstica en el Perú: el caso Lima. *Boletín Documental sobre la Mujer de CIDHAL.*
1983   La trabajadora doméstica (Lima, Peru). Lima: Perú-Mujer. Mimeographed.

Fitzgerald, E. V. K.
1976   *The State and Economic Development: Peru since 1968.* Cambridge: Cambridge University Press.

Gálvez, Thelma and Rosalba Todaro
1983   La especificidad del trabajo doméstico y la organización de las trabajadoras de casa particular. Paper presented at the Latin American Studies Association conference, Mexico City.

García Castro, Mary
1982   ¿Qué se compra y que se paga en el servicio doméstico?: el
               caso de Bogotá. In *Debate sobre la mujer en América
               Latina el el Caribe*, edited by Magdalena León, pp. 99–122.
               Bogotá: Asociación Colombiana para el Estudio de la
               Población.
García, Brígida, Humberto Muñoz, and Orlandina de Oliveira
1982   *Hogares y trabajadores en la cuidad de México*. México,
               D.F.: El Colegio de México and Instituto de Investigaciones
               Sociales, Universidad Autónoma de México.
Gianella, Jaime
1970   Marginalidad en Lima metropolitana. Lima: Centro de
               Estudios y Promoción del Desarrollo (DESCO).
Gogna, Mónica
1981   El servicio doméstico en Buenos Aires: características de
               empleo y relación laboral. Buenos Aires: Centro de
               Estudios e Investigaciones Laborales (CEIL) and Consejo
               Nacional de Investigaciones Científicas y Técnicas (CON-
               ICET). Mimeographed.
Goldsmith, Mary
1983   Relaciones de poder en la organización de las empleadas
               domésticas en la Ciudad de México. Paper presented at the
               Latin American Studies Association conference, Mexico City.
González Salazar, Gloria
1976   Participation of women in the Mexican labor force. In *Sex
               and Class in Latin America*, edited by June Nash and Helen
               Icken Safa, pp. 183–201. New York: Praeger.
Gutiérrez, Ana
1983   *Se necesita muchacha*. (Mexican edition of the book *Basta*,
               issued in Peru by the Sindicato de Trabajadoras del Hogar,
               Cusco.) México, D.F.: Fondo de Cultura Económica.
Henríquez, Narda
1980   Migración y problemática urbana. In *Problemas pobla-
               cionales peruanos*, edited by Asociación Multidisciplinaria
               de Investigación y Docencia en Población, pp. 97–129.
               Lima: AMIDEP.
Hewett, Valerie
1974   Migrant female labor in Colombia: an analysis of urban
               employment in domestic service. Bogotá: Corporación Cen-
               tro Regional de Población. Interim Report.
Heyman, Barry Neal
1974   Urbanization and the Status of Women in Peru. Ph.D. dis-
               sertation, University of Wisconsin, Madison.
Jelin, Elizabeth
1976   The bahiana in the labor force in Salvador, Brazil. In *Sex
               and Class in Latin America* edited by June Nash and Helen
               Icken Safa, pp. 129–46. New York: Praeger.

1977   Migration and labor force participation of Latin American women: the domestic servants in the cities. *Signs* 3, no. 1 (Autumn): 129–41.

1982   Women and the urban labor market. In *Women's Roles and Population Trends in the Third World* edited by Richard Anker, Mayra Buvinić, and Nadia H. Youssef, pp. 239–80. London: Croom Helm. Also published in Spanish in Estudios CEDES 1, no. 6 (1978) by the Centro de Estudios de Estado y Sociedad, Buenos Aires.

Katzman, David M.
1981   *Seven Days a Week: Women and Domestic Service in Industrializing America.* Urbana: University of Illinois Press.

Kotliarenco, María Angélica, and Soledad Rodríguez
1982   Infancia y pobreza: estudio exploratorio en niñas chilenas. Santiago, Chile: UNICEF.

Lauderdale Graham, Sandra
1982   Protection and Obedience: the Paternalistic World of Female Domestic Servants, Rio de Janeiro, 1860–1910. Ph.D. dissertation, The University of Texas, Austin.

Lockhart, James
1968   *Spanish Peru, 1532–1560: A Colonial Society.* Madison: University of Wisconsin Press.

Lomnitz, Larissa de
1975   *Como sobreviven los marginados.* México, D.F.: Siglo XXI Editores, S.A. Published in English as *Networks and Marginality: Life in a Mexican Shantytown.* New York: Academic Press, 1977.

MacEwen Scott, Alison
forthcoming Economic development and women's work: the case of Lima, Peru. In *Sex Segregation in Urban Labour Markets in the Third World,* edited by Richard Anker and Catherine Hein. Geneva: International Labour Office.

Macisco, John J., Jr.
1975   *Migrants to Metropolitan Lima: A Case Study.* Santiago, Chile: Centro Latinoamericano de Demografía.

Martínez, Hector, William Prado, and Jorge Quintanilla
1973   El éxodo rural en el Peru. Lima: Centro de Estudios de Población y Desarollo.

Massiah, Joycelin
1982   Women who head households. In *Women and the Family,* edited by J. Massiah, pp. 62–130. Cave Hill, Barbados: Institute of Social and Economic Research, University of the West Indies. Women in the Caribbean Project, Volume 2.

McGee, T. G. and Y. M. Yeung
1977   Hawkers in Southeast Asian cities: planning for the bazaar economy. Ottawa: International Development Research Centre.

McHale, Magda Cordell, and John McHale, with Guy F. Streatfield
1979   *Children in the World*. Washington, D.C.: Population Refer-
                ence Bureau.

Mead, Margaret
1963   Anthropology and the camera. In *The Encyclopedia of
                Photography*, edited by Willard D. Morgan, pp. 166–84.
                New York: Greystone Press.
1975   Visual anthropology in a discipline of words. In *Principles
                of Visual Anthropology*, edited by Paul Hockings. Paris and
                The Hague: Mouton Publishers.

Mercado, Hilda
1978   La madre trabajadora: el caso de las comerciantes am-
                bulantes. Lima: Centro de Estudios de Población y Desar-
                rollo. Serie C, No. 2.

Merrick, Thomas W.
1977   Household structure and poverty in families headed by
                women. Paper presented at the joint conference of the
                Latin American and African Studies Associations, Houston.

Merrick, Thomas W. and Marianne Schmink
1983   Households headed by women and urban poverty in Brazil.
                In *Women and Poverty in the Third World*, edited by Mayra
                Buvinič, Margaret A. Lycette, and William Paul
                McGreevey, pp. 244–71. Johns Hopkins University Press.

Migration Today
1982   Women in Migration: Special Double Issue, 10: 3–4.

Morice, Alain
1981   The exploitation of children in the "informal sector": pro-
                posals for research. In *Child Work, Poverty and Underde-
                velopment*, edited by Gerry Rodgers and Guy Standing.
                Geneva: International Labour Office.

Moser, Caroline
1980   Why the poor remain poor: the experience of Bogotá
                market traders in the 1970s. *Journal of Inter-American and
                World Affairs* 22, no. 3. (August): 365–89.
1981   Surviving in the suburbios. *Institute of Development
                Studies Bulletin* 12, no. 3 (July): 19–29.

Nash, June
1975   Certain aspects of the integration of women in the develop-
                ment process: a point of view. New York: World Conference
                of the International Women's Year, Conference Background
                Paper. E/CONF.66/BP/5.
1976   A critique of social science roles in Latin America. In *Sex
                and Class in Latin America*, edited by June Nash and Helen
                Icken Safa, pp. 1–21. New York: Praeger.
1982   Implications of technological change for household level
                and rural development. Paper presented at the Conference
                on Technological Change and Rural Development, Univer-
                sity of Delaware.

Nash, June, and Helen Icken Safa, editors.
1976   *Sex and Class in Latin America.* New York: Praeger.
1985   *Women and Change in Latin America: New Directions in Sex and Class.* South Hadley, Massachusetts: Bergin and Garvey Publishers, Inc.
Nett, Emily M.
1966   The servant class in a developing society: Ecuador. *Journal of Inter-American Studies* 8, no. 3 (July): 537–52.
Oballe de Espada, Aída
1971   La comercialización minorista tradicional a nivel de Lima metropolitana. Lima: Ministerio de Agricultura.
Oficina Interacional de Trabajo
1978   Participación laboral femenina y diferencias de remuneraciones según sexo en América Latina. Santiago, Chile: Programa para América Latina y el Caribe (PREALC), No. 13.
Orlansky, Dora and Silvia Dubrovsky
1978   *The Effects of Rural-Urban Migration on Women's Roles and Status in Latin America.* Paris: UNESCO.
Österling, Jorge P.
1981   La estructura socio-económica del comercio ambulatorio: algunas hipótesis de trabajo. *Revista Economia* 4, no. 8 (December): 65–102.
Pérez-Ramírez, Gustavo
1978   Unveiling women in statistics. *Populi* 5, no. 1.
Piho, Virve
1975   Life and labor of the woman textile worker in Mexico City. In *Women Cross-Culturally: Change and Challenge*, edited by Ruby Rohrlich-Leavitt, pp. 199–245. Paris and The Hague: Mouton Publishers.
Prates, Suzana
1983   Organizaciones de apoyo a la mujer pobre en Montevideo: ¿Solución o reforzamiento de la postergación? Paper presented at the Latin American Studies Association conference, Mexico City.
Quijano Obregón, Aníbal
1971   Polo marginal de la economía y mano de obra marginada. Lima: Taller Urbano Industrial, Universidad Católica.
República del Perú, Instituto Nacional de Estadística
1976   Primer censo de ambulantes para Lima metropolitana. Lima: INE.
República del Perú, Ministerio de Indústria y Turismo
1975   Caraeterísticas socioeconómicas de la población ocupada en el sector industrial: estudio muestral a nivel nacional. Lima: Centro de Investigación, two volumes.
República del Perú, Oficina Nacional de Estadística y Censos
1972   VII Censo Nacional de Población.
Rodgers, Gerry, and Guy Standing, editors
1981   *Child Work, Poverty and Underdevelopment.* Geneva: International Labour Office.

Rodríguez Heredia, René
1979   Peru. In *Children at Work*, edited by Elias Mendelievich.
               Geneva: International Labour Office.
Rogers, Barbara
1980   *The Domestication of Women: Discrimination in Developing Societies*. London: Kogan Page.
Rubbo, Anna, and Michael Taussig
1978   Up off their knees: servanthood in Southwest Colombia.
               Female Servants and Economic Development, pp. 5–29.
               Ann Arbor: University of Michigan Occasional Papers in
               Women's Studies, no. 1.
Rutte García, Alberto
1973   *Simplemente explotadas: el mundo de las empleades domésticas de Lima*. Lima: Centro de Estudios y Promoción del Desarrollo (DESCO).
Safa, Helen Icken
1976   Class consciousness among working-class women in Latin
               America: Puerto Rico. In *Sex and Class in Latin America*,
               edited by June Nash and H. I. Safa, pp. 69–85. New York:
               Praeger.
1977   The changing class composition of the female labor force
               in Latin America. *Latin American Perspectives* 4, no. 4
               (Fall): 126–36.
1983   Women, production and reproduction in industrial capitalism: a comparison of Brazilian and U.S. factory workers. In
               Women, Men, and the International Division of Labor,
               edited by June Nash and María Patricia Fernández-Kelly,
               pp. 95–116. Albany: State University of New York Press.
Saffioti, Heleieth I. B.
n.d.   Domestic employment and capitalism. Mimeographed.
1969   *A mulher na sociedade de classes: mito e realidade*. São
               Paulo: Quatro Artes.
1978   *Emprego doméstico e capitalismo*. Petrópolis: Vozes.
Sagasti, Heli Ellen Ennis de
1972   Social Implications of Adult Literacy: A Study Among
               Migrant Women in Peru. Ph.D. dissertation, University of
               Pennsylvania.
1974   La mujer vendedora ambulante. Lima: Report to the Ford
               Foundation. Mimeographed.
Sant'Anna, Anna M., Thomas W. Merrick, and Dipak Mazumdar
1976   Income distribution and the economy of the urban household.
               Washington, D.C.: The World Bank, Working Paper No. 236.
Sara Lafosse, Violeta
1980   El status de la mujer y sus implicaciones demográficas. In
               Problemas poblacionales peruanas, edited by Asociación
               Multidisciplinaria de Investigación y Docencia en
               Población, pp. 293–331. Lima: AMIDEP.

Sara Lafosse, Violeta, Carmen Chiara, and Amelia Fort
1981   Valor del trabajo de la mujer en el agro y en la producción domiciliaria para la indústria de confecciones. In Fondo de las Naciones Unidas para la Infancia, *Participación económica y social de la mujer perunana*, pp. 13–178. Lima: UNICEF.

Schellekens, Thea, and Anja van der Schoot
1984   Todos me dicen que soy muchachita. Trabajo y organización de las trabajadoras del hogar en Lima, Perú. Ph.D. dissertation, Catholic University, Nijmegen, Holland.

Schmink, Marianne
1977   Dependent development and the division of labor by sex: Venezuela. *Latin American Perspectives* 4, nos. 1 and 2 (Winter and Spring): 153–79.
1979   Community in Ascendance: Urban Industrial Growth and Household Income Strategies in Belo Horizonte, Brazil. Ph.D. dissertation, University of Texas, Austin.
1982   Women in the urban economy in Latin America. Project on Women, Low-income Households and Urban Services in Latin America and the Caribbean. New York: The Population Council.

Scott Kinzer, Nora
1975   Sociocultural factors mitigating role conflict in Buenos Aires professional women. In *Women Cross-Culturally: Change and Challenge* edited by Ruby Rohrlich-Leavitt, pp. 181–98. Paris and The Hague: Mouton Publishers.

Sindicato de Trabajadoras del Hogar del Cusco
1982   *Basta: Testimonios*. Cusco: Centro de Estudios Rurales Andinos "Bartolomé de Las Casas."

Smith, Margo Lane
1971   Institutionalized Servitude: Female Domestic Service in Lima, Peru. Ph.D. dissertation, University of Indiana.
1973   Domestic service as a channel of upward mobility for the lower-class woman: the Lima case. In *Female and Male in Latin America: Essays*, edited by A. Pescatello, pp. 191–207. Pittsburgh: University of Pittsburgh Press.
1977   Construcción residencial y posición social del servicio doméstico en el Perú contemporaneo. In *Asentamientos Urbanos y urbanización socioproductiva en la historia de América Latina*, edited by J. E. Hardoy and R. P. Schaedel, pp. 363–85.
1978   Personal communication Buenos Aires: Ediciones de la Sociedad Interamericana de Planficación (SIAP).

Standing, Guy
1981   *Female Labour Force Paticipation in Kingston, Jamaica*. Geneva: International Labour Office.

Standing, Guy, and Glen Sheehan
1978   *Labour Participation in Low-Income Countries*. Geneva: International Labour Office.

Strasma, John
1976   Agrarian reform. In *Peruvian Nationalism: A Corporatist Revolution*, edited by David Chaplin. New Brunswick, New Jersey: Transaction Books.

Suárez, Flor
1975   La movilidad ocupacional en Lima metropolitana. Lima: Dirección General de Empleo, Ministerio de Trabajo.

Suárez, Flor, Vilma Vargas and Joel Jurado
1982   Cambio de la economía peruana y evolución de la situación de empleo de la mujer. Lima: Ministerio de Trabajo y Promoción Social and UNICEF.

Sutton, Constance
1977   The power to define: women, culture and consciousness. In *Alienation in Contemporary Society: A Multi-Disciplinary Examination*, edited by R.S. Bryce-Laporte and C.S. Thomas, pp. 186–98. New York: Praeger.

Testa-Zappert, Laraine
1975   Women in the urban labor force: the case of Peru. Typescript.
1976   Socialization, Social Class and Economic Development: The Case of Peru. Ph.D. dissertation, University of Michigan, Ann Arbor.

Tinker, Irene
1974   The widening gap. *International Development Review* 16, no. 4: 40–42.
1976   The adverse impact of development on women. In *Women and World Development*, edited by I. Tinker and Michèle Bo Bramsen pp. 22–34. Washington, D.C.: Overseas Development Council.

Vargas de Balmaceda, Vilma
1981   Diagnóstico laboral de la mano de obra del hogar. Typescript.

Villalobos de Urrútia, Gabriela
1975   Diagnóstico de la situación social y económica de la mujer peruana. Lima: Centro de Estudios de Población y Desarrollo.
1977   La madre trabajadora: el caso de las obreras industriales. Lima: Centro de Estudios de Población y Desarrollo.

Webb, Richard
1974   Income and employment in the urban, modern and traditional sectors of Peru. Washington, D.C.: Urban Poverty Task Force, The World Bank. Mimeographed.

Weiss, Carol I.
1976   Migration, urbanization and family size in Peru. Mimeographed.
Wolf, Eric R., and Edward C. Hansen
1972   *The Human Condition in Latin America.* New York: Oxford University Press.
Worth, Sol
1976   Margaret Mead and the shift from "visual anthropology" to the "anthropology of visual communication." Paper presented at the Margaret Mead Symposium, American Association for the Advancement of Science meeting, Boston.
Worth, Sol, and John Adair
1975   *Through Navajo Eyes.* Bloomington: Indiana University Press.
Youssef, Nadia Haggag
1974   *Women and Work in Developing Societies.* Berkeley: University of California, Population Monograph Series No. 15.
Youssef, Nadia Haggag, Mayra Buvinić, and Ayse Kudat
1979   Women in migration: a third world focus. Washington, D.C.: International Center for Research on Women.
Youssef, Nadia Haggag, and Carol B. Hetler
1983   Establishing the economic conditions of woman-headed households in the third world: a new approach. In *Women and Poverty in the Third World*, edited by Mayra Buvinić, Margaret A. Lycette, and William Paul McGreevey, pp. 216–43. Baltimore: Johns Hopkins University Press.

Index

About the Authors

Chilean anthropologist Ximena Bunster is a graduate of the Universidad de Chile, and has a M.A. and Ph.D. from Columbia University. She was a full professor of anthropology and sociology at the Universidad de Chile and professor of anthropology at Catholic University in Santiago, but left both positions in 1973 and has since served in visiting roles in numerous U.S. institutions—including Rutgers, Texas, Connecticut, Maryland, the University of Pennsylvania and, Denison. While at Clark University, she also became coordinator of its Women's Studies program. Dr. Bunster's research and writing cover such topics as Latin American society and culture; underdevelopment; working conditions of women and children in developing societies; peasant societies; and the anthropology/sociology of women and of human rights.

Elsa Chaney received her Ph.D. in comparative politics at the University of Wisconsin in 1970. Since that time she has divided her working life between teaching and practical work in the field, centered around women in development concerns in the Caribbean, South America and Africa. She has worked on both rural development and income-earning projects for women. Her field work in Peru for this book was preceded by an earlier stay in that country, where she interviewed 167 women active in local and national politics for her book *Supermadre: Women in Politics in Peru and Chile*.